Emerging from
Communism

Emerging from Communism

Lessons from Russia, China, and Eastern Europe

edited by Peter Boone,
Stanislaw Gomulka, and
Richard Layard

The MIT Press
Cambridge, Massachusetts
London, England

This book was set in Palatino on the Monotype "Prism Plus" PostScript Imagesetter by Asco Trade Typesetting Ltd., Hong Kong.

Printed and bound in the United States of America.

Library of Congress Cataloging-in-Publication Data

Emerging from Communism : lessons from Russia, China, and Eastern
  Europe / edited by Peter Boone, Stanislaw Gomulka, and Richard
  Layard.
      p.   cm.
    Papers based on a series of meetings among members of the Centre
  for Economic Performance at the London School of Economics.
  Includes bibliographical references (p.   ) and index.
  ISBN 0-262-02447-0 (hc : alk. paper)
    1. Structural adjustment (Economic policy)—Europe, Eastern.
  2. Post-communism—Europe, Eastern. 3. Europe, Eastern—Economic
  policy—1989– 4. Structural adjustment (Economic policy)—Russia
  (Federation) 5. Russia (Federation)—Economic policy—1991–
  6. Structural adjustment (Economic policy)—China. 7. China—
  Economic policy—1976– I. Boone, Peter. II. Gomulka, Stanislaw.
  III. Layard, P. R. G. (P. Richard G.) IV. London School of
  Economics and Political Science. Centre for Economic Performance.
  HC244.E484   1998
  338.947—dc21   98-23560
                                                         CIP

Contents

Preface   vii

1   **Why So Much Pain? An Overview**   1
    Richard Layard

2   **Output: Causes of the Decline and the Recovery**   13
    Stanislaw Gomulka

3   **Inflation: Causes, Consequences, and Cures**   43
    Peter Boone and Jakob Hørder

4   **Privatization and Restructuring in Central and Eastern Europe**   73
    Saul Estrin

5   **Bank Restructuring and Enterprise Reform**   99
    Sweder van Wijnbergen

6   **Unemployment and Restructuring**   123
    Richard Jackman

7   **Why China Grew**   153
    Wing Thye Woo

8   **Why China Grew: The Role of Decentralization**   183
    Chenggang Xu and Juzhong Zhuang

Notes   213
References   219
Index   233

Preface

This book comes from the Emerging Markets Group, which is a part of the Centre for Economic Performance at the London School of Economics. The Centre for Economic Performance covers most aspects of applied economics, and in 1989 it established a group working on transition economies, led by Stanislaw Gomulka. As time passed, increasing numbers of us became involved in one way or another in the reform process in Eastern Europe and Russia. This book is a combined effort, based on an iterative series of meetings among members of the group in which we attempt to distill what we have learned.

We should like to thank the Economic and Social Research Council, which supports the Centre, for allowing us to branch out in this way, as well as the European Union's TACIS program, which has supported our work in Russia; the World Bank, which had a major joint program with the Centre; and the Know-How Fund.

We should also like to thank Vera Rich for careful editing, Sarah Grainger for excellent assistance, and Terry Vaughn of MIT Press for unfailing support.

1 Why So Much Pain? An Overview

Richard Layard

The collapse of Communism in Europe is the world's most important event since the end of the Second World War. At the same time China has taken major steps in the direction of capitalism. But everywhere the transformation is only partly accomplished, and in Cuba it has not even begun. Sensible strategies for the future depend crucially on learning the right lessons from what has been done so far.

The most striking fact is that in Eastern Europe and Russia the reforms were accompanied by huge falls in output—followed in Eastern Europe by some recovery, especially in Poland (see table 1.1). By contrast, in China output has grown steadily at a rate never seen in Europe. The main challenge facing us is to explain these facts. If free markets and private ownership are meant to increase economic opportunity and welfare, why has their introduction been accompanied by such pain in Eastern Europe and Russia? And why no output fall in China? Were fundamental mistakes made in the European model of change that could be avoided in future?

1.1 Eastern Europe and Russia

Six facts stand out about the European reform process, compared with the Chinese.

State Power Was Weak

The European reforms followed the collapse of Communist rule and the introduction of democracy. The new governments were both weak and determined, above all, to prevent the return of Communism. These facts largely explain what followed.

Table 1.1
Growth, inflation, and unemployment, 1989–96

	Change in GDP (%)		Change in prices (%)		Unemployment
	1989–96	1993–96	1989–96	1995–96	1996
Poland	4	23	16,270	55	13
Czech Republic	−9	12	212	19	3
Hungary	−13	5	479	59	11
Russia	−49	−25	508,010	321	9
China	108	54	118	22	3

Sources: GDP—EBRD, (1996); IMF, *World Economic Outlook* (Oct. 1996). Inflation rates—EBRD (1996); IMF, *World Economic Outlook* (Oct. 1996); OECD, *Economic Outlook* (Dec. 1996). Unemployment—OECD, *Economic Outlook* (Dec. 1996); ILO, *Yearbook of Labour Statistics* (1995).
Note: Unemployment rate for China is for 1994.

Price Liberalization Was Rapid

Most of the reform governments inherited budget deficits, and thus an excess of monetary demand over the value of output at current controlled prices. Queues were lengthening. Since governments lacked the authority to undertake a monetary reform and no longer had the power to control prices, they had little option but to free most prices within one or two years of taking power. This rapidly made the system of state orders inoperable, and both prices and quantities became basically determined by market forces. In addition, the reformers opened up foreign trade to market forces, and the system of state trading between the former Communist countries was largely abolished in 1991.

As a result, the opportunities facing enterprises changed at an incredible speed. Enterprises dependent on raw materials faced huge increases in the real cost of their inputs, and at the same time many found that the demand for their products had disappeared or shifted elsewhere to cheaper producers.

If capital and labor could have been redeployed rapidly, there would have been no reason for aggregate output to fall. But this redeployment cannot be done overnight. The formation of new relationships in conditions of uncertainty always takes time, in business as in private life. And when the participants are quite unused to writing contracts that determine the profits and survival of a business, the process takes even longer. As a result there is massive unused capacity during the adjustment process.

The speed of change has been greater where some commercial culture already existed. Thus the slowest adjustment has been in the former Soviet Union, which suffered seventy-five years of central planning and absence of markets, and fastest in Poland and China, where agriculture was always mainly private (except for shortish periods in China).[1] In Poland the new private sector has grown rapidly since 1990 and now accounts for 20 percent of national output, whereas in Russia new enterprises are struggling to get started and local governments fail to protect new market entrants and overregulate the local economy. In Russia the revulsion against state control was much less than it was in Eastern Europe, where Communism was associated with oppressive foreign domination.

Military Demand Fell Rapidly

If deregulation was rapid, so too was the change in the pattern of government expenditure. There was a major collapse in the government's demand for defense production. (This also resulted from the weakness of the state—taxes were more difficult to collect.) Under Communism the defense and space effort probably accounted for around 20 percent of GDP in the Soviet Union (and 5–10 percent in the rest of the Warsaw Pact nations). Today, throughout the former Communist world, the figure is below 5 percent. Such a huge adjustment could not fail to cause a substantial fall in total output, especially in Russia.

There Was a Macroeconomic Shift, Raising Unemployment

Another reason for the fall in output was the necessary change in the macroeconomic balance of the economy. In Russia and much of Eastern Europe, Communist policy had been to let the level of monetary demand exceed the maximum value of production at the controlled level of prices. This ensured that almost anything that was produced could be sold.

Prices were controlled by fiat. But once they were freed, prices naturally shot up. Controlling the resulting inflation required monetary restraint, but this restraint worked only by generating sufficient slack in labor and product markets to offset inflation inertia. As these countries moved to free markets, unemployment, originally negligible, rose to the "natural rate." This inevitably involved falls in output.

This process of adjustment happened much more gradually in China, which liberalized its markets step by step and at the same time developed substantial urban unemployment. Inflation was continuously restrained and never exploded as it had in Eastern Europe and Russia.

Inflation Was High

In China monetary policy has generally been quite restrictive and inflation has usually been single-digit. By contrast, in Eastern Europe and Russia there have been episodes of very high inflation. These stem from the weakness of the state. The government no longer had its former power to collect taxes, and this was truer in federal states like Russia than in smaller ones like the Czech Republic. At the same time the pressure for continued subsidies remained high, and when the Ministry of Finance refused to provide them, the pressure shifted to the Central Bank, which often obliged with cheap credits. The combination of budget deficits and cheap credits fueled inflation.

Some countries resisted these pressures better than others, especially those which received strong early support from the IMF, as Poland, Hungary, and Czechoslovakia did. In Russia, Gaidar consciously agreed to inflationary credits as the price of remaining in power and pushing on with privatization.

The resulting inflation has been a major factor delaying the recovery. In high inflation it is impossible to plan for the future. Private investment rates are low, and capital flies abroad. Everyone waits for the uncertainty to clear. In Russia, unlike China, high inflation and political uncertainty have been major factors retarding output growth. Yet, as the Vietnamese experience shows, the control of inflation need not itself have any serious short-run output effects.[2]

Privatization Was Rapid

By historical standards, privatization has been extraordinarily rapid throughout post-Communist Europe. Two motives have been at work. One, political, has been to create a large enough class of capitalists to prevent the reelection of a Communist government. Henry VIII of England prevented the return of Catholicism by selling off the monasteries, and today's reformers have prevented the return of Communism by selling off state enterprises. The second, economic, motive is of course the belief that private ownership is an essential condition for efficiency in the long run.

However, in the short run, privatization yields slow returns. Managers devote excessive energy to organizing the claims on future output, and too little to making sure that output is produced and markets are won. Sometimes key parts of an enterprise are hived off, leaving the total output from the existing capital lower than before. In the end reorganization may pay off, but in the short run, output falls.

Conclusion

Thus it is no longer difficult to understand why output performance has been so disappointing in Eastern Europe and Russia. Much of the reform policy has been driven by the weakness of the government and by the desire to preserve freedom through preventing a return of the Communists. But ideas have also played a role. Many Western economists, including myself, advocated rapid change—partly because we understood the weakness of the government and partly because we believed that it would be better to suffer considerable pain and disorder for a short time than to have less pain over a longer period. The argument was that the sum of present and future welfare would be higher if change was rapid and the new, less distorted economy was established as soon as possible.

Were we right? The evidence is not yet fully in. Certainly there has been substantial pain. Yet, on the best available evidence, rapid reform had no effect, positive or negative, on the extent of the fall in output between 1989 and 1995, though it speeded up the whole process, thus bringing forward the recovery.[3] If this analysis is right, then rapid reform increases the (discounted) value of the whole path of output. But we are still very close to the beginning of the reform. There have so far been few cases of strong and sustained recovery (except for Poland) and some challenging cases (like Uzbekistan) where reform has been slow but the output fall so far has been relatively small.[4] Certainly output has fallen everywhere, however fast or slow the reform. While the bulk of the evidence is favorable to the case for rapid reform, we cannot yet prove that, if politics had permitted, a more gradual evolution would have been a mistake.

1.2   China

Certainly the Chinese experience is prima facie an argument in favor of gradualism. However, there were three key differences in initial conditions between China after the death of Mao and Eastern Europe and Russia after 1990. Only one of these differences was political.

The Chinese State Remained Strong

There was no upsurge against the ruling elite and thus no breakdown of state power. Budgets were generally consistent with low inflation.

China Was Predominantly Rural and Desperately Poor

The poverty of China offered remarkable possibilities for catch-up, and thus high economic growth, provided the economic framework was right. In some ways China in 1978 was like Europe in 1947—far behind the technological frontier and with a large reserve of excess labor in agriculture, ready for redeployment in the more productive industrial sector (especially the township and village enterprises). In this respect China was not unlike Korea and Taiwan in 1960. It could grow by huge transfers of people out of unproductive agriculture into the growing industrial sector, and industrial growth did not therefore depend, as it did in Eastern Europe and Russia, on redeployment of people within the urban economy. Growth was possible even though the state enterprises continued to receive uneconomic subsidies—because the state enterprise sector was small enough not to bankrupt the rest of the economy.[5]

Thus post-Mao China grew, just as did the non-Communist Far East. But this was by no means automatic: North Korea stagnated. So there really is something remarkable to be explained—that China grew even though its nonfarm economy was largely owned by governmental bodies. The clue to this was the high degree of decentralization of state structures.

The Chinese Economy Was Highly Decentralized

China's sensational economic growth since 1978 has come from five main areas.

1. *Agriculture.* Agriculture had been recollectivized in 1966 and was reprivatized in 1978. This therapy, which also involved free prices for a substantial share of output, was more drastic than anything yet applied to agriculture in Russia and Central Europe (outside Poland), and had immediate and spectacular effects. Like many of China's recent reforms, it began on an experimental basis in some areas and was then studied at the national level and recommended to the rest of the country.

2. *Township and village enterprises (TVEs).* These small-scale enterprises were set up by municipal governments on their own initiative. The ability

of local municipalities to father these enterprises reflects the strong decentralization brought about by the Great Leap Forward (1958–60) and the Cultural Revolution (1966–77). Even so, no one has fully explained the success of this sector, where corporate governance conforms to none of the models normally recommended in the West.

In some ways the Great Leap Forward and the Cultural Revolution were equivalent to the recent economic reform in Eastern Europe. They dismantled many of the bureaucratic controls and in the process caused considerable initial losses of output. But the decision-making framework that emerged was conducive to high subsequent growth—as it will eventually turn out to have been in Eastern Europe.

3. *State-owned enterprises.* Even in the state-owned enterprises in China, productivity and output have grown. This is a challenging difference between the Chinese and East European experiences. One reason may be that many of the state-owned enterprises are under the control of county, rather than provincial or central, governments. Probably more important, the scope for catch-up is greater—akin to that in Russia in 1960s. And the rest of the economy is growing.

4. *The new private sector.* By now the new private sector in towns is producing around 30 percent of the country's national output. This reflects an environment for new business that is in many ways easier (in terms of regulation) than in Russia or even Eastern Europe. Industrialized towns and cities vie with each other to create a more favorable business climate. Private business also benefits from the rapid growth of rural incomes.

5. *Foreign trade.* A final area is foreign trade. China exports 23 percent of its national output, an exceptionally high figure for such a large country with few natural resources. Due to an open trading policy (including special economic zones with tax breaks for foreigners[6]), the trade sector has grown extremely fast, leading to substantial input of foreign capital and know-how, often financed by overseas Chinese.

Thus there is no fundamental mystery about why China has grown so rapidly. It has pursued many of the policies recommended by economic liberals, and has grown like the rest of the Far East. The main difference regards TVEs and state-owned industrial enterprises. The latter have not been hit by sudden cuts in defense orders or in subsidies, and have therefore shared in the general growth.

1.3 The Book

Against this background, the members of the Emerging Markets Programme at the Centre for Economic Performance decided to set down what they believed they knew about the causes and consequences of the economic reforms followed in Eastern Europe, Russia, and China. The next five chapters are about Eastern Europe and Russia, and the last two about China.

Output

Gomulka reviews the various explanations that have been proposed for the output drop in Eastern Europe and Russia—some sensible arguments (already mentioned) and others less sensible. He goes on to discuss the conditions for recovery, stressing the importance of the de novo private sector and of sufficient domestic savings to finance adequate investment.

Inflation

One source of low output, and certainly of hardship, has been high inflation. What caused this? Boone and Hørder begin by asking why there were very different jumps in prices at the time of liberalization, from around 30 percent in Czechoslovakia to 250 percent in Russia. This range reflected the degree to which the public had lost confidence in money and was expecting further subsequent inflation. In most cases these expectations of further inflation proved well founded.

In general the rate of subsequent money creation was driven by the power of different interest groups—and not to any major degree by programs of social support. For example, in Russia the enterprise lobby was very powerful, and in 1992–93 extracted nearly 30 percent of GDP in credits from the government. In consequence, enterprises paid an inflation tax on their existing money holdings, but since they held only half the money stock, their net gain was nearly 15 percent of GDP. The household sector, and in particular pensioners, lost an equivalent amount.

So why did the great inflation come to an end? One reason was that inflation so increased velocity and reduced the holdings of real money that the level of inflation needed to generate a given transfer to industry rose and rose. Industry decided it was not worth the candle. Another reason was improved understanding of the inflation process.

How can further inflation be prevented? Many institutional arrangements can help, such as conditional IMF aid, constitutional budget processes, and, where appropriate, "poison pills," as when a currency board is put in place.

Privatization and Restructuring

While inflation has to be controlled in any economy, the more fundamental elements in economic transition are the establishment of free markets and the establishment of private ownership. Estrin examines the extent to which private ownership has so far contributed to improved performance.

There are, of course, two ways in which private ownership can develop: through the privatization of state enterprises as going concerns, and through the establishment of new privately owned firms (using newly created and older assets). And among privatized companies many patterns of ownership can develop, depending on the form of privatization that is adopted. Thus owners can be predominantly workers, managers, or outsiders. Most theories of corporate governance predict superior performance from companies where ownership is concentrated in few hands, thus short-circuiting the free rider problem. Thus it might be expected that privatized companies do best if ownership is concentrated in the hands of managers or of outsiders owning substantial blocks of shares.

Estrin attempts to test the impact of ownership patterns on enterprise performance. He shows that newly founded private firms do best of all. But so far no one type of privatization can be shown to have done better or to have restructured faster than any other. Only time will tell.

Banking Reform and Privatization

As economic reform proceeds, it becomes clear that some enterprises are in trouble. If the enterprises have substantial debts to banks, the banks too are in trouble—due to the non-performing loans. A major banking crisis looms. This was a threat in most of Eastern Europe, though not in Russia, where high inflation wiped out much of the debt.

Van Wijnbergen addresses the question of how the bad loans should be handled—or, more broadly, the role of the banks in the process of restructuring. The sharpest contrast is between the approaches adopted in the Czech Republic and in Poland. In the Czech Republic, the government took over the bad loans, replacing them on the banks' balance sheets by well-performing government debt. A public agency was then set up to try and collect the bad debts. The problem with this approach is that the agency's officials have inadequate incentive to recover the loans and to force the firms to restructure.

By contrast, in Poland the banks were left with their bad debts—which gave them a strong incentive to force restructuring in order to recover their money. Meantime, the banking crisis was averted by a once-for-all recapitalizing of the banks. This worked well and provides important lessons for other countries.

Unemployment and Restructuring

A major consequence of economic reform has been unemployment, a condition largely unknown under Communism in Europe. A key question is to what extent high unemployment is necessary to the process of restructuring. According to Jackman, it is not.

As he shows, the key change that all these economies have to make is a shift from manufacturing into trade, finance, and other services. The speed at which this is occurring and new jobs are being created in the new sectors is independent of the level of unemployment. This is perhaps not surprising because the new jobs are usually filled by people who are still working rather than by the unemployed.

Thus unemployment is explained by much the same factors that explain unemployment in nontransition countries. A country like Poland, which has open-ended unemployment benefits, has high unemployment, while a country like the Czech Republic, which has short-duration benefits and active policies to help the unemployed, has low unemployment.

Why China Grew

When we turn to China, everything is different. There is a long sequence of reforms from 1978 to the present. And there is steady growth. Does this show that gradualism is best? Wing Thye Woo argues that it does not.

In his comprehensive account, growth occurs for all the reasons given earlier in this chapter. One key factor is that the government never lost control. Thus inflation remained low. This in turn encouraged higher savings and a strong confidence in the future.

Thus, when the production function approach is used to account for the sources of growth, over half the growth is due to capital accumulation.

Another key factor is the reallocation of labor out of low productivity agriculture. Total factor productivity growth, though positive, is not particularly large—though exact measurement is difficult when so much of technological change is embedded in new capital.

A key issue is the role of the state-owned enterprises, which employ 18 percent of the workforce—the same as in 1978. Unlike state enterprises in Eastern Europe, their output grew. Why is this?

The state-owned enterprises have been given increased autonomy, but their rates of profit have declined. In consequence they have received increasing subsidies, which are a growing drain on the budget.

Xu and Zhuang argue that there are further reasons for the relative success of state-owned enterprises in China. Their average size is smaller than in Europe, and they are controlled by more localized political structures than was typical in European Communism. Thus, in China total factor productivity growth was negative in centrally owned state enterprises but was positive in those under local control.

However, the main growth of industrial production came from the new private sector and the TVEs. Though their pattern of ownership is ill-defined, this did not limit their ability to motivate both managers and workers—given the relatively disciplined framework of society. Thus a clear key to China's success has been decentralization of public and collective enterprises, linked to an economy that is in many ways as capitalist as the newly capitalist countries of Eastern and Central Europe.

2 Output: Causes of the Decline and the Recovery

Stanislaw Gomulka

2.1 Introduction

In the 1990s the percentage falls in total officially measured output in most transition economies of Central Europe (CE) and the Former Soviet Union (FSU) have been the largest anywhere in modern peacetime history —greater even than the falls that developed economies experienced during the Great Depression of the 1930s. The falls are much smaller, though still formidable, after reasonable corrections to the official data are introduced. This phenomenon is interesting theoretically, and important socially, primarily because of its magnitude, but also because it was largely unexpected. Moreover, these output falls took place against the background of rapid growth in China and Vietnam, which had begun fundamental changes of their economic systems earlier, in a gradual manner, and whose experiences contributed, in the 1980s, to expectations of immediate improvements from the more radical reforms in CE.

These contrasting experiences have given rise to a fierce debate between proponents of two rival hypotheses, one emphasizing the impact of inherited initial conditions on output decline and the other giving more weight to the deliberate choice of reform policies during transition itself.

Differences in initial conditions are a natural candidate for explaining the wide intercountry variation in output performance during transition because, in fact, the economic, institutional, and political conditions did vary strongly among the countries concerned at the start of transition. This variation was caused partly by differences in the level of development, as reflected by the GDP per capita and the sectoral compositions of output and employment (table 2.1). Differences in institutional and political factors were also large—first and foremost the sudden fall of Communist regimes in CE and the FSU, but not in China and Vietnam. This fall led to the almost immediate collapse of the Council for Mutual Economic

Table 2.1
China and Russia: Level of GDP per capita and composition of employment during transition

	China			Russia	
	1978	1985	1994	1990	1994
GDP per capita at PPP ($)	1000	1600	2510	6960	5260
As proportion of U.S. level (%)	5.3	7.8	10.8	31.5	22.6
Employment share (%)					
Agriculture	71	62	58	13	15
Industry	15	17	18	42	38
Services	14	21	25	45	47
State sector	19	19	18	90	44

Sources: World Bank and IMF databases and World Bank staff.

Assistance (CMEA), the Warsaw Pact, and the USSR itself at the outset of transition, which in turn had a powerful influence on trade flows and arms production, as well as on the speed and the content of transition reforms.

A radical transition reform may be viewed as a large block of innovations. Any innovation represents a Schumpeterian creative destruction phenomenon: a costly disruption to the existing economic arrangement in the short run but, usually, a beneficial spurt of efficiency and growth in the long run. Many of the reform measures were forced by initial conditions, but some were a matter of choice. Hence it makes sense to ask whether all the decline in output has been inevitable. The answer to this question by the proponents of the second hypothesis is often phrased in terms of microliberalization reforms having been either too fast or too slow, and macrostabilization policies having been either excessively tight or excessively loose. This line of inquiry has, however, failed to provide a method of deciding which policies were forced by initial conditions and which were discretionary. Nor has it offered a convincing solution to the extremely complex problem of disentangling the direct and indirect effects on output of identifiable supply and demand shocks (Gomulka 1991; Borensztein et al. 1993; Kornai 1994; Rosati 1994; Berg 1995; Williamson 1995; Blanchard 1997).

In this chapter I shall argue that, on present evidence, the large output falls and the high speed of transition in CE and the FSU were related to each other, but each was caused mainly by a unique set of initial, inherited conditions: the large accumulation of deep structural problems under the earlier system, especially in the industrial sector, and the sudden collapse of the USSR, the Warsaw Pact, and the CMEA at about the same time. As Balcerowicz (1995) has argued, in these circumstances the strong radicalism of liberalization policy measures and institutional reforms ought to have been, and largely was, commensurate with the extreme gravity of the economic crisis. Moreover, the evidence suggests that the speed of macroeconomic stabilization had a significant effect on the time profile of decline and recovery during transition, but had little impact upon the magnitude of the cumulative fall of output. In particular, virtually the only effect of a restrictive (loose) macroeconomic policy was to hasten (delay) the fall in output and the start of recovery (Gomulka 1994; Kornai 1994; Aslund et al. 1996).

Kornai (1994) proposed the term "transformational recession" to indicate that the large falls of output during the initial period of transition were directly related to the change of economic system rather than to transition policies. The evidence and the arguments presented in this chapter confirm this broad evaluation, but with an important modification intended to differentiate the countries of CE and the FSU from China and Vietnam—namely, that the falls were related not merely to the change of economic system but also to the speed of that change, and that this speed in the countries of CE and the FSU was in turn related to the initial conditions of much deeper (economic and political) crisis. The four major specific causes were (1) sharp changes in relative prices (in response to price and trade liberalization, changes of taxes and subsidies, changes in terms of international trade, and border charges); (2) the elimination of excessive real aggregate demand to establish buyers' markets; (3) the collapse of captive markets within the former CMEA area; and (4) the collapse of the arms industry and of state-financed investments in housing, energy, agriculture, and infrastructure. This explanation of output falls is reinforced by our critical review of eight other potential causes suggested in the literature of the subject and by downgrading them to minor importance.

This chapter is also concerned with the issues of recovery and long-term growth. From the evidence to date, it would appear that the single most important factor underlying the considerable variation in the pace of recovery, in those countries of CE and the FSU that had begun to experience it by 1996, has been, on the supply side, the initial size and the subsequent growth of the proper private sector, as distinct from the privatized one, typically involving new domestic entrepreneurs and foreign investors. The speed of trade and price liberalization, and the extent and the quality of privatization of typically medium and large state enterprises, were also important (Pohl et al. 1997; chp. 4, this book). Since both recovery and growth have progressed most in Poland, the chapter provides a discussion of the "Polish model of transformation."

In transition economies (other than China and Vietnam, where there is still an exceptionally large pool of underutilized labor in agriculture), an early recession is helpful to recovery and growth, since it releases some of the poorly utilized physical and human capital of the initially dominant state sector for reallocation, and this assists both the growth of the initially small de novo private sector and the general restructuring of the (former) state sector.

In section 2.2 we review the stylized facts. Section 2.3 discusses the special case of Poland, and sections 2.4–2.6 review the various interpretations of the decline in output in the FSU and CE. Section 2.7 discusses two models of the postreform recovery. Section 2.8 takes up the factors that influence long-term growth and, therefore, the prospect for transition economies to catch up to the world's most developed economies. Section 2.9 sums up and draws conclusions.

2.2 Stylized Facts

The explanations offered in this chapter are clearly dependent on my understanding of what the basic facts are. Despite the poor quality of the data relating to outputs in transition economies, it is useful to present what may be called nine "stylized facts." The aim is to separate the discussion concerning "facts" from that concerning "explanations."

1. The variation in officially measured GDP falls from the prereform top levels to the lowest levels during transition has been large, ranging from moderately high for Poland (15 percent), Hungary (18 percent), and the Czech Republic (21 percent), to very high for Russia (40 percent), the Baltic Republics (55 percent), and Ukraine (60 percent), and extremely high for the Trans-Caucasian Republics (75 percent) (see figure 2.1 and table 2.2). Correcting the official data for underreported activities and methodological errors (holding gains due to inflation ignored or not eliminated fully, undercoverage, inadequate account of improved quality and availability) reduces these falls: in Poland, to about 7 percent compared with the level in 1989 (Czyzewski et al. 1995), and to about 10–12 percent if 1988 is taken as the base year (Rajewski 1993; Czyzewski et al. 1995); to 15–25 percent in CE outside Poland; to 25–35 percent in Russia (Koen 1996; World Bank and Goskomstat 1995); and to perhaps 30–40 percent in the FSU outside Russia.

2. The maximum falls in the volume of officially measured gross industrial output have been greater than in total GDP: about 40–50 percent in

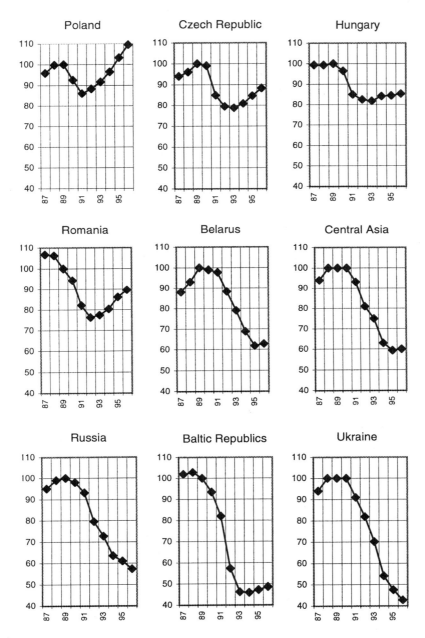

Figure 2.1
Measured GDP in transition economies, 1987–1996 (1989 = 100)
Source: Table 2.2.

Table 2.2
Real GDP in selected countries and regions (1989 = 100)

	87	88	89	90	91	92	93	94	95	96
Poland	95.9	99.8	100.0	92.6	86.1	88.3	91.7	96.5	103.2	109.4
Czech Republic	94.1	96.0	100.0	99.0	85.0	79.5	78.8	80.9	84.8	88.4
Hungary	99.4	99.3	100.0	96.5	85.0	82.5	81.8	84.2	84.5	85.4
Romania	106.7	106.2	100.0	94.3	82.2	76.2	77.4	80.4	86.1	89.6
Belarus	88.1	93.1	100.0	99.0	97.8	88.4	79.0	68.8	61.8	62.8
Central Asia	94.0	100.0	100.0	100.0	93.2	81.0	75.0	62.9	59.3	60.0
Russia	95.1	99.0	100.0	98.0	93.1	79.6	72.7	63.5	61.1	57.4
Baltic Republics	101.9	102.8	100.0	93.5	82.1	57.3	46.3	46.0	47.2	48.6
Ukraine	94.0	100.0	100.0	100.0	91.0	81.9	70.2	54.1	47.6	42.8

Sources: 1987–95, Central Statistical Office, Warsaw, *Quarterly of International Statistics 4* (3–4) (May 1996); 1996, IMF, *World Economic Outlook* (May 1997).

CE and 50–60 percent in the FSU. The official statistics for gross industrial output are probably more reliable than those for GDP. However, some industrial output before transition would be contributing little positive value added at new prices, so the falls in value added probably have been smaller than those in gross output.

3. Falls in investment expenditures, especially in inventories and housing, have been greater than falls in GDP. Defense expenditures on equipment and materials also have declined sharply as a proportion of GDP, especially in the FSU. Consequently, during the period of falling output, private consumption has, in most transition economies, declined only moderately. The overall standard of living has declined even less, because of the elimination of shortages (Roberts 1995), but it has declined sharply for some people and increased sharply for others.

4. The patterns of recession and recovery have been, in the years 1989–95, largely of the L-curve type (sharp falls followed by slow recovery) rather than of the initially hoped-for J-curve type (small falls followed by fast growth). The notable exception—apart from the obviously special case of East Germany—is Poland, where recovery started earliest and has been sharpest.

5. In Polish industry the initial falls were almost uniformly large in nearly all sectors. However, in terms of individual products, product groups, and enterprises, the variation in output changes has been extraordinarily large (figure 2.2). This points to changes in microeconomic circumstances having played the principal role in output falls.

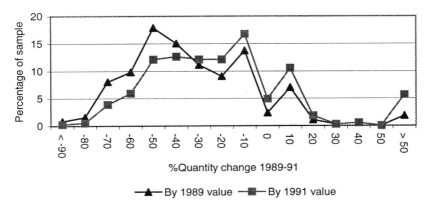

Figure 2.2
Extraordinary dispersion of output change in Poland 1989–1991 at the product level: 590
industrial product groups
Source: Mark Schaffer, personal communication.

6. Transformational recessions differ from recessions experienced by market economies in that, in a cross-country comparison, larger output falls during transition were associated with higher rather than lower inflation. This points to a limited role in output falls of stabilization-oriented policies, and to an important role of (supply-side and demand-side) shocks that induced both large output falls and high inflation rates.

7. Transformational recessions also differ from standard ones in that the falls in investment/GDP ratios, while considerable, have typically been smaller than is usually the case in market economies. These recessions are therefore "investment-led" to a lesser extent (Rostowski 1997). This also indicates that their origins are mainly structural, the result of microeconomic factors rather than macroeconomic policies.

8. Structural changes during both recession and recovery have been deep and in the desired direction: from arms, government services, energy, and heavy industries to financial services, trade, information-processing, and manufactured consumer goods. However, the pace and sustainability of overall recovery are still, and will continue to be, strongly dependent upon recovery in manufacturing.

9. The sectoral composition of GDP in current prices changes during transition in favor of services and away from manufacturing. To a great extent this is due to the relatively larger contractions of manufacturing during recessions, but it is also partly due to faster productivity gains in

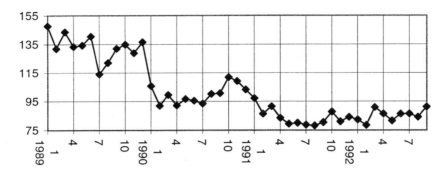

Figure 2.3
Poland's industrial output during the contraction phase (average monthly output in 1990 = 100)
Source: Central Statistical Office, Informacja I-III Quarters, Warsaw, 22 October 1992.

the manufacturing sector, and therefore declining relative prices of manufacturing products, during recoveries.

2.3   The Instructive Case of Poland

The four major events that precipitated large output falls were (1) rapid price and foreign trade liberalization, (2) the collapse of the CMEA and the dollarization of trade within the former CMEA area, (3) the breakups of the Soviet Union, Yugoslavia, and Czechoslovakia, and (4) the dissolution of the Warsaw Pact with the consequent large fall of defense spending, especially in the FSU. In most transition economies these four groups of events took place more or less simultaneously, making it extremely difficult to separate out their individual impacts on output. The exception is Poland, where there was a year's gap between the first two events and where the last two had only a minor impact.

It will be seen from figure 2.3 that, in addition to a gradual fall during 1989, there were two distinct and sharp falls in the volume of industrial output, measured by sales in constant prices, at the beginning of 1990 and 1991. The first fall, by close to 30 percent, occurred within just a few weeks of the Big Bang of January 2, 1990. This was clearly linked to the price liberalization measures and corrective price increases, coupled with the removal of subsidies and tight macroeconomic policies. The measures reduced almost instantly, and by a large magnitude, the purchasing power of wages and other income as well as real accumulated savings. Real aggregate demand fell sharply. On the supply side, the price revolution of

Table 2.3
Changes in Polish industrial output by cause (percent of total output of previous year)

Factor	1990	1991
Stabilization	−9.6	7.4
CMEA collapse		
Direct	−1.4	−2.2
Indirect	−1.2	−1.8
Structural	−20.0	−5.8
Non-CMEA trade	+8.0	−5.6
Total effect	−24.2	−8.0

Source: Czyzewski et al. 1995.

January 2, 1990, turned many activities—again virtually overnight—into loss makers if their goods were to sell at market-clearing prices, or producers of unwanted goods if priced at unit costs. Under the old regime of controlled prices, large subsidies and widespread forced substitution had sustained the production of such goods, which, under the new economic regime, had to be discontinued rapidly.

The second fall, also by 30 percent, was spread over a few months of 1991 and reflected a profound collapse of exports to the former CMEA area as well as sharp terms-of-trade losses following dollarization of the remaining trade with the FSU. Between the two falls, there was a considerable recovery in industrial sales, by about 20 percent, which must be linked to a substantial easing of macroeconomic policies and a sharp increase in real incomes in the second half of 1990. The recession reached a trough in the period May–September 1991, with industrial sales (and output itself) equal to 60 percent of the average level in 1989.

Macroeconomic policy (especially fiscal policy) was probably excessively tight in the first half of 1990 and excessively loose in the second half. Taking this into account, the liberalization and stabilization components of the Big Bang would account, table 2.3 suggests, for about 25 percentage points of the 40 percent cumulative fall, and the collapse of the CMEA trade for the remaining 15 points.

To estimate the separate effects of stabilization, price liberalization, and the CMEA collapse on industrial output more accurately, three Polish experts on national accounting proposed a new method (Czyzewski et al. 1995). Applying it, they produced the estimates in table 2.3.

Such estimates may be strongly dependent on the degree of aggregation (32 industrial branches were used in this particular exercise). Their authors nevertheless dismiss stabilization as a major cause of the fall and

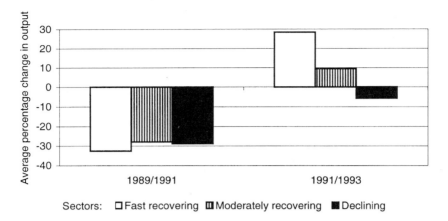

Figure 2.4
Polish industry's output: uniform falls (1990–1991) and non-uniform recoveries (1992–1993)
at the sectoral level
Source: Zukowski 1996.
Notes: *Fast* recovering sectors are defined by Zukowski (1996) as those in which the increase
in output exceeded the industrial average increase of 11.5 percent, by a factor of at least 1.5,
in the period 1991–1993. These included metal products, precision instruments and apparatus, transport equipment, electrical engineering and electronics, chemicals, wood products,
weaving, and apparel printing. *Moderately* recovering sectors are those in which the increase
in output exceeded the industrial average of 11.5 percent by a factor of between 0.5 and 1.5.
They comprised fuels; building materials; glass products; pottery, china, and earthenware;
paper; textiles; and food processing. *Declining* sectors comprised coal-mining, power, iron
and steel, nonferrous metals, machine-building, and leather.

attribute some 80 percent of the total fall to structural changes, associated
mainly with changes in relative prices, and to the aggregate effect of the
price liberalization, and about 20 percent of the fall to the collapse of the
CMEA.

The falls were fairly uniform at the level of sectors (figure 2.4) but, as
noted in section 2.2 (figure 2.2) extremely diverse at the disaggregated
level of product groups. This diversity points to the crucial role played in
output falls by changes in relative prices and shifts in supply and demand
functions. Figure 2.5 shows that, indeed, outputs declined (recovered)
most in sectors where relative prices increased (declined) most.

2.4   The Aggregate and Structural Effects of Price Liberalization

An immediate fall of output in response to a radical price liberalization is
probably the most striking feature of the "transformational recession."
There are two aspects of the phenomenon: aggregate and structural.

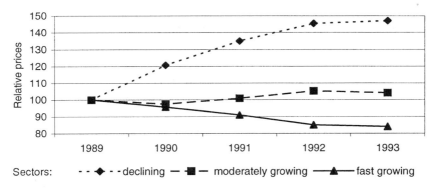

Figure 2.5
Polish industry: the negative relationship between changes in output and in relative prices
(1989 = 100)
Source: Zukowski 1996.
Notes: *Fast* growing sectors are defined by Zukowski (1996) as those in which the increase in
output exceeded the industrial average increase of 11.5 percent, by a factor of at least 1.5, in
the period 1991–1993. These included metal products, precision instruments and apparatus,
transport equipment, electrical engineering and electronics, chemicals, wood products, weaving, and apparel printing. *Moderately* growing sectors are those in which the increase in output exceeded the industrial average of 11.5 percent by a factor of between 0.5 and 1.5. They
comprised fuels; building materials; glass products; pottery, china, and earthenware; paper;
textiles; and food processing. *Declining* sectors comprised coal-mining, power, iron and steel,
nonferrous metals, machine-building, and leather.

The aggregate aspect of price liberalization lies in the elimination of
excessive real aggregate demand. Under the earlier regime of widely controlled prices, real incomes and real aggregate demand were kept artificially high. Outputs were then constrained by resources, not demands.
Even initially unwanted goods would eventually be sold as substitutes for
desired goods that were in short supply (so-called forced substitution).
With these initial conditions a sudden price liberalization results in prices
increasing faster than nominal incomes for a while, so that real purchasing
power declines. This decline was necessary in all transition economies in
order to transform sellers' markets into buyers' markets. This systemic
change was aimed at eliminating both shortages and forced substitution,
and at enhancing competition between suppliers. These were essential
goals to achieve if markets were to take over the role of the main coordination mechanism from the planners.

In a market economy some unemployment of labor (and other resources) is necessary to enable it to respond flexibly to changes in
demands and supplies under conditions of limited mobility of resources.
This open unemployment of inputs is the cost societies pay for the benefit

of wide choice in free markets at low inflation. The rate of that structural or natural unemployment may vary between countries and over time, but it is certainly much higher than the near-zero rate that characterized centrally planned economies. It is this immediate and necessary fall in the rate of employment of resources, by anything in a range of (say) from 5 to 10 percent, together with the corresponding fall in output, that we may call the *aggregate effect of price liberalization*.

The *structural effect of price liberalization*, on the other hand, is related to the negative impact on outputs of sharp changes in relative prices. These changes occur as a result of reducing or eliminating product-specific subsidies, reducing the (initially extremely large) variation in rates of turnover taxes, increasing (typically by a large factor) relative energy prices and interest rates, and introducing a uniform exchange rate together with a usually large devaluation. These changes were typically introduced as a package and implemented over a relatively short period of time, sometimes on a single day. As a result, almost immediately, households had to spend relatively more on essentials, such as food, energy, transportation, and housing, and were therefore forced to economize on clothing, footwear, household appliances, leisure, and culture.

Supply-side shocks are those that involve, as a result of changes in input prices and tax (subsidy) rates, significant shifts in supply functions for specific products. These shocks typically lead to changes in the quantities demanded, but these latter changes originate on the supply side and should not be confused with those caused by falls in real aggregate demand. Demand functions for products may also undergo shifts, due to changes in tastes, real incomes, and real wealth (e.g., real accumulated savings). The results of such shifts are new equilibrium prices and quantities. However, there is typically an asymmetry in the speed of adjustment of these prices and quantities to equilibrium magnitudes: instant adjustment of prices and demands and slow adjustment of supplies. Elsewhere I phrased it thus: "The new relative prices required that a corresponding change in the whole product composition of the economy's supply side took place. But because of the presence of various rigidities, some resources had to become unemployed before they could be redeployed to produce what, with new prices, is in demand and is profitable" (Gomulka 1992). In other words, a radical price liberalization may be viewed as a reform that imposes on the economy, within a short period of time, a large block of "innovations" causing, as any innovations do, the Schumpeterian phenomenon of "creative destruction": declines in most outputs in the short run and increases in the long run.

The recessionary impact of price liberalization would be reduced if relative wages could be adjusted at a stroke to compensate partly or fully for changes in nonwage costs and taxes/subsidies, so that relative prices change less or remain unchanged at prereform levels. However, this compensation would require that wages became product-specific, even within the same enterprise for the same category of workers. For this to be sustained, a complete failure of labor markets to arbitrage would be needed. It would in any case be economically inefficient and socially impossible (wages in many situations would have to be negative or near zero) to maintain wage differences of this kind for any prolonged period of time.

For nations the speed of price liberalization is a choice variable. In China this liberalization has been introduced gradually, over some 15 years, rather than in the course of a few days or months. A gradual liberalization releases resources at a rate slow enough for most of them to be reemployed elsewhere almost immediately. However, for the more developed transition economies a fairly rapid reallocation of labor and other resources may still have been the better social choice. Without an early shake-up to release resources, it would have been impossible for the de novo private sector to develop as quickly as it did. In contrast, in China and Vietnam there existed, and still exists, a large pool of underemployed labor in agriculture that can provide workers for employment in the nonstate sector. The speed of early adjustment in prices and outputs is thus related also to initial conditions of this kind, with consequences for the subsequent rate of recovery, and even for long-term growth.

The much more rapid pace of price liberalization in the more developed socialist countries was, however, prompted less by such long-term considerations than by the powerful influences of other initial conditions: the double collapse of central planning and the Communist power, the presence of large (macro and micro) imbalances, and the apparent expectations of national electorates that strong policy measures could and should be implemented by new governments to remove shortages. These initial conditions were quite different in China and Vietnam. Thus both short-term and long-term considerations favored the choice of gradual price liberalizations in those two countries, but rapid liberalizations in the former socialist countries of CE and the FSU.

2.5 The Knock-on Effects

Reduction and sometimes elimination of the production of goods that, given their higher relative prices and lower real incomes, were no longer required in the original quantities or were unprofitable have had knock-on effects on demands for wanted and profitable goods. These effects arise because of limited mobility of capital and labor. For example, the elimination of subsidies to agricultural machinery and fertilizers led instantly to large price increases and a near collapse of demands for these farm inputs. Their manufacturers responded by reducing employment and the real wages of their workers and by purchasing less inputs from suppliers. The suppliers were usually unable to export their (now surplus) products, and they could not immediately invent and produce alternative goods for domestic or export markets. Therefore, they too reduced employment and the real wages of their workers. This chain reduction of outputs and purchasing power led, in turn, to the reduction of demands for consumer goods that were genuinely wanted. The only exceptions to this rule were cases when the relative prices of the needed goods declined substantially, so that the substitution effect dominated over the income effect; when the goods concerned were essential, so that the fall in real income did not matter; or when the goods were attractive enough to be salable at a profit to foreigners.

The above argument still holds good, even with the modification that the lost subsidies are returned to households and firms in the form of reduced taxes. The reason is that these tax reductions would not significantly affect the demands for the agricultural inputs mentioned above or, for that matter, for any goods that were exposed to the original price shocks. Therefore, the negative original output falls and their knock-on effects still occur. The same argument applies in discussing the output implications of reduced government spending (e.g., on defense goods) coupled with reduced taxes. The asymmetry here is the same as before: the negative output effect of reduced spending is heavily concentrated on specific products while the positive output effect of reduced taxes is widely dispersed. Therefore, the demands for these specific products fall, and hence most of the resources of labor, capital, and intermediate inputs locked in their production become temporarily unemployed. Crucial in the argument is, thus, the assumption that mobility of resources between products is small in the short term.

That price shocks are capable of causing output falls under limited mobility of resources has been demonstrated theoretically. Gomulka and Lane (1997) present a model of developments in a two-product economy in which relative prices change as a result of an exogenous increase in the price of an imported input. It shows that the result is an immediate decline of both outputs and that the decline may be by the same proportion. Similar results have been obtained by Blanchard (1997).

Table 2.4
Shares of industrial value added in GDP shares of, and of CMEA exports in, NMP, 1988; shares of inter-FSU trade in GNP, 1990; and index of lowest real GDP

Country	Shares in NMP			Index of lowest GDP (start of transition = 100)	
	Industry	CMEA exports	Inter-FSU trade	1995	1996*
Bulgaria	48	40	0	73	70
Czechoslovakia	50	21	0	78	78
Hungary	29	20	0	80	80
Poland	40	10	0	86	86
Romania	49	10	0	72	72
Russia	39	6	11	72	70
Ukraine	43	6	24	60	56
Kazakhstan	36	6	21	65	65
Lithuania	45	6	41	43	43
Latvia	38	6	37	55	55
Estonia	35	6	30	68	68

Sources: Shares in NMP of industry and CMEA exports—P. Marer et al., *Historically Planned Economies* (Washington, DC: World Bank, 1992); shares in GNP of trade within FSU—D. Michalopoulos and D. Tarr, *Trade in the New Independent States* (Washington, DC: World Bank, 1994); index of lowest real GDP—de Melo and Gelb (1996); shares of industrial value added in GDP in the CIS and Baltic states—*Economic Survey of Europe in 1995–1996* (New York and Geneva: United Nations, 1996), 61.
* Takes account of the estimates of GDP changes in 1996 (EBRD 1996).
Notes: Industrial shares for countries of the FSU are for 1991. Industrial value added, exports, gross domestic product (GDP), and net material product (NMP) are in current prices. The FSU export share, 6 percent, is assumed to apply for all former Soviet republics. For inter-FSU trade, the averages of export and imports are used. To translate the share of industry in NMP to one in GDP for the five CE countries, it was assumed that GDP = 1.2 NMP.

The greatest concentration of unwanted, no longer wanted, unprofitable, or no longer profitable goods was in industry. It is therefore not surprising that falls in industrial output have been larger than those of GDP. In that sector the knock-on effects probably also have been large, especially in the countries that suffered most from the collapse of regional export markets.

We can perform a simple test of this hypothesis, based on data in table 2.4. The results are the following (t-ratios in parentheses):

$$Y^{min} = 103.4 - 0.54 \text{ IN} - 0.17 \text{ CMEA} - 0.78 \text{ FSU} + \text{error term} \qquad (2.1)$$
$$\phantom{Y^{min} = } (9.2) \quad (2.0) \qquad (0.84) \qquad\qquad (6.0)$$

Observations = 11, $R^2 = 0.87$, SE = 5.3,

Table 2.5
Lowest GDP: Actual and "predicted" by equation (2.1)

	Actual	Predicted	Residual
Bulgaria	70	70.7	−0.7
Czechoslovakia	78	72.9	5.1
Hungary	80	84.4	−4.4
Poland	86	80.2	5.8
Romania	72	75.3	−3.3
Russia	70	72.8	−2.8
Ukraine	56	60.5	−4.5
Kazakhstan	65	66.6	−1.6
Lithuania	43	46.2	−3.2
Latvia	55	53.1	1.9
Estonia	68	60.2	7.8

where Y^{min} is the index of lowest GDP during transition until and including 1996 (100 is the GDP at the start of transition), IN stands for the share of industrial value added in net material product (NMP) before the start of transition, CMEA denotes the share in NMP of CMEA exports in 1988, and FSU stands for the average of intra-FSU imports and exports as a percentage of GNP in 1990 for a particular country. This test confirms that GDP falls were larger in the countries that, at the start of transition, had a larger industrial sector and traded more within the FSU (see also table 2.5). The size of intra-FSU trade turns out to be especially significant. This variable may well be the main reason why the fall of output in Russia has been lower than in most other former republics of the FSU.

Equation (2.1) is only a rough indicator of the true impact of these three variables. Detailed analysis of the losses caused by the collapse of the CMEA trade has produced more precise estimates. In particular, Rosati found the losses to be in the range of 3–4 percent of GDP for Poland and the former Czechoslovakia, 6 percent for Hungary, and 13 percent for Bulgaria (Rosati 1994, 1995). Similar results were reported earlier by Rodrik (1992).

2.6 The "Other Explanations" of Output Falls

The thesis that in CE and the FSU the four principal common causes of output declines in the early phase of transition were (1) radical price and foreign trade liberalizations, (2) the elimination of excessive aggregate demand, (3) the collapse of captive markets within the CMEA area, and (4) the near collapse of selected state purchases (i.e., arms, energy, housing, infrastructure) can be challenged on two fronts. First, it can be argued that there are no empirical or theoretical estimates of the output effects of these four causes that are sufficiently reliable to command consensus. Second, it can also be noted that there are several competing explanations of the decline. The case for the "four main causes" will be much strengthened if it can be shown that these "other explanations" cannot be considered important causes in all or most transition economies.

For Calvo and Coricelli (1993), the villain is a credit crunch. Following a Big Bang, nominal interest rates were sharply increased, and either inflexible state-owned banks were supposed to deny firms funds for the purchase of inputs or else the firms themselves began reducing borrowing for fear of insolvency. In both cases supplies fell, leading to falls in incomes and demands. The two economists suggest that "trade was destroyed for lack of market institutions, not simply as a consequence of textbook changes in relative prices or movement along transformation frontiers." This thesis has been tested on Polish industrial data by Berg and Blanchard (1994) and Schaffer (1992). Both studies firmly rejected it as a significant explanation. Polish firms had accumulated significant inventories of inputs prior to the Big Bang, yet the falls of production followed it immediately, leading to increases of stocks of final products. The stocks of inventories of inputs were found not to be correlated with output falls across industries. Schaffer (1994) also reports evidence showing that, as a proportion of sales, spending on materials went up in the first quarter of 1990, not down, which again is consistent with building up stocks and not consistent with a "credit crunch" preventing firms from buying materials. The Calvo-Coricelli analysis is also difficult to reconcile with the fact that substantially different monetary policies across countries have led to similarly large falls in industrial outputs (Bofinger 1994).

Kornai (1994) argues that it is not possible to isolate one single main cause for the transformational recession. He nevertheless places at the top of his list the impacts of price and foreign trade liberalizations on aggregate demand and on product-specific supplies and demands, the factors regarded in this chapter as main causes. However, he also regards as important three other factors: (1) disruption of coordination, (2) a hardening of the firms' budget constraints, and (3) the backwardness of the financial sector. These are plausible causes, but have they been really important?

In Hungary and Poland formal central planning was dismantled well before the reforms of the early 1990s, so in these two countries there was little disruption of coordination during transition. Yet industrial output fell by about 40 percent, which is not much less than in other transition economies. Considerable hardening of the firms' budget constraints did take place almost immediately, especially in CE and the Baltic Republics. However, both before and immediately after the Big Bang, enterprise profitability tended to be high and firms' bankruptcies were rare. In Poland this was especially the case in the first year of transition. The substantial elimination of subsidies was a reflection of tighter budget constraints. But we have discussed this aspect already, regarding it as an element of the price reform. It contributed to output falls through changes in relative prices and their impact on demands, not through bankruptcies. Finally, it is true that the backwardness of the financial sector did not help channel resources efficiently, but had it done so, this would probably have caused some additional disruption in the short run.

Still another possible cause was a shift in consumer preferences away from low-quality goods (Charemza 1993). The liberalization of foreign trade did indeed offer consumers a larger selection of imported goods, and this may have affected preferences. However, the early drastic devaluations in most transition economies (East Germany and Hungary were the exceptions) restricted consumer imports in the early phase of transition, yet output falls were largest in that initial period.

The dislocation of the traditional channels of input supplies has also been suggested as a possible cause (Williamson 1995). This factor may have been significant occasionally in the FSU, following the breakup of the Soviet Union. However, price liberalizations have generally helped to eliminate supply bottlenecks in most transition economies. Some traditional trade intermediaries have become underemployed, mainly because enterprises have chosen to trade directly among themselves.

A purely "classical" explanation of the recession was suggested by Bofinger (1994). In the pretransition period, Bofinger maintains, enterprises were maximizing outputs rather than profits, and so they were over-employing labor and other resources. Real wages were, as a result, higher than labor marginal productivities. A switch to the maximization of profits led to a gradual shedding of labor and an immediate reduction of output.

There are two major problems with this explanation. First, by 1989 most enterprises in Hungary and Poland were no longer subject to central plans and, being in most cases financially self-dependent, were concerned about profits more than about output. Yet industrial output falls in the two countries were on the same large scale as in neighboring Czechoslovakia and most other transition countries. The explanation also predicts an increase in profits and profit margins in response to reform. The data contradict this, for in most cases, profits and profit margins have declined.

An entirely "nonclassical" view of the recession, one inspired by Keynesian-Kaleckian theory, was suggested by Bhaduri and Laski (1992), among others. They note that "Some multilaterate institutions recommend indiscriminately austerity, especially in government spending, ... for the former communist economies trying to make a transition to the market system." In their view, "The economic disaster of pursuing the orthodox remedy of 'austerity only' is now far too apparent in East Europe.... By restricting demand in almost every possible way—through an extremely tight money policy, reduced government expenditure in an attempt to reduce budget deficit, and restraint on wages—these economies have been precipitated in an economic depression which can be compared only with the Great Depression of the 1930s in the capitalist world."

This particular explanation was based on early evidence from Poland and the former Czechoslovakia. However, the explanation was largely disproved by the subsequent experiences of those transition countries, such as Russia and Ukraine, that initially adopted highly expansionary monetary and fiscal policies but to no avail. As noted in the Introduction, the cumulative cross-country evidence implies that macropolicies have been capable of significantly influencing the time profile of output contraction, but not of greatly affecting its eventual magnitude. This evidence is simply too strong to allow any other conclusion. Moreover, this conclusion still holds if comparisons are restricted to the countries of the FSU only, or to the countries of CE only.

2.7 Two Models of Transformation and Recovery

By 1997, the GDP levels have stabilized in most countries of the FSU, particularly in Russia and Ukraine, and recovery has started in all countries of CE. The strongest recoveries have taken place in Poland, Slovenia, Slovakia, Estonia, and the Czech Republic, as well as in Albania and Armenia. The most interesting cases, however, are Poland and Hungary. Despite a common record of early reforms, they adopted significantly different policies, amounting to two different models of transformation and recovery. The Polish recovery is also interesting in its own right, because it started earliest and has been, until 1997, the strongest among transition economies. As such, it is indicative of the forces of recovery and growth that are still in the early development stage elsewhere. The Hungarian recovery, on the other hand, in spite of the long history of reforms and the large inflow of foreign direct investment during transition, has been disappointingly slow. In 1997, Poland is the only country of the region that, in fact, has passed the recovery phase. Indeed, in 1996 the levels of measured GDP, manufacturing output, and private consumption were already significantly above the prereform levels. By these measures most other countries of CE are unlikely to complete their recoveries before the year 2000, and most countries of the FSU will probably need another five to ten years of the twenty-first century to reach their prereform volumes of output.

The reforms adopted by Poland and the responses to them on the supply side have been sufficiently different to justify the term "Polish Model of Transformation." Its ten major characteristic features are listed below.

1. Strong price and trade liberalizations at the outset of transition.

2. Low entry barriers to new private enterprises and the imposition of fairly strict budget constraints for state enterprises.

3. Rapid privatization of small businesses and relatively slow, but high-quality, privatization of medium and large-scale state enterprises, designed to attract strategic investors capable of deep restructuring and introduction of new products.

4. In the legal system, adoption of an old and sound commercial code, and the inheritance of a legal system capable of enforcing contracts.

5. In the financial sector, strong supervision and tough regulation of the banking sector, the securities market, and the stock exchange; a solid financial restructuring of banks and enterprises that held underperforming debt (see chp. 5, this book); and restructuring designed to minimize moral hazards and induce privatization.

6. In the welfare state, readiness by the government to accept high unemployment as the price of rapid restructuring; low unemployment benefits but relatively high pensions and other social transfers.

7. In fiscal and monetary policies, relatively low budget deficit of the government and a moderately restrictive monetary policy of the central bank; a fairly rapid introduction of a modern and effective tax system entailing a radical shift from profit taxes to VAT and other indirect taxes.

8. The insistence on, and securing of, a substantial reduction of foreign debt, both sovereign and commercial.

9. An exchange rate policy of anticipated crawling peg, designed to provide stability to real effective exchange rates.

Table 2.6
Structure in current prices and level of Polish industrial output, in 1992 prices, 1989–95, by ownership

Structure (%)	1989	1990	1991	1992	1993	1994	1995
Total	100	100	100	100	100	100	100
Public	83.8	82.6	73.0	69.2	65.0	60.6	54.8
State				68.3	62.5	57.2	50.6
Cooperatives, etc.	8.8	5.3	5.0	4.7	4.2	3.5	3.2
Private	7.4	12.1	22.0	26.1	30.8	35.9	42.0
Privatized	0	0.5	2	4	6	8	10
Emerging (de novo) private	7.4	11.6	20.0	22.1	24.8	27.9	32.0
Level (1989 total = 100)							
Total	100	75.4	69.2	71.0	75.2	84.7	92.6
Public and privatized	83.8	62.7	51.9	52.0	53.6	58.1	60.0
Cooperatives, etc.	8.8	4.0	3.5	3.3	3.2	3.0	3.0
Emerging (de novo) private	7.4	8.7	13.8	15.7	18.4	23.6	29.6

Sources: Central Statistical Office, Warsaw, various issues of *Rocznik statystyczny*; share of output by privatized businesses, author's estimates based on employment statistics. For 1993, Schaffer (1996) estimates the share at 6 percent.

10. A rapid expansion of business schools and an extremely rapid spread of modern information technology in the business sector, mass media, and administration.

Concern for proper corporate governance has slowed the pace of privatization. However, in other transition countries, faster privatization of state enterprises did not always, or immediately, lead to recovery, though by and large it has been conducive to investment, restructuring, productivity, and profitability (Pohl et al. 1997). In most of these other countries, control over the majority of enterprises was given to insiders—workers and managers—and they face competing incentives that more often than not lead them to delay restructuring. Existing state enterprises also tended to be large and capital-intensive. Their restructuring is therefore expensive. Insiders in those enterprises generally lack finance of their own to supplement typically small profits.

The available evidence clearly indicates that the Polish recovery has been driven, on the supply side, by a very rapid expansion of the domestic new, or emerging, private sector (table 2.6). The collapse of demand for unwanted traditional goods and the imposition of financial discipline forced state enterprises to sell surplus capital assets to private firms at giveaway prices. Private entrepreneurs began to establish new enterprises based on old capital assets to produce new and wanted goods at a profit.

This asset privatization, as it is called, has increased capital mobility and was probably a major reason why, on the demand side, the recovery was led initially by private consumption and not, as originally expected, by investments and/or net exports. Only later, in 1994–95, did the classical model of recovery and growth begin to apply, with net exports and investments playing the dominant role. This was also helped by the fact that in the 1980s, about two million Poles, some 15 percent of the non-agricultural labor force, were, for periods ranging from several months to several years, guest workers in Western countries, particularly Germany and the United States. They were learning new skills, establishing trade contacts, selling goods, and saving capital. It so happens that about two million new businesses have been established since 1989, most of them during the first two years of transition.

This unintended pattern of privatization has had further positive side effects: the more successful private firms are now in a position to participate, as strategic investors, in the privatization of medium and even large state enterprises. Also, with the overall improvement of the economy, the remaining state enterprises are able to attract stronger interest from foreign investors and can be sold at higher prices.

What also distinguishes Poland is the fact that the country happened to have a sizable private sector at the start of transition, much larger than that of any other postsocialist country. Polish private agriculture, however, proved irrelevant in instigating recovery. The urban private sector has been the main driving force of recovery in manufacturing, not just in trade and services.

The rapid growth of the urban private sector also helped recovery indirectly. It did this by absorbing the surplus labor of the state sector and by supplying markets with new products. In these ways, private enterprises have increased the competitive pressures on state enterprises and induced their restructuring effort.

The recovery of the Polish urban sector has been led by an exceptionally strong recovery in manufacturing, some 70 percent increase of output in the period 1991–96. Data in table 2.6 portray the crucial contribution to that increase of the emerging (de novo) private sector. In the period 1991–95 its output increased by 115 percent, accounting for two-thirds of the total increase of the industrial output during that period. For manufacturing alone, the share was about half. This de novo private sector output also increased during the contraction phase (1989–91) by 85 percent, reducing the initial fall of total industrial output by about six percentage points. This aggregate, industrywide evidence suggests that the earlier case studies, such as Pinto et al. (1993), which highlight the restructuring gains in some state and former state enterprises should be interpreted with care. Examples of significant, even large improvements do exist, but most (former) state enterprises appear to lack sufficient finance and/or business leadership to overcome typically large inherited constraints quickly. A similar conclusion has been reached, on the basis of evidence from samples of enterprises, by Belka et al. (1994) with reference to the former Czechoslovakia, Hungary, and Poland; by Schaffer (1996) with reference to Poland; and by Richter and Schaffer (1996) with reference to Russia.

An early important decision for Poland to take was whether to attempt a substantial debt reduction. The arguments against such a step concerned the possible large adverse impact on long-term credibility and foreign direct investment. There was also the risk that the attempt might fail. These arguments persuaded Hungary to reject the debt reduction option.

However, in 1989 and 1990, Poland's external position was extremely poor, and the prospects of a rapid improvement were unclear. The decision to seek a debt reduction was in those circumstances inevitable. In the event, the comparative benefits of that decision have been greater than initially hoped and the costs lower than initially feared. Hungary did benefit from considerable foreign interest in direct investment. This led it to adopt a privatization strategy based on direct sales to foreign firms. But the large inflow of privatization revenue has been used in Hungary to reduce the cost of transition rather than to reduce the external debt or domestic investment (Kornai 1997). In Poland macroeconomic policies had to be tighter and privatization has been more domestically based. The early fiscal tightness was in part necessitated by the absence of foreign direct investment during the prolonged debt reduction negotiations (1990–94), and in part by conditions imposed by official creditors through the IMF. As a result, the debt reduction became an investment for future growth recovery and external credibility. It led, in particular, to the adoption of a more prudent fiscal policy and a tighter incomes policy.

Another important feature of the Polish model of transformation has been the concern to redirect and expand foreign trade and to obtain a solid and lasting improvement of the external position quickly. This concern led the Polish authorities to devalue the zloty relatively strongly at the start of transition. Moreover, since late 1991 an economic doctrine has been adopted according to which the exchange rate policy should be subordinated mainly to the need to secure and maintain solid external equilibrium, while monetary and incomes policies should address the inflation problem. The result of this doctrine has been that the real effective exchange rate was set at a competitive and stable level. The stability of the rate was achieved through the transparent instrument of daily devaluations at a preannounced rate linked to anticipated inflation, with the exchange rate being corrected further, when necessary, by additional small and infrequent devaluations or appreciations. This exchange rate policy must have somewhat retarded the progress of reducing inflation, but may have helped the recovery of output.

The combination of a competitive exchange rate and tight fiscal and monetary policies has also been adopted by the Czech Republic and, in 1995–96, by Russia to obtain positive net exports and to induce industrial recovery. An important by-product of the policy is an increase of reserves of foreign exchange. This increase helps to restore the confidence of potential foreign and domestic investors in the local currency and the economy. That confidence in turn reduces capital flight and stimulates savings and investment, including foreign direct investment. A virtuous cycle of this type leads in due course to a surplus on capital account. Once this happens, an appreciation of the real exchange rate and acceptance of a trade deficit become appropriate policy responses. Net imports then supplement domestic savings in financing investment and therefore help to increase long-term growth.

2.8   National Savings, Public Finance, and Long-Term Growth

Among newly industrialized and other less developed economies, there is a cluster of highly successful economies, mainly in East Asia and including China; a cluster of highly unsuccessful ones, mainly in Africa; and a large third intermediate group, consisting of most of Latin America, India, CE, and the FSU. In all these three clusters the per capita growth has been, and continues to be, driven mainly by technology transfer from the developed part of the world. The variation in the accumulation of capital, both physical and human, and in the growth of foreign trade has been, apparently, the key factor underlying the intercountry variation in that transfer, and therefore also the rate of growth.

The standard growth theory of the Solow-Swan type concentrated on the contribution of capital accumulation to growth, regarding changes in population and technology as given. The theory predicted that if only a small fraction of the labor force was gainfully employed, so that there was a large labor reserve to begin with, then the growth rate of output would be proportional to the rate of investment. However, once the labor reserve was exhausted, diminishing returns to capital would set in. The consequence of this was that the long-term growth rate would be independent of the investment rate, determined instead by the rate of population growth and the rate of technological change, both exogenously given.

The theory of economic growth changes radically once the neoclassical assumption of unrestricted and costless access to any technological information is rejected and the reality of an extremely uneven distribution of technological know-how among countries is acknowledged. In this case the rate of economic growth of technologically less advanced countries is dependent primarily on the factors that influence the rate of international technology transfer. Our present understanding is that this transfer can be influenced above all by the choice of economic system and the size of investment. In this way, the rate of the technological change becomes an endogenously determined variable.

A simple way of modeling the full impact of capital accumulation on growth is to assume that technology (T) is labor-augmenting and that the level of technology adopted is proportional to the capital/labor ratio chosen. That is,

$$Y = F(K, TL) \tag{2.2}$$

and

$$T = a(K/L). \tag{2.3}$$

The proportionality assumption is implied by the empirical observation of little international variation in the capital/output ratio.

In writing equation (2.3) we still assume that technology is free, but that its absorption requires fixed capital. This assumption presupposes that there is, outside our emerging economy, a technology reserve pool to which there is free access, and that within our economy there is a sufficient "social capability" to absorb it gradually.

The new approach lies in regarding T as a choice variable rather than exogenously given. This reflects the perception that each country has its own production function with a distinct aggregate level of technology (figure 2.6).

If the production function F displays constant returns to scale, combining equations (2.2) and (2.3) implies

$$Y = F(K, aK) = K/v, \tag{2.4}$$

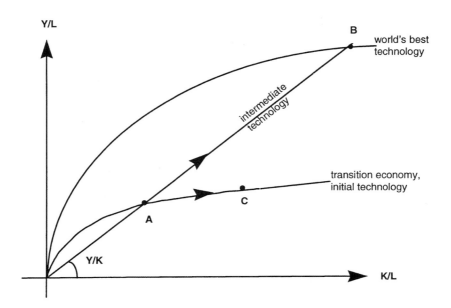

Figure 2.6
Production function for transition (A) and developed (B) economies and the turnpike growth path (AB)

where $v = 1/F(1, a)$, a constant capital/output ratio. In this case, output becomes proportional to capital stock; hence equations (2.2) through (2.4) are known as the AK Model (Barro and Sala-i-Martin 1995). It follows that the growth rate of output, g_Y, equals the growth rate of capital and

$$g_K = \frac{\dot{K}}{K} = \frac{sY - \delta K}{K} = \frac{s}{v} - \delta,$$

where s is the savings rate. Hence

$$g_Y = s/v - \delta \tag{2.5}$$

and

$$g_T = s/v - \delta - n, \tag{2.6}$$

where n is the given growth rate of employment. This "new growth" theory approach, originally inspired by Arrow (1962) and later reinterpreted by Romer (1986) and Lucas (1988), among others, again promotes the rate of investment to the key growth determinant. This time, however, the labor reserve pool is replaced by the technology reserve pool.

Decreasing returns to capital may not set in as long as this technology reserve is substantial and the social capability of transition countries to absorb it is high.

The AK-type models were designed to help to understand economic growth in developed economies. However, empirical testing has produced strong evidence "that the *AK* models do not provide a good description of growth in advanced economies" (Jones 1995). This growth can indeed be explained much better by R&D-based models in which the rate of innovation is related to the rates of growth of R&D inputs, as in the Phelps-Gomulka model (Phelps 1966; Gomulka 1970, 1971, 1990), among others.

But in contrast to economies of the world's technology frontier area, transition economies do not need to rely on their own R&D activities to advance technologically. Following the change of economic system, the formerly socialist countries already have or are about to develop a large absorptive capability. They have almost open frontiers for people and goods with developed economies, and they have obtained easy, almost costfree access to the technological know-how of these other countries. Hence an AK-style model may be applicable to transition (and other emerging) economies for much of the period in which their catching up takes place. The question is: What else do these transition countries need to do, in addition to adopting a market-based economic system, to become as successful as continental Western Europe had been in the 1950s and the 1960s, or as most of the East Asian countries have been since the late 1960s?

If equations (2.5) and (2.6) hold even approximately, the main focus of attention must be on the investment/GDP ratios. These ratios have been, and remain, in the range between 30 percent and 40 percent in East Asia including China, but are typically between 15 percent and 20 percent in transition countries of the FSU and CE. On the other hand, in transition countries (other than China and Vietnam) the shares of total public expenditures typically remain between 40 percent and 50 percent of GDP; these shares have been, and still are, much lower in the dynamic NICs, ranging generally between 20 percent and 40 percent of GDP. Moreover, a large component of public spending in the formerly more developed socialist countries is the expenditure on social transfers, which finance consumption, rather than on education or infrastructure, which may promote growth. Large public spending requires a heavy burden of taxation, and this adversely influences incentives for work and investment. Moreover, large social transfers, in particular high state pensions, reduce the incentive to save.

A significant change in the distribution of GDP, away from publicly financed consumption and in favor of investment, may therefore be the single most important and most difficult task of economic policy in many transition countries during the next decade or so. If government spending in those countries is to be comparable with that of low-income members of the European Community, or that prevailing in developed Western Europe in the 1950s, it will have to be in the range of 30 percent to 40 percent of GDP (i.e., some ten to fifteen percentage points lower than in 1997). This gives an indication of the magnitude of the redistribution required.

2.9 Concluding Remarks

Mutual interactions of demand-side and supply-side causes of output falls make a precise identification of their separate contributions to total falls virtually impossible. However, after reviewing the evidence and arguments, we must, I think, conclude that the main root cause of output depressions has been that the product composition of the supply side of transition economies at the start of reforms was substantially different from that needed under the new conditions. A need therefore arose for extremely large-scale and time-concentrated restructuring, and was brought into the open by large and swift shifts in demand and supply functions. These were themselves mainly the result of rapid price and foreign trade liberalizations (in the FSU, also of much lower military spending), taking place in conditions of limited (interproduct, interenterprise, and intersectoral) mobility of resources. Since the required microadjustments were large and the various rigidities severe, the product compositions of the supply side of these economies could initially change mainly through severe and highly product-differentiated contractions. Hence, the depressions were deep and, as argued by Winiecki (1991), unavoidable. Whenever, as in the FSU, the real aggregate demand was initially not reduced to correspond to the level of the (much reduced) aggregate supply, the countries concerned suffered very high inflation as well as great depression. This conclusion suggests that it is misleading to compare transformation recessions of the 1990s with the Great Depression of the 1930s. Aggregate output contractions may be similar, but in terms of structural causes, the appropriate comparison is with the post-1945 experiences of Germany and Japan.

With respect to long-term growth, this chapter is similar to related studies (such as Barbone and Zalduendo 1996; Fischer et al. 1997; Sachs and Warner 1996). It recommends economic policies that promote high domestic savings and foreign direct investment, low inflation, and free international trade with a view to accelerating international transfer of technologies and skills to transition economies from the world's technology frontier area. The radical reform program of the 1990s has brought about much of the institutional structure needed to conduct such policies.

The countries of CE and the FSU also have human capital that, in quantity and quality, is similar to that which the most successful emerging economies of East Asia, Western Europe, and Latin America have or had at a similar level of GDP per capita. International statistics suggest that the growth rates of such economies can be high, provided the macroeconomic environment is stable and the microeconomic one is liberal and competitive. Since 1950 most Latin American countries have mainly failed to create such an environment. The countries of CE and the FSU therefore know the model they should not follow. On the other hand, the East Asia model relies on a specific culture, which helps to keep social transfers at very low levels and, therefore, also the tax burden. This has helped to raise national savings to very high levels. But that model may prove difficult to adopt for countries that developed and experienced the culture of a large welfare state for several generations.

The transition countries of CE and the FSU are therefore probably likely to adopt the West European practice of the 1950s and the 1960s, with the key ratios being 20 percent to 30 percent for the investment/GDP ratios and 35 percent to 45 percent of GDP for government spending. With these ranges for these two ratios, the trend growth rates of GDP would be in the range of 4 percent to 7 percent, rather than the 7 percent to 10 percent observed in East Asia.

Acknowledgments

This chapter benefited greatly from the critical comments of three anonymous referees, particularly with respect to sections on recovery and growth. Also helpful were comments of my students, colleagues, and seminar participants at the London School of Economics, the Central European University, and Oxford University. I would like to thank in particular Peter Boone, Dieter Bös, Antoni Chawluk, Richard Layard, Mark Schaffer, Richard Ericson, and Chris Scott. Computer-friendly charts and tables were compiled, and econometric tests conducted, by Joanna Gomulka. I am also indebted to Sarah Grainger and Pat Nutt for skillful secretarial assistance.

3

Inflation: Causes, Consequences, and Cures

Peter Boone and Jakob Hørder

3.1 Introduction

The economic reform process in Eastern Europe and the former Soviet Union was preceded by the collapse of the entire political system in the socialist countries. After decades of socialism, the one-party system broke down and new political leaders emerged. This breakdown meant that many of the checks and balances on political decision making were lost. In this chapter we argue that this is a key fact that is needed to understand the subsequent pattern of inflation and liberalization across these countries.

One of the first economic implications of the breakdown of the political system was a loss of confidence in domestic money. Under the socialist system, domestic money was the main instrument for savings. When the USSR broke apart, there were fifteen central banks suddenly able to create ruble money. In most of Eastern Europe, political turmoil led to rapid increases in the money supply as governments issued credits to their supporters. The result was initially creeping inflation, which soon spiralled into outright price explosions as people realized that continued inflation would erode the value of their savings. As a consequence, they reduced money balances, purchasing goods and foreign exchange. Thus the initial price jumps, which were very often much larger than economists and policy makers had anticipated, reflected not the past "monetary overhang," but rather sudden losses in confidence due to political turmoil.

After these initial large price jumps, some countries were able to contain inflation through orthodox stabilization programs. But many countries embarked on policies that for several years kept inflation high. As shown in figure 3.1, these same countries tended not to liberalize their economies (as measured by the World Bank index of liberalization). This begs the

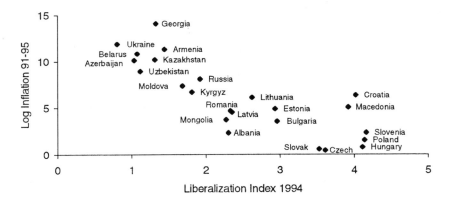

Figure 3.1
Inflationary performance and liberalization

question: why did some countries choose not to implement full liberalization and stabilization while others implemented both very quickly? One possible answer is that gradual reforms would lead to better economic outcomes. But in fact empirical evidence suggests that at best the slow reformers were no worse off in terms of their total output decline. Furthermore, their policies have prevented necessary structural adjustment so that these economies have taken much longer to recover from the recession.

In this chapter we argue that the real reason underlying the lack of reform in some countries was, once again, the breakdown in the political process. In the vacuum that followed the political breakdown, the old elites and rent seekers captured the political initiative in these countries. To sustain their powers, and sequester incomes, they issued credits and maintained distortionary policies and, as a result, acquired enormous assets. In Russia in 1992, revenues from net credit issue alone equalled 32.7 percent of GDP. Other countries in the CIS earned similar incomes from credit issuance. When such large funds are available, it is no surprise that the politicians who wanted stabilization faced enormous and sometimes violent opposition from those fighting to gain access to these resources. Whenever the pro-reform lobby lost the battle, high inflation was maintained and distortionary policies continued for several years.

This explanation, relying on political factors, also helps explain the illusionary "fiscal crisis" in many of these countries. While the total revenues (including seigniorage) of many governments in the CIS and Eastern Europe have remained high, these countries have not maintained social programs such as pensions and health care at adequate levels. In this chapter we argue that this is yet another consequence of the underlying political crisis. When the government is controlled by old elites and rent seekers grabbing for resources, it is no surprise that the politically weak, and particularly those who should benefit from social programs, do not gain from the policies being implemented. The result has been much greater poverty than would otherwise have occurred.

If our arguments are correct and factors related to the breakdown of the political system affected the size of the initial price jump, whether the country stabilized or experienced continued high inflation, and the distributional consequences of the pursued policies, then we can draw several lessons from the break-up of the communist system and the diverse performance of the different economies. It seems that some countries tackled the breakdown differently from others and that the way chosen had a severe impact on the subsequent economic performance. Thus we argue that the economic performance of any former socialist economy was heavily influenced by political choices in that economy and not entirely determined by structural factors. The lessons learned from the different choices made and the reasons for these choices can be useful when designing policies in future situations of political breakdown and near anarchy. First, it is clear that stabilization programs must focus on measures that help reinstate political checks and balances, and promote coordination of decision making. We argue that democratic reform is an essential part of this. But in addition we discuss several economic mechanisms that can be implemented to promote stabilization. These include a macroeconomic version of a "poison pill," that is, a policy initiative that tends to reduce inflation, and once introduced is difficult to reverse. Currency boards are one example of such policies. Other examples of policies that can help enforce long-term stabilization are: conditional foreign assistance targeting political coordination, preemptive policy strikes, and the design of detailed budgetary processes.

This chapter is organized as follows. Section 3.2 discusses what factors caused the initial price jumps and the eroding confidence in the stability of domestic money. Section 3.3 examines the rationale for continued high inflation in many countries, and presents evidence that rent seeking and support for the old elite were the prime causes of this. Section 3.4 discusses why countries, after several years of high inflation, have subsequently returned to low inflation. Section 3.5 uses the analysis of the experience of the former socialist economies to draw lessons for future stabilization policies. Section 3.6 concludes.

Table 3.1
Inflation in the former socialist economies

	Year of peak	Highest level	Level in 1994	Level in 1995
Albania	1992	226	28	9
Armenia	1994	5458	5458	179
Azerbaijan	1994	1500	1500	536
Belarus	1994	2200	2200	73
Bulgaria	1991	335	89	70
Croatia	1993	1516	98	3
Czech Republic	1991	57	10	10
Estonia	1992	1069	48	30
Georgia	1994	18000	18000	164
Hungary	1991	34	19	29
Kazakhstan	1994	1980	1980	177
Kyrgyzstan	1993	1209	280	49
Latvia	1992	951	36	27
Lithuania	1992	1020	72	25
Macedonia	1992	1925	654	18
Moldova	1992	1276	327	25
Mongolia	1992	321	145	65
Poland	1990	586	32	32
Romania	1993	256	131	33
Russia	1992	1353	220	184
Slovakia	1991	61	14	11
Slovenia	1992	201	20	10
Tajikistan	1993	2195	2195	240
Turkmenistan	1993	3102	2400	2500
Ukraine	1993	2735	842	342
Uzbekistan	1994	746	746	254

Source: As reported in Aslund et al. 1996. Original data from de Melo et al. 1995 and World Bank, *Country Economic Memorandums* (various issues).

3.2   The First Price Jump

The inflation experience of every country under consideration can be divided into two components. In all the former socialist economies reform began with an increase in the rate of inflation. The rise in official prices that occurred after price liberalization in part reflected a general monetary overhang. But once the overhang was cleared, subsequent inflation was driven by other underlying factors.

The initial price-jump episodes in the former socialist economies had surprising features. Table 3.1 shows the pattern of inflation after reforms began for twenty-six countries. The highest price rise generally took place at the start of reform programs, when price liberalization occurred. These price rises were generally far greater than policy makers initially forecast, and caused immediate social hardships because the value of past savings was greatly eroded overnight. For example, at the start of the Polish stabilization program it was estimated that prices would rise by 35 percent in January 1991, while the actual increase was 70 percent.[1] In Russia the IMF estimated that prices would rise by 50 percent after the January 1992 price liberalization.[2] But instead prices rose by a startling 250 percent. The large rise in prices can be explained by a severe loss of confidence in money as a savings vehicle just before the reforms. This can be understood by examining the pattern of money demand, money supply, and parallel market prices. Under the planning system the government maintained strict control over money circulation so that the demand and supply of domestic money, measured at official prices, were more or less equal. With stable prices, households were willing to hold money for both savings and transaction purposes. Money-market equilibrium in this simple setting is thus:

$$\frac{M_t}{P_t} = m(y_t, \pi_t, E_t\pi_s \forall s > t).$$

The important point here is that the demand for domestic money contains both a transactions component, which is affected by output (y_t) and the short-term cost of holding money (π_t),[3] and a savings component, which is affected by the expected future rate of inflation ($E_t\pi_s \forall s > t$).[4] If we invert this equation, we can find the price level that is consistent with individuals being willing to hold the outstanding domestic money. If official prices are set too low, then money demand would be less than money supply and parallel market prices would rise to reflect the excess money supply. As official prices are liberalized, they jump to the level of parallel prices. This is one interpretation of how a monetary overhang might cause an initial price jump.

However, there seems to be more to the price jump than just the realignment of official and parallel prices. In all countries, liberalization was preceded by an explosion of parallel market prices.[5] Several factors affected parallel market prices at the time. The gradual opening of parallel markets and reduced legal restrictions on transactions should have lowered parallel prices, because greater supply on the parallel market should have reduced the relative price differential with official markets. Here the sharp rise in parallel prices must be attributed to an alternative source. We believe the main cause was a fairly sudden loss in confidence in domestic money as a means of savings (i.e., an increase in $E_t \pi_s \forall s > t$). In every country the money supply grew relatively slowly during this period, but the threat of high inflation coming from price liberalization, and a well-founded belief that the authorities would lose control of monetary policy, would certainly have been enough to cause a flight from monetary savings. With a legacy of high savings in domestic money, any loss of confidence could lead to a manyfold increase in prices. In many countries the result was an explosion of parallel prices some time before liberalization. Hence it seems that the initial price jump partly reflected a realignment of official and parallel prices, but also a reduction in people's confidence in domestic money.

Some people have argued that this price jump was avoidable. For example, Goldman (1994) argues that the initial inflation could have been prevented by an appropriate monetary reform, such as dividing all bank accounts and cash by three. If the authorities had reduced enterprise and business deposits by a greater factor than household savings, then the losses of pensioners and households could have been reduced. But this measure might have exacerbated the situation for other reasons. Such a monetary confiscation could well have reduced people's confidence in money even further, causing prices to rise in any case or necessitating even greater monetary reform. In addition, monetary reform would not have changed the basic incentives to cause higher inflation in the future. As discussed below, money confiscation would not change the incentives for issuing money in the future. And in fact, enterprises would have had even greater reason to demand new credits for "working capital," which might well have precipitated even higher inflation.

The loss of confidence in domestic money that seemingly exacerbated the size of the initial price jump could have been caused by the population's anxieties over the possible economic policies to be pursued in the future. The subsequent experience of the majority of the former socialist economies shows that these fears were justified.

3.3   Subsequent Inflation

In most countries inflationary performance after the initial price jump was dismal. As shown in table 3.1, even in 1994 inflation was still running at well over 50 percent per annum in eighteen of the twenty-six countries. There was no technical reason why these countries could not have maintained lower inflation—after the initial price jump it was completely feasible to reduce inflation to 1 percent or 2 percent per month within weeks of the start of reforms. Even with substantial official price increases after the initial price liberalization, it would be possible to adjust relative prices so that monthly inflation remained low. This means that the subsequent high inflation was due to the choice of the responsible authorities rather than an inevitable result of the reform.

Economic Rationale for High Inflation

There are two basic categories of explanations for why the authorities chose to permit high inflation. The first takes the view that policy makers rightly or wrongly perceived it to be beneficial to the economy. The initial economic collapse, the changed economic system, and subsequent political turmoil meant that government revenues fell sharply at the start of reforms. In the short run, with few alternative means to raise tax revenues, seigniorage became one of the easiest sources of financing. An optimizing policy maker would want to equate the marginal benefits of higher government expenditures to the marginal cost of financing them. If benefits seemed high, or if inflation were perceived not to be costly (or even not caused by money issue!), then increasing money issue and inflation would be a justifiable response.

According to this explanation, the countries with the greatest economic problems, and hence the worse fiscal constraints, would be those that would benefit most from seigniorage revenues. We would expect the countries with the largest external and internal shocks (such as the dissolution of the CMEA), countries with relatively greater need for restructuring, countries at war, and those with the sharpest fall in fiscal revenues to have the highest inflation rates. In these cases inflation would be costly, but it would serve a useful purpose in financing productive expenditures.

A related justification of inflation is proposed by Calvo and Coricelli (1992), who argue that the legacy of imperfect financial markets—which meant that government credit was the only source of financing available to enterprises—made credit policy especially important in former socialist economies. They contend that, after the initial price jump, enterprises were faced with extremely low real working capital balances. This limited their ability to produce and hence contributed to the output decline. In this model, a less restrictive monetary policy would have led to higher output. Thus, if Calvo and Coricelli are right, we would expect loose monetary policy to be correlated with greater output. Figure 3.2 plots the

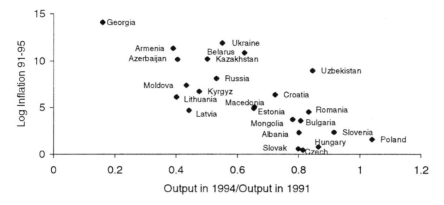

Figure 3.2
Inflation and cumulative output decline

relation between the cumulative output decline (1989 to 1995) and inflation (1990 to 1995) in twenty-two former socialist countries. The most striking observation here is the strong negative relation between output growth and inflation. The data do not seem to support Calvo and Coricelli's hypothesis. In fact, as was pointed out by Bruno and Easterly (1995), the data, if anything, seem to suggest that stabilization actually improves rather than worsens output performance.[6] This is perhaps taking the argument somewhat too far. As has already been pointed out, the observed negative correlation might also reflect the reverse situation. That is, countries with severe shocks (low output growth) may have had more to gain from seigniorage financing (high inflation) than countries where the output shocks were smaller.

A closer examination of figure 3.2 seems to support this hypothesis. As can be seen, countries from the CIS and countries at war have higher inflation rates than other countries. To examine the main country characteristics that correlate with high inflation, we present, in table 3.2, some results from cross-country regressions where cumulative output decline is regressed on inflation, with a dummy reflecting whether the country was in the ruble zone (former USSR), and a dummy for countries at war.

The results show that, after controlling for ruble zone and war, there is no longer a significant correlation between growth and inflation. This fact suggests that tight credit policy was not a key factor explaining the output decline in these countries. However, these results also suggest that pro-stabilisation policies did not serve to reduce the output decline. A reasonable interpretation of these regressions is that monetary policy

Table 3.2
Output and inflation: OLS regressions, dependent variables

	Output 1995/output 1990				Growth rate of output, 1995			
Log (price level 1995/ price level 1991)	−0.048* (0.01)	−0.006 (0.01)			−3.470* (0.57)	−3.400* (0.83)		
Cumulative liberalization index			0.133* (0.03)	0.007 (0.03)			3.517* (0.78)	3.307* (1.43)
Former USSR		−0.340* (0.09)		−0.348* (0.08)		−0.281 (2.38)		−0.600 (3.45)
War		−0.183* (0.07)		−0.191* (0.05)		−0.101 (2.08)		−0.144 (2.26)
R²	0.65	0.80	0.48	0.79	0.64	0.64	0.47	0.47
N	23	23	25	25	23	23	25	25

Source: de Melo et al. 1995.
Notes:
* Significant at 5% level.
t-statistics are in parentheses.
War and Former USSR are dummy variables set to 1 for countries involved in war and members of the former USSR, respectively.
Cumulative Liberalization Index, from de Melo et al. 1995, measures the degree of liberalization of the economy as described in the text. The index ranges from 0 to 4.

had little overall impact on the subsequent economic decline. This does not imply that monetary policy had no effect on the timing of the decline and of the return to growth. Figure 3.3 plots the correlation between inflation and growth in 1995 alone, and table 3.2 shows some regression results controlled for the effects of wars and ruble zone membership. This plot and the regressions show that in 1995, even after controlling for these variables, there was a strong negative correlation between inflation and growth. The countries that had the highest growth rates were all countries that had stabilized. Those that had continued high inflation in 1995 had the lowest growth rates. These countries might have avoided large output declines early on—but at the cost of large recessions later on.

The main effect of monetary policy in the former socialist economies thus seems to have been the timing of the start of the recession. If one probes a bit deeper, one finds that this was due to its effect on restructuring policies. Aslund, Boone, and Johnson (1996) show that countries that reduced inflation tended to have more rapid growth of the private sector, greater institutional change as proxied by the EBRD indices, and more

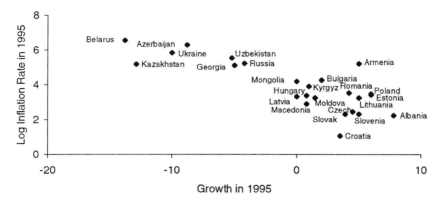

Figure 3.3
Inflation and output growth

rapid growth of services. Lack of stabilization in part reflected a policy of continued subsidies to the state sector. The countries with high inflation were able to raise extremely large amounts of seigniorage.

As shown in table 3.3, these levels of seigniorage generally far exceeded levels in Latin America and were truly enormous. In Russia seigniorage equalled approximately 33 percent of GNP in 1992. The primary beneficiaries of seigniorage in the CIS countries, Romania, and Bulgaria were enterprises. With negative real interest rates, this was an important source of finance for enterprises, which kept the state sector producing and slowed down the reforms that would be induced by hard budget constraints. Why then did the policy makers in some countries choose to delay restructuring by maintaining lax monetary policies, while others opted for immediate stabilization and thus plunged directly into recession? Our analysis seems to suggest that it was not because continued lax policies provided the economy with better options after a couple of years of delayed stabilization. The data, if anything, support the opposite view: economies that delayed stabilization suffered more subsequently.

Politics and the Credit Process

We might conclude from all this that the policy makers who did not stabilize were simply in error. They initially thought that loose credit would give enterprises time to adjust, and that this in turn would limit the ultimate output declines and restructuring costs. In retrospect, credit policy has had little impact, so the policy measures were at best unhelpful and

Table 3.3
Seigniorage and natural resources

	Real value of net credit issue[1] (% GNP, 1992)	Major natural resource exports outside FSU[3] ($ million of cotton, oil, and gas)
Estonia	0.2	0
Hungary	0.4	0
Poland	6.4	0
Romania	6.4	0
Latvia	11.9[2]	0
Albania	14.4	0
Lithuania	19.7[2]	0
Kyrgyzstan	29.1[2]	0
Moldova	32.6[2]	0
Russia	32.7[1]	24,200
Ukraine	34.5	small
Kazakhstan	35.7	1,000
Belarus	42.8	0
Turkmenistan	63.2	840
Uzbekistan	na	673

1. The data show the change in net credits to government plus gross credits to the rest of economy by the monetary authority, measured as a fraction of GNP. These are calculated on a quarterly basis. To calculate quarterly GNP, we allocated annual nominal GNP according to the quarterly pattern of producer price indexes (or consumer price indexes when producer prices were unavailable). The estimates will tend to overstate the real value of credits if there are long lags in credit allocation, and when quarterly inflation is high. The high measure for Turkmenistan reflects this. The Russian measure is calculated using monthly data, so the inflation bias should not be large in this case. Data from IMF, *Economic Trends* for various countries and *International Financial Statistics* for CIS countries; *Russian Economic Trends* (various issues); and *Ukrainian Economic Trends* (Oct. 1994).
2. These estimates are based on credits from commercial banks and the monetary authorities, and will therefore be substantially larger than credits from the monetary authority alone. To the extent that governments also directed commercial bank loans, and given negligible nominal interest rates during this period in most countries, this may be a better measure of the resources available to the authorities that control credit issue.
3. Data from IMF, *Economic Trends*.

turned out to be costly due to social costs of continued inflation. But this view completely ignores any political explanations of inflation, although these seem far more reasonable than economic arguments or explanations based on ignorance. Under the Soviet system, the link between monetary variables and demand was well understood. While policy makers were unfamiliar with free prices, they had for seventy years been well aware that economic balance required stringent control on credit and money issue. And while officials such as the Russian Central Bank Chairman Viktor Gerashchenko argued that issuing money was not inflationary, he may have done so more to support his policy of liberal credits to the industrial lobby than out of a real belief in a statement that by the end of 1992 was very clearly not true of Russia by the end of 1992. Even in Ukraine, notorious for its lack of professional economists, Oleh Havrylyshyn argues that ignorance and lack of careful consideration of stabilization policies were not the primary reasons for the choice of loose credit policies:[7]

... progress in reforms is not hampered primarily by a lack of understanding about the objective measures of stabilisation and adjustment that need be taken. What is most lacking is a sufficiently large constituency that is both committed ... and able to see through [such measures] ... the 30 March Economic Reform Programme of the Ukrainian Cabinet of Ministers was no less sensible or orthodox than the Russian Letter of Intent to the International Monetary Fund of February 1992. In practice, the main difference was a reformist Russian cabinet ... the Ukrainian government allowed a huge expansion of credits to the economy starting in mid-1992, revealing its lack of commitment to the stabilisation goals set out in March. The Russian government did the exact same thing ... because it was unable to convince the public body on the need for monetary constraint.

Does the answer to the question then lie once again in the breakdown of the political system, and was subsequent high inflation caused more by a lack of political consensus than by wrong economic judgments or ignorance by the policy makers in the economies concerned? There are several reasons to think so. The most fundamental can be gleaned from reexamining table 3.3. The credit issues that occurred in these countries bordered on the obscene. The amounts are truly enormous, and even if one accepts that some industries needed subsidies, and that households deserved better social programs, the 32.7 percent of GNP seigniorage in Russia is far greater than that needed to pursue a careful and well-targeted program. In the first year of reforms, over 80 percent of Russian enterprises reported profits, while in Poland all of the top 500 enterprises reported profits. This was in part due to accounting methods, but it was also attributable to the ability of enterprise directors to suppress wages, given their relative power over employees. Most enterprises had substantial scope to sell inventories and to sell foreign exchange to provide financing. But with highly negative real interest rates, and large profits to be made from credits, it is no surprise that they all demanded such credits. In fact, a program that targeted a few politically sensitive enterprises could well have been worked out at a cost of only 3–5 percent of GNP.[8]

Likewise, a properly designed social support program would have been very cheap. The IMF estimated that an extensive social safety net, together with increased benefits to pensioners and health care provisions, would have cost roughly 3 percent of GNP in 1992. Thus in combination an enterprise support program and a social safety net would cost only 8 percent of GNP, less than one-quarter of the 33 percent of GNP seigniorage raised in 1992. These figures indicate that monetary policy was simply out of control in Russia and the other high-inflation countries during the early stage of reform. A more careful examination of credit policy provides additional evidence that the process was hijacked. Although there is little evidence on the pattern of credit issue by country, Russia's experience provides what appears to be a common trend. In 1992, there was no centralized program for monetary policy, and orders for new credits frequently came from the parliament, government, and president. The benefactors of these huge credits were not those groups that suffered the most social damage: for example, pensions remained relatively low and access to them was very limited. Subsidized credits were given to the agroindustrial complex, northern territories, and major industries. In June 1992 Gaidar, after trying to implement a tight credit policy, yielded to the demands of the industrial lobby to protect the privatization program. He alluded to this directly in his Lionel Robbins Lectures[9]:

... So we were ready to begin the process of privatization. Unfortunately, it coincided with a civil crisis during which pressure mounted to weaken monetary policy and increase drastically the budget deficit. When we could no longer withstand the pressure, we loosened monetary and financial policy.

This pattern of large credits to the industrial lobbies and agriculture has repeated itself throughout the CIS countries, Bulgaria, and Romania. In a few cases, such as Estonia, Poland, and Czechoslovakia, where reformists managed to maintain a social consensus (at least for some time) with the population, industry's demands for credits could be resisted. But in countries where reformists were weak, or where no reformists came to power, the social consensus necessary to fight off large industrial concerns and combat inflation was not strong enough or simply nonexistent.

A related reason for the lack of monetary discipline is corruption. There is substantial evidence that corruption and bribery were rife in Ukraine and Russia and particularly in Central Asian countries during the first few years of reforms. Handelman (1994) documents the Chechnya scandals of 1992, in which gangs obtained promissory notes authorized by the regional branch of the Russian Central Bank in Chechnya. These were subsequently honored by commercial banks in other parts of Russia, and in one arrest some $200 million worth of cash was collected. Triesman (1995) examines the allocation of preferential credits in the Moscow region. Although these credits were ostensibly aimed at improving food supplies, he shows econometrically that the only variable providing a significant explanation of whether an enterprise received funds is its director's "connections with Moscow city authorities." No variables related to food supplies or other factors reflecting the stated purposes of the credits were explanatory. In Ukraine, although there is no recorded evidence of central bank corruption, there have been analogous incidents. For example, a former prime minister has been charged with embezzling several hundred million dollars. In such an environment, it is understandable that officials can come under enormous pressures to issue credits for personal gain.

The sheer size of potential seigniorage has in itself made inflation almost inevitable. The amounts available were so substantial that any one person would have been under enormous pressure to break credit limits. It would have taken a set of determined politicians, a government with a strong political base, and a weak opposition to prevent inflation in a country as large as Russia. In smaller countries where increases in money issuing would lead directly to inflation through exchange-rate depreciation raising import prices, the benefits of inflation would have been smaller. In such a situation a determined reformer would face less opposition. In the Czech Republic a strong leader was able to build consensus. And in Poland, Balcerowicz was, ironically, unopposed in the first few months largely because his government represented the major force that would have benefited from industrial credits, that is, the Solidarity trade union. In all these cases personal leadership undoubtedly played a key role in weighing the balance of forces in favor of stabilization.

To conclude, it seems that the countries that experienced continued high inflation did so because rent seekers had captured the political process following the breakdown of political institutions. This, rather than structural explanations and explanations based on ignorance among policy makers, seems to have been the reason for the high inflation. This view is

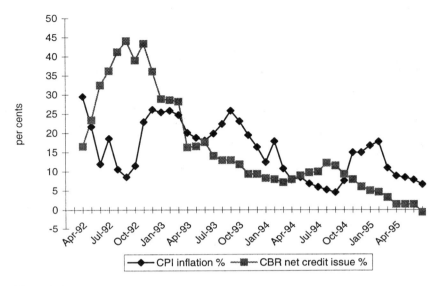

Figure 3.4
Revenue from credits and CPI inflation (March 1992–June 1995)

supported by the sheer size of the seigniorage revenue extracted and by its distribution.

3.4   Why Has Inflation Fallen in Most Countries as of 1996?

But if there were such great pressures for inflation, what then has allowed countries to stabilize over time? As seen from table 3.2, by 1995 after several years of high inflation more than half the countries had managed to reduce it below 50 percent per annum, and virtually every CIS country is now on track to bring inflation down to 2–3 percent per month sometime in 1997. There are many possible explanations. Figure 3.4 illustrates one key reason for the case of Russia. Seigniorage declined rapidly from the unprecedented highs in 1992 to much smaller levels in 1995. This is true even while the inflation rate remained as high as that of 1992. The main reason appears to be the rapid development of financial markets, which helps people avoid the inflation tax. When the payments system was slow, and there were few alternatives to holding funds in rubles, enterprises and households became hostages to the inflation tax. As agents found means to conserve on money balances, they avoided the inflation tax and money velocity rose. The levels of seigniorage gained in

1992 would certainly lead to hyperinflation in Russia today, so the benefits from inflation have been reduced sharply.

A second reason for the fall in inflation is foreign financial assistance and the desire of politicians to become part of the world economic system. Substantial bilateral and multilateral aid to CIS countries has been conditional on agreeing on a monetary program with the IMF in which low inflation is a key requirement. It is no surprise that every country that has stabilized has taken advantage of IMF loans when embarking on a program. There is still some dispute as to whether these benefits are marginal or significant. Sachs (1994) argues that such short-term assistance can provide key support for a political leader fighting off the interest groups who favor high inflation. Alternatively Gomulka (1994) argues that assistance can play only a minor role, and political determination at the start is key. No doubt the answer depends on the specific situation in the economy. In Russia, during the first year of reforms, the potential gains from seigniorage were far greater than any conditional aid offered.

In addition, IMF programs required price and trade liberalization that would have seriously reduced the scope for gains, which in our view were worth well over $20 billion for various interest groups. It is not surprising that this scope had to be reduced, and that opposition to high inflation had to increase, before the government could credibly sign on to an IMF program.

A third reason for the reduction in inflation lies in the improvements in the political system that have taken place, particularly in the former ruble zone countries. This includes both the organization of political parties and improvements in the policy-making process. In countries where there are free elections, inflation has become one of the key concerns of the population. Granville and Shapiro (1996) report that a 1 percent reduction in inflation will reduce the number of Russians under the poverty line by 700,000. In opinion polls Russians report inflation as their second major concern after unemployment. If these opinions are channelled into the formal political system, then they are bound to affect the politicians' desire to increase their control over inflation.

Another reason why a well-functioning political process reduces inflation is that it increases coordination among policy makers. After the initial collapse of the political system, rules for decision making were largely absent. In a few countries where one clear leader emerged, decisions could be made coherently,[10] taking into account all relevant costs and benefits. But all too often, a number of decision makers with competing interests became involved in policy making in a situation without well-functioning rules for policy implementation. Aizenman (1989) and Hørder (1996) analyze the effects of this in a theoretical framework. If many different agents gain effective control over money issue—for example, if the central bank responds to demand from the parliament, government, and president—then the equilibrium outcome would be high inflation. Each group will try to sequester credits for their own benefit, and will consider only the costs specifically attributed to itself. Alternatively, when there is one clear group or individual responsible for credit policy, then that person bears the full burden and blame for the costs of inflation.

An example where the absence of a well-functioning decision-making process caused inflation is the conduct of monetary policy in the CIS in 1992. After the break-up of the former USSR, each of the CIS republics was effectively able to issue ruble credits. It was only natural that many of them would expand credit issue, knowing that the inflation costs would be spread across all the republics while they themselves gained the immediate benefits of seigniorage. This situation was brought under control only in July 1992, when clear limits on credits from the Russian Central Bank to other republics were put in place. Even then it took another year before these credits were fully stopped. In 1992 some 10 percent of GNP in monetary credits were given by Russia to the other republics.

Lack of a well-functioning political process can also lead to indecision which, again, can result in high inflation. Alesina and Drazen (1991) present a theoretical model showing that when different decision makers (or groups of decision makers) are able to veto decision making, it can be individually rational for each of them to refuse agreements that would bring about stabilization. They put off taking decisions in the hope that other groups will agree to better terms. In such a situation, the stock of government debt can grow substantially, or a high inflation equilibrium can be sustained, while each interest group waits, hoping that someone else will concede to paying higher taxes, or will accept a reduction in credits received, to halt inflation. The lack of agreements over budget plans, and the inability of governments to work out decisive stabilization programs, probably reflected this type of indecision. Improved political processes and rules help prevent the inflation caused by such a "war of attrition" by penalizing those who are hijacking the process.

It seems that in most cases where countries did not stabilize initially, the factors supporting continued high inflation have been eroded by subsequent economic and political developments. It appears that even in the former socialist economies that chose inflationary policies, stabilization has occurred, albeit with a substantial delay. While this is a positive development, there are still lessons to be learned from the early stabilizers as to what high-inflation countries could have done differently to promote early stabilization and thus reduce the hardship suffered by the population at large.

3.5   Lessons for Stabilization

When there is political chaos and uncertainty, it is tempting to argue that economic policies and strategies will play little role in determining whether a country stabilizes. But the lesson from the former socialist countries is that this is at most only partially correct. There is no doubt that large seigniorage revenues, a well-organized opposition in favor of loose credit policies, and a corrupt environment reduce the chances that a politician interested in stabilizing an economy will succeed. But there are lessons and examples from the CIS that show stabilization is still possible even in these extreme environments. The aim of this section is to examine some of these lessons.

How economic policies affect outcomes is determined largely by the nature of political leadership in the economy. The economic policies implemented in the former socialist economies were not determined purely by this historical legacy of institutions and fundamental economic factors. If this had been the case, then how could we explain the enormous differences in the economic policies actually implemented? Was Albania predestined to join the group of rapid stabilizers, while Romania and Bulgaria stayed behind with high inflation? And why did Kyrgyzstan manage to stabilize early and generally follow liberal macroeconomic policies while all its neighbors were mired in interventionist policies with high inflation?

The success or failure of all these countries reflected in part differences in the political leadership. In Ukraine, there was undoubtedly an opportunity to enter into serious reforms right from the start. President Kravchuk won the support of the population for his strong nationalist stance, but there was little discussion of his economic priorities. A determined president could have called for economic reform and built a strong political base through popular support. If Kravchuk had been a spirited reformer as well as a nationalist, then he might have succeeded. Likewise, among the Central Asian Republics, President Akayev of Kyrgyzstan is the only example of a president determined to implement radical market reforms. He continuously fought with the parliament and government to gain power over economic policies and implement reforms. It was his popularity, and a series of referendums that he soundly won, that gave him the political support needed to implement stabilization. It is easy to imagine that without his determination, and with a person more like Nazarbayev of Kazakhstan in power, Kyrgyzstan would never have chosen, much less implemented, such a program.

In this section we look at the options facing a pro-stabilization leader who at a given moment has the opportunity to design an economic reform program. Since a key problem faced by reformers is the reversal of their stabilization attempts, the question we pose is: what policy options help ensure that reforms can continue? There is an extensive literature on stabilization and the optimal design of economic programs. This focuses mostly on Latin America and is concerned with issues such as wage controls, other price controls, and the choice of an optimal exchange rate regime at the start of stabilization. We do not focus on such issues both because they are already well discussed in this literature, and because they are somewhat less relevant in the formerly socialist countries, where there was often no need for wage and price controls. In these countries trade unions and workers seemed to have weak bargaining power relative to enterprise directors. In Eastern Europe there were few strikes and no evidence that wage demands would fuel inflation as they did in Latin America. In Poland, for example, workers elected enterprise directors in state enterprises, and wage controls were implemented to limit wage growth in the first few years of the program.

Instead, we focus on the political arena, where clear patterns across countries have emerged in terms of links between political developments and economic reforms. Several options and issues are worth considering. These relate to the underlying causes of inflation described in the previous section. We concentrate on four major policy options that we label: (1) poison pills, (2) preemptive policy changes, (3) conditional assistance, and (4) deadlines and reform of the political process. There is very little theoretical work on these issues, and therefore our discussion may at times be superficial. We believe, however, that these examples provide insights into important issues and can serve as valuable starting points for future research.

Poison Pills

The leaders of stabilization programs often claim that they have only a short period of time to carry out policies before opposition builds up and it becomes difficult to conduct reform. This is what Balcerowicz refers to as the "period of extraordinary politics" or what is sometimes called a window of opportunity. An extreme example was the situation faced by the Gaidar team. When they came to power, different members of the team stated that they were unlikely to last even six months. As shown in the empirical results, tight monetary policy speeds up industrial decline and restructuring and hence the industrial lobby is a natural opposition to stabilization. Loose credit helps postpone the eventual decline. This raises the possibility that short-term stabilization may be politically self-sustaining. Once a country embarks on a stabilization program that lasts long enough for real restructuring to start, enterprises opposed to reform will lose power as their size declines and their level of employment is reduced. This will naturally reduce their political power, since the threat of employment cuts and strikes is now less punishing. This in turn will strengthen the pro-stabilization forces and lead to a continuation of the stabilization policies. However, in addition to relying on such self-sustaining policies, a pro-reform policy maker acting in a window of opportunity can introduce a so-called poison pill to sustain sound macroeconomic policies.

In corporate finance poison pills are a well-known invention to prevent corporate takeovers. Some countries have implemented similar devices in their economic policies. One example of an economic policy with poison pill features is a currency board. In Estonia the central bank governor, with the support of the government, announced a fixed exchange rate and introduced a currency board system in July 1992, just before elections. By doing so, the governing politicians effectively changed the incentives of subsequent governments. The poison pill aspect of a currency board is that it is extremely difficult to reverse without risk of financial turmoil. Under the rules of operation, the Bank of Estonia must always buy or sell foreign exchange on demand at a given exchange rate from all domestic entities. There are no provisions for suspension of foreign currency sales. The exchange rate is pegged and there are onerous procedures for changing it. Parliament must approve any change in the exchange rate, and this ensures a real risk of news leakage (and hence a run on foreign reserves) prior to an agreement being reached in parliament. Unless there is wide consensus on changing the rules, it would be dangerous for any one group to open a Pandora's box by trying to change the system.

A currency board locks in a number of important macroeconomic polices needed for stabilization. First, by law the Bank of Estonia is not permitted to issue domestic credit. It can only issue base money through foreign exchange purchases. Second, the currency is fully convertible for current account transactions. And since the central bank must buy and sell foreign exchange resulting from current account transactions, the money supply will adjust to ensure balance-of-payments' equilibrium. With the exchange rate fixed, domestic prices will be anchored by import competition. Third, since the central bank cannot issue credits to the government or to commercial banks, the system forces an immediate adjustment in the budget, industry, and the banking sector. The government can spend only its tax revenues and must rely entirely on non-inflationary financing —ensuring that subsidies will be cut and price controls can be scaled back, as they are not needed. Enterprises will not receive credits from the central bank and hence restructuring cannot be postponed. Finally, the banking system cannot be bailed out. While in many countries commercial banks with poor loan portfolios maintained liquidity by borrowing from the central bank, in Estonia these banks ran into severe problems early on and were forced into bankruptcy. Because the government could not afford to bail out the banks, depositors lost a fraction of their accounts. This had the positive result of forcing households to recognize the risks inherent in each bank, and encouraging them to place their money in safer banks. In an environment where many new banks are being established (for example, some 2,500 banks were formed in Russia in 1992), this is an important start to limiting moral hazard problems in the banking system.

A second example of a poison pill also comes from Estonia. After fixing the exchange rate, the Bank of Estonia sold futures contracts up to eight years ahead, at low fees, promising to sell foreign exchange at 8 kroons per DM. We do not know the total amount of sales, but this is a very clear form of poison pill. Any central bank governor who in the future chooses to devalue the currency will face losses on these outstanding futures contracts. The intriguing aspect of the currency board system is that it changes the political payoffs to policy reversals. Figure 3.5 shows a simple sketch of how the payoffs might change. Suppose that in the first stage of a game the government is unsure of whether it will stay in power in the second stage, and if it does not, an alternative group that relies on antireform support will come to power. Suppose further that if reforms last long enough (here, two periods), they will not be reversed because the major proponents of reversal will be sufficiently weakened. The payoffs to alternative policies are shown in figure 3.5. If in the second stage of the game the opponents come to power, the net payoff from reversing reforms is B-A when there is a poison pill, or B when there is no poison pill. This makes it clear that there are two key criteria necessary for a poison pill to work:

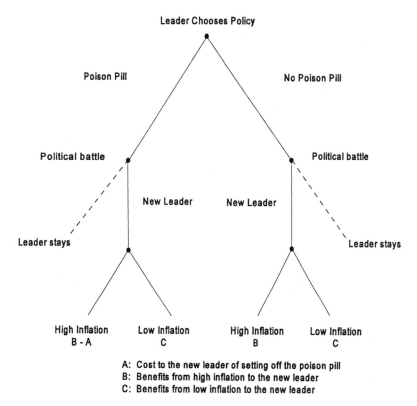

A: Cost to the new leader of setting off the poison pill
B: Benefits from high inflation to the new leader
C: Benefits from low inflation to the new leader

Figure 3.5
The impact of a poison pill on the subsequent inflation choice

1. the opponents must perceive and pay a penalty when they reverse reforms;

2. the opponents' perceived penalty must be greater than the perceived net gains from policy reversal.

Note that the effects of a poison pill may also be painful for other members of society. Therefore the risk of a poison pill is that if (1) and (2) are not satisfied, its application may backfire. If the opponents choose to reverse policies in spite of the poison pill, then as the pill is invoked all members of society will bear the costs. A second problem arises if the new government is able to blame the costs of invoking the pill on the previous government. Then even though the costs of the pill are potentially large, they may still not be borne by the persons in power. Hence the poison pill might fail to prevent policy reversal and indeed lead to a worse outcome than in a situation where there is policy reversal but no poison pill.

In Estonia the currency board was popular as it immediately stabilized prices after the spell of high inflation experienced while Estonia still used the ruble. It seems reasonable that the public would have attributed any failure of the system to the actual government that tried to reverse policies (witness the recent Mexican default or Turkey's early experience under Ciller). Given the relatively small amounts to be gained from breaking the rule, it is quite possible that once the currency board was in existence, opponents to stabilization coming to power would decide to maintain the system. Although the currency board seems to have worked in Estonia, it is not clear whether such a system would be politically effective in a larger country such as Russia. As mentioned above, in Russia the total benefits of breaking off pro-stabilization reforms were seigniorage revenues equal to 32.7% of GNP in 1992. Likewise, the banking sector and the industrial sector in Russia—the two groups most likely to oppose a currency board—were much larger than in Estonia. Estonia also had an advantage because ethnic Russians (many of whom had no voting rights) made up a disproportionately large portion of the population in the industrial sector. This made it easier for the government to implement stabilization that primarily hurt industry.

Preemptive Policy Changes

It is also possible, at least in theory, that partial or preemptive policy changes may change the payoffs to political actors so that reforms are maintained. In Ukraine, there was a power vacuum in the autumn of 1993 after a coal miners' strike triggered a political battle between the parliament and president. The result was a compromise agreement to hold new elections for both parliament and presidency. As the various groups waited for the elections, in December 1993 the governor of the central bank launched a single-handed attempt to reduce inflation from hyperinflationary levels. He virtually stopped credit issue and there was an immediate decline in inflation and output.[11] The policies met with substantial criticism from President Kravchuk, and he vowed to fire the governor once elections were over. In a surprise result, Kravchuk lost the election to former Prime Minister Kuchma, and once Kuchma came to power he faced the choice of reversing the stabilization or agreeing to it. As many of the costs of stabilization had already been borne, and the IMF had promised to approve aid if stabilization was maintained, Kuchma after his election faced a very different situation from that of December 1993. The past costs of stabilization were already sunk, and any reversal would mean his having to repeat the exercise again at some future date. By making a preemptive attack on inflation, the central bank governor had changed the incentives enough for the new president to eventually decide to continue the relatively tight monetary policies.[12]

A similar pattern was seen in Serbia. After an episode of hyperinflation in 1993, in January 1994 the minister of finance announced a stabilization program with a pegged exchange rate. At the same time the government announced that the budget deficit would be 15 percent of GNP. Without other sources of financing, this deficit could be financed only through money issue. Because the authorities had built up sufficient reserves to more than cover outstanding M1, the pegged exchange rate was credible for approximately four to five months, provided the budget deficit was implemented as planned. After this time the outstanding stock of base money would have surpassed foreign reserves, and with continued money issue people would have expected an exchange rate collapse. As in the Ukrainian case, the initial public support for the stabilization changed the nature of the political game. The pro-stabilization ministers within the government were strengthened by the early support and the success of the program as inflation fell. It then became clear that unless the budget was adjusted, the program would break down. In April of that year the cabinet finally agreed on a reduced deficit, and hence failure was avoided. Once again it seems likely that the early stabilization, and the subsequently changed payoffs to those supporting and opposing budget cuts, proved to be sufficient to shift the balance of opinion in favour of budget cuts by April.

It should not be surprising that preemptive actions on the part of a small group with some temporary power over exchange rate policy, or monetary policy, can change subsequent incentives for political actors. But in practice it is not clear whether these incentives will be enough to prevent the reversal of reforms. Many countries have stabilized for a temporary period and then reversed reforms. In Ukraine the decision to maintain course was in part due to the change of leadership, and was also helped by other factors such as the IMF money available provided reforms were maintained. In Serbia the decision to stop financing the war ensured that the budget could be kept in reasonable balance, and fingers had already been burned from the severe hyperinflation in 1993. Preemptive strikes probably work in an environment where the costs and benefits of inflation are nearly balanced. If there are strong forces opposing the necessary stabilization policies, however, then high inflation may be unavoidable.

Conditional Assistance

There are many advocates of conditional foreign aid and both economic and political arguments in its favor. As described in section 3.2, during the economic crises in former socialist countries budget revenues fell and there were legitimate demands for broad social programs. In such a situation inflation may be a logical choice by government officials. If, on the other hand, a government could borrow to cover temporary spending needs and revenue shortfalls, then it could avoid the social costs of inflation. Indeed many of the requests for aid by recipient countries were formulated along these lines. However, as we have previously argued, the understanding of fiscal crisis in many of the former socialist economies misses the nature of their underlying problems: the breakdown of the political system, and lack of well-directed financing, was at the heart of so-called fiscal crises.

A related reason for economic aid is to cover balance-of-payments needs. In the former socialist countries, imports fell drastically when the CMEA trading regime ended and state orders were halted. There were also problems with developing a viable interstate payments system early on. Given the level of exports, foreign aid can support higher output and wages by limiting the decline in imports. But here aid can only have a small impact: at best it will be several percent of GNP, and such amounts are small compared with the declines in real GNP and purchasing power reported for CIS countries.

Because the direct economic impact of foreign aid would most likely be small, one main role of foreign aid should instead be to support weak governments that aim to introduce and maintain good policies (Sachs 1994). In this case small amounts of funds may be helpful if they translate into greater political power. In many CIS countries the liberal factions of governments had only limited control over state resources. When foreign assistance was made conditional on introducing policies they preferred, it could possibly tip the balance of political power in their favor. However, given the large amounts of resources that were up for grabs in many countries (see table 3.3), it is no surprise that aid was ineffective at the start of reforms in many countries. The essential issue is whether there are enough net benefits from aid to the groups in power so that once they have received the aid, they will still be willing to implement the policies that were a condition of aid being granted. Since IMF programs require that the amount of credits issued are cut and that trade restrictions and other rent-seeking policies are halted, this will only happen when the net benefits of the policies favoring rent-seeking groups decline, and only then will the political balance tip in favor of reformers. Thus the role of foreign aid in promoting initial reforms may be limited.

Aid may be more helpful in a role of ensuring policy coordination. When inflation and general economic breakdown is caused by a lack of coordination of policies across different interest groups, then the process of negotiations and conditional aid that the IMF begins may actually help bring this lack of coordination to an end. For example, IMF programs demand that the government limit foreign borrowing. In Mongolia and Ukraine, where there were brief periods where any ministry could take on foreign loans (and did!), such simple rules could have helped coordinate overall fiscal and monetary strategies. The difficulty here is that each interest group with veto powers over these decisions must be willing to accept the conditions. Since typically the IMF deals only with the central bank and government, they may not be able to reach consensus if the parliament or other authorities feel they will get no benefits from foreign assistance. Countries can enter into such aid programs only if they are committed to reform, so it is impossible to tell whether aid plays a critical role in the process of reform or is marginal or ineffective. Virtually every CIS country has now entered into some sort of IMF program. In response to early criticism, the IMF introduced special financing in 1993 with reduced conditionality. This ensured that a large number of countries started programs, but it is not clear whether these programs actually speeded up the process of stabilization. One important role that early loans can play is to open up a clear dialogue with potential recipients. This allows them to make a better assessment of their own benefits and costs of reforms, as well as providing technical assistance on program design. Because dialogue also leads to small steps in the direction of reform, it may have acted as a preemptive action as described above, which in turn made it more desirable for governments to continue the steps with broader IMF programs later on.

Budget Process and Deadlines

In former socialist countries, poor economic policies were often due to lack of coordination or rational indecision rather than because some single agent in absolute control chose them. Alesina and Drazen (1991) argue that wars of attrition, where one party has a veto right over decisions needed to stabilize the economy, can result in long periods of socially costly inflation. Their model permits the introduction of mechanisms changing the incentives of each group so that they are more willing to make early agreements and concessions. In Aizenman (1989) and Hørder (1996), lack of coordination among policy makers drives the inflation process. If each ministry has, in effect, the opportunity to issue credits—say by pre-committing to spending and building up arrears—and if each of the spending agencies fails to take into account the actions of other ministries, there is a potential for high subsequent inflation.

These arguments suggest that rules that force coordination and speed up decision making may help ensure that stabilization is sustainable. Indeed, in many countries lack of coordination between agencies was an important factor causing inflation. In Ukraine, until 1994, the parliament had the legal right to make special demands for emergency credits and spending. This meant that the government, parliament, and central bank were all effectively able to issue credits. In Russia in the first year after liberalization, there was no clear process for credit coordination and the situation was further exacerbated by the right of both the government and president to grant tax waivers and make spending promises, and of the parliament to legislate similar changes. High inflation ensued. Once credit policies and overall budgetary policies were coordinated, inflation fell. The lesson to be drawn from these experiences is that procedures and rules enforcing political coordination can play a key role in ensuring that stabilization is successful. The specifics will depend on the country in question, but the following are some basic rules:

1. There should be an ultimate arbiter able to penalize groups who do not make decisions. Such penalties should be mandatory, although discretion may be exercised as to which group is penalized.

2. There must be a mechanism ensuring participation and encouraging agreement between all major political groupings in the process.

3. There should be clear costs that can be attributed to each group when the process breaks down and deadlines are not met, and there must also be means to resolve the crisis if no ultimate agreement can be obtained (an election).

4. There should be a mechanism for ensuring implementation of the budget as planned and legal requirements preventing deviations except

for emergencies. There must be a single arbiter responsible for deciding when deviations are legitimate.

Even when such procedural rules are included in a stabilization program, there may still be a problem of adherence. Such rules can work only as part of a program accepted as legitimate by most political groups. If there is a window of opportunity when a leader can implement such rules, then they may in turn become difficult to change later on, thus locking in a stable budget-making process that prevents wars of attrition or inflation driven by uncoordinated policy making.

3.6 Conclusion

We believe that the loose monetary policies and continued high inflation in the former socialist economies were primarily a reflection of the political breakdown, the institutional breakdown, and widespread corruption in these economies. Close examination of those policies has shown that credits and budget expenditures were directed to strong political lobbies rather than to reduce the social costs of adjustment. Since these lobbies were generally large industrial enterprises and the former political elite, the ultimate impact of high inflation was to retard structural adjustment. The enterprises that fought hardest for credits were undoubtedly those requiring the greatest structural reforms and downsizing in the transition process. By giving credits to these groups, loose monetary policies simply delayed the onset of the output decline and may have had the perverse effect of strengthening the antireform lobby. However, in each country the scope for rent seeking and seigniorage declined over time as reforms progressed. So by 1995 the benefits of loose credit policies were markedly reduced, and it is no surprise that virtually every country has now entered into a stabilization program.

These political explanations for high inflation provide lessons for stabilization programs in the future. When instability is caused by political breakdown, and a lack of checks and balances on leaders, then programs should be directed at these problems. This means focusing on policies that force or encourage coordination. Most important, democratic change can play a key role in ensuring that politicians are held responsible for their actions, and that the public's interests are channelled into the formal political process. The lesson from the CIS countries is that when a political system fails to do this, high inflation and enormous rent seeking can result. This means that more political rules and conditionality should be incorporated into initial stabilization programs.

In addition, there are more specific actions that leaders who face a narrow window of opportunity can take to coordinate economic policy and prevent reversal of reforms. We discussed how poison pills, preemptive policy strikes, checks and balances on budget processes, and conditional foreign assistance should be key ingredients in policy programs introduced in such a situation. These policies would need to be introduced alongside more standard and well-discussed fiscal measures (see, for example, Sargent 1983).

What does this bode for the future paths of inflation of Eastern European and the CIS countries? We are optimistic. Since in many of these countries political processes are gradually being redefined, and the benefits of seigniorage and rent seeking have fallen, the causes of high inflation have now been reduced. This suggests that in most of these countries we will not see recurring high inflations and instability, as observed for example in Latin America, in the future. Wherever there is a repeated breakdown of the political system, for example in war-torn areas and where there is civil disorder, there may very well be further episodes of similar inflations. In these cases, the lesson from the former socialist countries should provide guidelines as to how to prevent long episodes of disruption.

4 Privatization and Restructuring in Central and Eastern Europe

Saul Estrin

4.1 Introduction

Public ownership of the means of production was one of the central tenets of Communism, and a defining characteristic of all the countries ruled by Communists, including, within the industrial sector, China. This meant that private ownership was rare anywhere in Communist countries, and virtually nonexistent outside agriculture. Any exercise listing the reforms required to change Communist economies into capitalist ones would therefore have to place "privatization" high on the agenda.

The conceptual issues raised by privatization in Central and Eastern Europe do not differ fundamentally from those in the Western debate (see, e.g., Vickers and Yarrow 1988). The framework is that of principal-agent theory, which suggests that there may be significant efficiency gains from private ownership. However, rather than such ownership changes taking place in the relatively small public sector of an otherwise privately owned and market-oriented economy, it is occurring in countries in transition from generations under Communism and central planning. Privatization is therefore only one element in a wider program of reform, matched in significance by, for example, price liberalization, institutional and legal development, the removal of trade restrictions, and macroeconomic stabilization. This has altered the case for privatization, strengthening the arguments for speedy and widespread ownership changes.

The context of economic reform has led the countries of Central and Eastern Europe to innovate in their methods of privatization. In the absence of developed capital market institutions and with a drastic shortage of domestic savings, completely new ways of privatizing large segments of the economy have had to be developed. One of the important aims of this chapter is to examine the ownership consequences of these new methods—mass privatization—and to tentatively explore whether they might be expected to yield the efficiency gains apparently obtained by privatization in the West (see, e.g., Boardman and Vining 1989).

The chapter contains five further sections. In section 4.2, the literature comparing state and private ownership as governance mechanisms and the particular problems posed by privatization in the transitional context are briefly summarized. We then go on, in section 4.3, to discuss methods of privatization, an area in which the governments of Central and Eastern Europe have been highly innovative. The outcome of the privatization processes, in terms of who has actually ended up owning firms, for several of the most prominent countries—including Russia, Poland, Hungary, and the Czech Republic—is the subject of section 4.4. We turn to the impact of privatization on enterprise performance in section 4.5, which outlines both theoretical predictions and summarizes the empirical evidence to date. Conclusions are drawn in section 4.6.

4.2   Why Privatize in Eastern Europe?

In most firms of any size, ownership is separated from control. Private owners can be assumed to be interested in increasing their net worth. Managers, on the other hand, will want to use firm-specific rents to achieve their own personal goals—job security, pay, fringe benefits, perks, managerial power, and so forth. The conflict of interest causes problems for efficiency because of the asymmetry of information available to the two sides; private shareholders do not know enough about the firm to know whether managers are acting efficiently, or even honestly. If managers were given a free hand, one would assume that efficiency and profitability would suffer.

A market system offers a number of ways to resolve this conflict of interest. Clearly competitive product markets limit firm-specific rents, and therefore the extent of the damage unconstrained managers can wreak; hence the stress in the Western literature on combining privatization with liberalization. Private ownership also means that the behavior of the firm becomes subject to the scrutiny of capital markets, at least provided ownership titles are not too widely dispersed for the costs of monitoring to outweigh the benefits. Managerial decision making is monitored by competing traders in equity markets, whose conflicting judgments on potential company performance are summarized in the share price. If the managerial team is thought to be incompetent or inefficient, the share price will be reduced, putting pressure on managers to improve their performance. These pressures come in part via managerial incentives in the form of shareholdings and bonus payments. They also come from the way that the managerial market operates, with managerial performance in part assessed by movements in share prices. A persistently poor capital market showing can also encourage a takeover bid by a different management team.

Few of these mechanisms carry over to state ownership. Ownership and control are still separate, with the resulting conflict of interest and informational asymmetry between managers and the state. However, the state as owner may have multiple objectives—for example, creating employment in depressed regions, holding prices below average costs as an element of a prices and incomes policy, or satisfying service criteria. Profits can become secondary. Managerial discretion will be further increased if the government's various objectives for state-owned firms conflict or are frequently changed. The government as owner cannot rely on the highly motivated scrutiny of managerial performance provided by competitive capital markets. Monitoring of public-sector managers is in the hands of civil servants, who may not have the expertise, and certainly do not have the private incentives, of capital market traders.

These arguments have a strong resonance for Central and Eastern Europe before reform (see, e.g., Brada 1996). The owner of enterprises was effectively the Communist Party, which also controlled the state. The central planning system in principle provided a clear objective for firms—output growth—and a rigorous system of monitoring (see, e.g., Ellman 1989). However, the system also suffered from serious problems of information and incentives (see Kornai 1980), which led to extremely low levels of efficiency and innovation by Western standards, as well as poor quality standards.

However, the economies of Central and Eastern Europe are not obviously fertile territory for the application of policies that rely on the operation of competitive markets. Product markets are relatively imperfect in many countries and capital markets are severely underdeveloped (see, e.g., EBRD 1995).

The prospects for privatization yielding the expected productivity benefits in the short term are therefore not propitious (see Nuti 1995). As a consequence, in the early years of economic reform, there was intense discussion of whether microeconomic restructuring could at first be motivated by price liberalization and free trade. Perhaps privatization could be left until the track records of existing state-owned firms had become established, until the stock of domestic savings in private hands was sufficient to ensure the success of a competitive bidding process for the assets, and until capital markets were more developed. This would allow the use of an auction system in privatization to allocate assets to the highest bidders (bidding in the belief they would be able to earn the highest returns from them). The government would also be able to maximize its revenues from the privatization process.

But this approach assumes that the state can manage its assets effectively in the intervening period. In practice, the collapse of Communism has left state-owned firms with few or no resources, a weak internal structure to handle the new demands of the marketplace, and few mechanisms for the state to enforce governance. Most firms were effectively controlled by their employees—managers or workers or both.

In these circumstances, the option value of continued state ownership was low. The authorities had to create new structures if they sought to influence enterprise decisions to prevent a gradual dissipation of the net worth of the enterprise sector: by workers or managers raising their wages and emolument, by workers maintaining employment in the face of declining demand, or by managers stealing profitable assets. In most countries, governments had neither the interest nor the capacity to rationalize. An alternative to the gradual disappearance of the state's assets, probably into the hands of the former Communist *nomenklatura*, was rapid privatization (see Estrin 1994).

Given the experience of Communist rule, the population in many countries put little faith in the views of the state as an independent agent acting to maximize social welfare. More cynical interpretations of public ownership were prevalent, with the dangers of rent-seeking and corruption from continued state ownership being stressed (see, e.g., Frydman and Rapaczynski 1994; Boycko et al. 1995). This powerful urge to "depoliticize" the enterprise sector was for many observers the most significant motivation for speedy and widespread privatization.

4.3 Privatization Methods

Methods of privatization have not been a major issue in Western economies. Some form of auction method has typically been used, whereby the state seeks the highest attainable price the market will bear and potential purchasers value the assets according to their ability to generate returns from them. In the United Kingdom, which was in the forefront of early Western privatizations, a range of methods was used, from public tender through stock markets to sealed bids, according to the type of firm and the character of potential buyers (see Vickers and Yarrow 1988). A similar approach should in principle have been applied in transitional economies, where it is even more important—given the shortage of entrepreneurial talent at the start of reform—that assets get into the most efficient hands.

However, any attempt to organize public offerings in Central and Eastern Europe as a way to privatize the bulk of the economy faces insurmountable practical problems. At the aggregate level, the stock of private savings is far too small to purchase the assets of the industrial sector at prices that reflect future expected profitability. The market could clear only at very low prices, or extremely slowly. For example, it was calculated that at prereform savings rates it would take more than a century for the government to sell the assets of the Czechoslovak industrial sector (valued at their historic cost).

Governments could still, of course, seek to use auctions or public tenders to sell a few selected firms, either to domestic purchasers or to foreigners. This happened in most countries, especially those of Central Europe, where progress in reform as a whole was more advanced. Foreign owners would clearly be outsiders to the existing managerial structures, and could be expected to introduce some form of Western governance apparatus to the enterprise. Sales to domestic customers could be to insiders or outsiders, with managers and workers being the most obvious buyers. Only Hungary has been willing or able to sell an appreciable share of former state-owned assets to foreigners, and has attracted a disproportionate share of foreign direct investment as a consequence (see Meyer 1995). However, the preponderance of foreign ownership in the viable parts of Hungary's industrial sector has given rise to considerable public disquiet. Some governments, notably in Romania, have encouraged the emergence of insider-owned firms with ownership centered in trusts controlled by managers and/or workers. These management and employee buyouts (MEBOs) have also been an important element in the Polish privatization (see Estrin 1994), though there the assets have typically come onto the market through liquidations, and in Russia (see Boycko et al. 1995).

An alternative approach has been restitution to former owners. This has the advantage of immediately re-creating a property-owning middle class and reestablishing "real owners" of industrial firms. However, it is also highly regressive, leading to instantaneous concentrations of wealth in the hands of those whose sole claim to such privilege is the circumstances of their parents or grandparents before World War II. It also entails tremendous complexities that make the procedure very slow in practice. For example, suppose that a factory has been built on a plot of land formerly owned by a farmer. Does he receive the land, and therefore rental for the factory? Or should he be compensated for the value of the property at the time of its seizure, and if so, how is such a valuation to be made some 50 years later? This discussion raises the deeper question of how to distribute the assets accumulated during the Communist era, when consumption levels were held down for a generation to allow capital accumulation. Since the taxes were imposed on everyone, the argument that the distribution of assets should be egalitarian is a powerful one. Nonetheless, restitution has been an important element in privatization in several Central European countries, notably the former East Germany, Hungary, the former Czechoslovakia, and Bulgaria.

In most transition countries, however, policy makers concluded that conventional privatization methods could not deliver the required scale of privatization in the relevant time frame. They therefore developed "mass privatization." This involves placing into private hands through vouchers the "savings" required to purchase state assets.

Mass privatization avoids the problems of enterprise valuation. Most important, it allows large numbers of firms to be sold speedily while in principle permitting an egalitarian distribution of the former government assets. However, governments forgo most, if not all, potential revenues from privatization.

Table 4.1 presents information on the 18 countries that have introduced mass privatization. The most conspicuous absentee is Hungary, and none of the former Yugoslav economies is included except Slovenia. In the former Soviet Union, Azerbaijan, Turkmenistan, and Uzbekistan have not introduced mass privatization programs. The table reports the year that voucher distribution began and provides information about three aspects of the design of such schemes:

1. The form in which the vouchers are issued. There are two questions here: Should they be bearer or registered? Should they be tradable? (Bearer shares are always tradeable.) Underlying this is the question of who receives the vouchers. Equity suggests that they should be distributed to the entire population, but in some of the newer countries created by the disintegration of the Soviet Union, questions of nationality, ethnicity, and seniority have been relevant.

2. How should firms be sold? The shares may be brought to market continuously, as firms become ready, or in waves involving the simultaneous offer of 25 percent or more of companies eligible for privatization. The latter approach allows buyers to compare options but is administratively much more demanding. In the ambitious Czechoslovak scheme, for exam-

Table 4.1
Mass privatization programs in Central and Eastern Europe and the Commonwealth of Independent States

Country	Year voucher distribution began	Are shares issued in waves or continuously?	Are vouchers bearer, tradable, or nontradable?	Is investment in funds allowed, encouraged, or compulsory?
Albania	1995	continuously	bearer	encouraged[a]
Armenia	1994	continuously	bearer	allowed[b]
Belarus	1995	continuously	bearer	encouraged[c]
Bulgaria	1995	waves	nontradable	encouraged
Czech Republic	1992	waves	nontradable	encouraged
Estonia	1993	continuously	tradable[d]	allowed[e]
Georgia	1995	continuously	tradable	allowed[b]
Kazakhstan	1994	waves	nontradable	compulsory
Kyrgyzstan	1994	continuously	bearer	allowed[f]
Latvia	1994	continuously	tradable	allowed[e]
Lithuania	1993	continuously	nontradable	allowed[e]
Moldova	1994	waves[g]	nontradable	encouraged
Poland	1995	waves	tradable	compulsory
Romania[h]	1992	continuously	bearer	compulsory[i]
Romania	1995	waves	nontradable[j]	allowed
Russia	1992	continuously	bearer	encouraged
Slovak Republic	1992	waves	nontradable	encouraged
Slovenia	1994	continuously	nontradable	allowed
Ukraine	1995	continuously	nontradable	allowed

Source: Estrin and Stone 1996.
[a] By July 1996 only one or two funds had applied to receive vouchers.
[b] Although a legal entitlement exists to invest vouchers in funds, in practice this option was limited.
[c] The results of the first voucher auction were canceled in March 1995, and fund licenses were suspended from then until August 1996.
[d] Vouchers were nontradable at the outset of the program, but cash trading was legalized in the spring of 1994.
[e] Citizens could exchange vouchers for other things, such as apartments or land.
[f] Citizens could invest their vouchers in housing as well as shares. They can sell their vouchers to funds, but no formal mechanism exists for them to subscribe to funds.
[g] Although the design of the Moldovan program was based on the offer of companies in waves, the waves were small in the early stages, and thus had many of the characteristics of a continuous issue.
[h] In 1991 Romania introduced a scheme based on the distribution of certificates of ownership in five private ownership funds. In 1995 a supplementary mass privatization program was introduced involving the distribution of coupons that could be exchanged for company shares or fund shares, after which the funds are to be transformed into financial investment companies.
[i] Under certain circumstances, certificates of ownership in funds could be exchanged for company shares.
[j] Certificates of ownership were bearer; coupons were registered and nontradable.

ple, shares in enterprises were transferred in waves comprising hundreds of firms simultaneously. (Czechoslovakia did not break up until after the first wave of mass privatization.) A computerized system was set up to mimic a general equilibrium market-clearing process.

3. What kind of capital institutions should be built into the process? Mass privatization transfers ownership rights but leaves the character of future capital markets open. In some schemes, capital market intermediaries are an integral part of the program; in others they are allowed or actively encouraged. In the Czech and Slovak Republics and Russia, the vouchers could be exchanged directly for shares in companies. Financial intermediaries, though only encouraged to participate, by the end of the process controlled a majority of shares in Czechoslovakia. Investment funds also emerged spontaneously in Russia, though their shareholdings are more modest. In the Polish scheme, citizens' vouchers were exchanged for shares in government-created investment funds that jointly own all the former state-owned enterprises.

4.4 Who Owns Privatized Firms?

It is clear that company behavior after privatization depends on more than whether a firm is state-owned or privately owned; it also depends in part on who has become the majority owner. One can categorize the emerging structures of ownership in four levels, summarized in figure 4.1 (see Earle and Estrin 1996). The simplest distinction is between state-owned and private firms. This underlies data such as the share of the private sector in employment and output. The most obvious problem is that this division lumps together privatized and de novo firms, despite the fact that the latter face very different economic problems. In general, de novo firms do not need to restructure and usually differ from privatized firms in size and character. One can instead consider a tripartite categorization of ownership into state-owned firms, privatized former state-owned firms, and de novo private firms. The dividing lines are necessarily somewhat arbitrary. We noted earlier that many firms which are categorized as de novo are in fact spin-offs of assets and management from the state sector. There is also debate about what constitutes a privatized enterprise. For example, in the Hungarian and Russian usage, a firm is privatized if any of its shares are held by nonstate owners. In both countries, a significant proportion of firms have sold a small or minority stake to private individuals or companies, and these are classed in the domestic literature as privatized, though

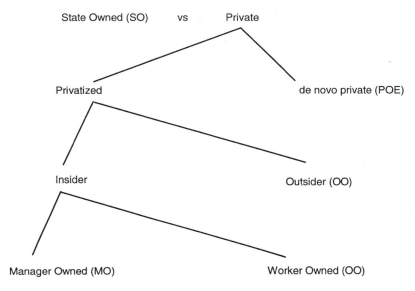

Figure 4.1
Alternate forms of majority ownership

the state remains the majority owner. In the empirical work that follows, we take privatization as implying that more than 50 percent of voting shares have been transferred into private hands.

The fact that most privatized firms have come into private hands via mass privatization means that we must also address the issue of who has become the majority owner. The simplest distinction is between privatized firms that are majority-owned by insiders and by outsiders. This gives us the third line in figure 4.1. Broadly, one might expect superior performance in restructuring and productivity from outsider-owned firms, provided that insiders are not able to block decision making (see Frydman and Rapaczynski 1994; Earle and Estrin 1996). We return to this issue in section 4.5.

At an even finer level of disaggregation, one might expect rather different behavior from firms that are majority-owned by their managers and by their workers, provided the latter are able to exercise effective governance over management. For example, one might expect worker-owners to resist layoffs or reductions in social benefits more vigorously than manager-owners.[1]

The evidence on emerging ownership patterns in the post-Communist countries is patchy and rather unreliable. However, the overall picture

Table 4.2
Private-sector share of GDP, 1996 (percent)

Albania	75	Latvia	60
Armenia	50	Lithuania	65
Azerbaijan	25	Moldova	40
Belarus	15	Poland	60
Bulgaria	45	Romania	60
Croatia	50	Russian Federation	60
Czech Republic	75	Slovak Republic	70
Estonia	70	Slovenia	45
Macedonia	50	Tajikistan	20
Georgia	50	Turkmenistan	20
Hungary	70	Ukraine	40
Kazakhstan	40	Uzbekistan	40
Kyrgyzstan	50		

Source: EBRD 1996.

is fairly clear. In all countries except the former Czechoslovakia and Hungary, privatization has led to majority ownership by insiders, typically workers or workers and managers together rather than managers alone. Hungary is an exception to this pattern because of the significant amount of foreign direct investment, though in the majority of privatized firms without foreign participation, insider control probably predominates. The Czech and Slovak mass privatization schemes have led to majority outside ownership of almost all firms.

This picture can be established with reference to the sketchy available evidence. In table 4.2 we present EBRD data on progress in privatization. The private-sector share is at least 50 percent in 15 countries and at least 70 percent in 5. Countries are distinguished more by location and date of reform than by privatization policy.

Earle and Estrin (1996) attempted, on the basis of data from the World Bank and Central European University Privatisation Project sources, to provide a guesstimate of insider ownership in five countries: the Czech Republic, Hungary, Poland, Romania, and Russia. Their work is summarized in table 4.3. Because of problems of data availability and comparability, these should be regarded as extremely rough approximations. Nonetheless, the overwhelming preponderance of insider privatization is clear.

Perhaps the best evidence on the emerging ownership structures in transitional economies comes from Russia, where the World Bank orga-

Table 4.3
Employee ownership resulting from privatization (est.)

Country (base group of companies for estimations)	Number of companies with employee control	Percent of privatizations	Average percentage held by all employees	Estimated total employment in EOs
Czech Republic	3	1	4.4	n.a.
Hungary	187	43	42.0	36,000
Poland	1,478	75	50.8	450,000
Romania	600	98	95	150,000
Russia	6,300	90	65	n.a.

Source: Earle and Estrin 1996.
Note: "Employee" is defined to include managers, because of the difficulty in obtaining information on ownership by different categories of employees. The sources and calculation of the estimates in the table are described below. Czech figures refer to companies privatized in the first wave of voucher privatization for which the approved privatization project granted more than 50 percent of shares to employees. Hungarian figures pertain only to the self-privatization program. Polish figures result from applying the proportion of employee-controlled firms in World Bank data on 21 firms in the liquidation program to the total of 1,999 Polish firms included in the program since 1991. The Romanian numbers refer to the results of a CEU survey of 66 privatized companies in the MEBO program. Those for Russia pertain to voucher-privatized companies; the proportion of 90 percent comes from a survey conducted by Blasi (1994) on the ownership structures of 127 companies in the program (applying this figure to the approximately 7,000 companies in the program yields an estimate of 6,300 employee-controlled companies). The estimate of all employees' stake in each country is based on all privatized companies in the base group (not only those with dominant employee control). All estimates are very preliminary.

nized a survey on a random sample drawn from a complete list of Russian industrial firms employing more than 15 people in 1991. The population was stratified by size and region, with sample replacement to maintain the stratified randomization. The ownership structure is summarized, along the lines of figure 4.1, in table 4.4. However, the Russian sample cannot be used to calculate the total share of the private sector (combining privatized and de novo firms) or the proportion of de novo firms because these were drawn from a different sample with the number of firms being predetermined. The table therefore excludes de novo firms. According to the sample, the Russian mass privatization has led around two-thirds of firms to leave the state sector. Of these, by far the most (83 percent) are majority-owned by insiders. Moreover, the bulk of these insider-owned firms are majority-owned by workers rather than managers. More recent data from Blasi et al. (1996) yield similar proportions.

Table 4.4
Outcome of Russian privatization (majority ownership in 1994, % firms)

State-owned	34
Privatized	66
Outsider	11
Insider	55
Manager-owned	12
Worker-owned	43

Source: Earle et al. 1995.

4.5   The Impact of Privatization on Company Behavior

In this section, we summarize theoretical predictions about the effects of privatization, comparing the effects of various majority ownership structures along the lines of figure 4.1. We then go on to survey the evidence from our own studies.

A Conceptual Framework

The Western literature strongly suggests that privately owned firms will perform better than state-owned ones. This proposition might be expected to hold in the transitional context, but three important provisos open up a richer empirical approach.

First, predictions about the behavior of firms are highly sensitive to the residual softness of the budget constraint. If budget constraints continue to be soft, it is unlikely that ownership changes in themselves will divert managerial behavior from the fruitful path of pursuing greater subsidies to the infinitely tougher task of restructuring. Conversely, the hardening of hitherto soft budget constraints is likely to lead to fundamental changes in enterprise behavior, perhaps as significant as those due to ownership changes. This is because, assuming that firms have no residual surpluses available—a reasonable assumption, given the macroeconomic environment in the early years of transition—managers will be forced to reduce costs, increase sales, and restructure their firms in order to survive.

Second, we have established that most privatizations have taken place through either the voucher method or MEBOs, with the consequence that most firms are majority-owned by insiders or dispersed outsiders. It is unclear what this implies about company performance. On the one hand, the Western literature emphasizes external capital markets as the disciplinary mechanism against inefficiency and rent-seeking. On the other hand, with managerial ownership at least, there is no separation of ownership and control, and hence no governance problem for capital markets to rectify. Insider control raises new agency problems, however, that seem likely to damage enterprise performance, notably restrictions on access to external finance. The fundamental problem for potential funders, whether of debt or of equity, is that they open themselves up to the threat of opportunistic behavior when governance is exercised by a factor of production other than by capital. A minority equity holder in an employee-owned firm, for example, cannot prevent the diversion of surplus from all owners to employee-owners via increases in wages and managerial remuneration. The Western empirical literature suggests that managerial ownership does improve performance up to a limit of around a 20 percent stake, a level far below that now observed in transitional economies. On balance, one might expect insider-owned firms to perform less well than outsider-owned ones, though perhaps better than state-owned enterprises.

However, one needs to be careful in defining good performance in the transitional context. Given the particular requirements for state-owned enterprises to restructure, the level and change in technical efficiency are not sufficient indicators, and profitability in the immediate postreform era is a seriously inappropriate as well as a poorly measured performance index. The contribution of privatization toward enterprise restructuring can be evaluated against three widely accepted objectives of the transformation process:

1. Developing a politically independent and market-oriented enterprise sector, "depoliticization"
2. Long-term enterprise restructuring
3. Short-term enterprise restructuring.

The balance of advantage by majority ownership type shifts according to the objective under consideration (see Earle and Estrin 1996). For example, insider ownership may weaken the prospects for long-term restructuring because of the inferior access to capital, but strengthen short-term restructuring because of superior knowledge of the market and technology.

What is the appropriate basis for comparison of performance in the three areas? We noted that in general we might predict that private firms perform better than state-owned ones. However, in the post-Communist economic environment, these sharp conceptual distinctions may not emerge empirically because outsider-owned firms may perform differently from

Table 4.5
Comparison of the impact of alternative ownership forms in attaining objectives of transition

	WO	MO	OO
Reorientation	++	+	+++
Long-term restructuring			
Unbundling	++	+	+++
Investment	+	++	+++
Short-term restructuring			
Nonlabor cost minimization	++	++	++
Labor cost minimization	0	+	++
Evolution of governance	++	+	+++

All entries are relative to the status quo (state ownership).
Notes:
+ denotes better
++ denotes much better
+++ denotes comparable to Western firms
0 denotes the same as the status quo

insider-owned ones, which themselves perform differently according to whether ownership is located primarily in the hands of workers or of managers. We need, therefore, to establish that all forms of private ownership are expected to dominate state ownership, and that outsider ownership is predicted to dominate all forms of insider ownership, with reference to the three objectives listed above. State ownership in this context is tantamount to a vacuum in property rights, with the firm effectively controlled by managers and/or workers and with few constraints on the capacity to decumulate assets through wage increases, perks, and theft.

Predictions about the capacity of different majority ownership arrangements to attain the three objectives listed above are summarized in table 4.5. All entries are relative to continued state ownership: + denotes a superior performance; ++, a highly superior performance; and +++, a performance comparable with Western firms. A minus sign denotes an inferior performance, and O, a performance the same as that of state-owned firms.

Depoliticization is viewed by many as a fundamental element of the transition process (see, e.g., Boycko et al. 1995; Frydman and Rapaczynski 1994). Relative to state ownership, in table 4.5 privatization in all cases will encourage some degree of depoliticization. Here property rights have been clarified, allowing a legal separation of state and enterprise, and a framework created that permits the interests of owners other than the state to influence enterprise decisions. This depends crucially, however, on hardened budget constraints. Among the forms of privatized firm, outside private ownership is likely to be best able to ensure depoliticization because the new owners are less likely to be part of the old order, especially if they are foreigners, and will probably have more restricted access to subsidy. Insiders, though they have some incentive to increase profits through their shareholdings, may have closer ties to the old bureaucracy and greater opportunity to pursue special concessions. Workers and managers may differ significantly here. Managers will typically be survivors from an earlier period, selected for their contacts and rent-seeking abilities rather than their managerial skills, while workers are a new and more diffuse group of owners. Managers may therefore be able to achieve higher returns from rent-seeking than can workers, because there are fewer of them among whom to share the spoils, and because their long-standing connections may make them more effective at rent extraction.

With respect to long-term restructuring, we focus on investment. Relative to state-owned firms, we predict investment to be greatest in outsider-owned firms, followed by manager-owned ones. Investment will be lowest in worker-owned ones, though investment levels may still be higher than in the current state sector.[2] The argument is based on the fundamental agency problems faced by minority investors in insider-controlled firms. These may be exacerbated in worker-owned firms by a chronic tendency to underinvest.

Short-term restructuring requires the firm to respond to the new post-liberalization relative prices by altering factor proportions, product mixes and production methods, quality targets, information systems, and so forth. All private firms have clear incentives to raise profits in these ways. It is useful, however, to distinguish between actions to minimize nonlabor costs or to increase revenues, and actions to reduce labor costs. Once again, there is no reason to assume outside owners behave in significantly different ways in either area from owners of Western firms. However, insiders might be expected to be rather less effective in this regard, at least initially, because of inexperience and possibly lack of expertise in these fields. The problem is likely to be more serious with regard to employment than other inputs or outputs, and, with respect to employment decisions, worse for workers than for managers as owners.

In summary, we predict that privately owned firms should perform better than state-owned ones in terms of productivity and in the three areas discussed above. We also predict that outsider-owned firms will perform better than insider-owned ones. Among insider-owned firms, managerial ownership is expected to lead to better performance with respect to investment and short-term restructuring. Worker ownership may yield relative advantages in terms of depoliticization.

Evidence on the Impact of Privatization

The evidence on the impact of privatization is surprisingly sparse. There are few studies, and the results are for the most part inconclusive (see, e.g., Pinto et al. 1993), though some new evidence is beginning to appear (see, e.g., Claessens and Djanjov 1997; Pohl et al. 1996; Kollo 1996). In this section, we summarize evidence from a series of World Bank–sponsored projects, covering the Visegrad countries plus Russia, in which enterprise-level information has been collected by survey methods.

Viability, Restructuring, and Privatization

Estrin at al. (1995) report the findings from a large case study project undertaken between 1990 and 1992. Up to 15 firms in Poland, Hungary, and Czechoslovakia were studied in detail, with the sample selected to control for size, industry, and competitiveness of markets. Using a variety of indicators of restructuring—for example, changes in product lines, quality control methods and changes in employment—firms' reactions to macrostabilization and market liberalization were categorized on a scale of 1 to 5. A score of 1 represents "passive" reactions and a 5 represents active restructuring across a broad front. Overall, the study found that only 17 percent of firms in the sample were reacting passively to the changed economic conditions, while 40 percent displayed very active responses. The figure suggests more enterprise-level restructuring during transition than is commonly believed, though there was no particular pattern to the responsiveness by sector.

Long-term responsiveness was indicated by whether or not firms had a long-term strategy for turnaround in place. Overall, one-third of sampled enterprises had no long-term strategy some three years into transition (in Poland). The proportion of firms with a long-term strategy was smaller than of firms undertaking some degree of short-term restructuring (60 percent as against 80 percent).

Estrin et al. (1995) went on to investigate the relationship between company viability, privatization, and restructuring. Viability was indicated by profitability, cash flow, and debt in 1992, and the changes in the 1989–92 period. Firms were categorized under three headings: viable, potentially viable, and nonviable. Viability can be taken to indicate the degree of the shock suffered by the firm. As table 4.6 makes clear, there is

Table 4.6
Short-term responses

	Poland	Czechoslovakia	Hungary
Steel	3	—	3
Textiles	3	3	5
Pharmaceuticals	2	3	5
Car parts	4	3	3
White goods	5	—	4
Heavy chemicals	1	3	3
Vehicles	3	4	3
Consumer electronics	3	4	3
Machine tools/engineering	3	3	4
Furniture	2	4	—
Glass	2	—	2
Footwear	2	5	—
Plastics	4	4	3
Textiles/garments	4	4	3
Food processing (brewing)	—	—	5
Food processing (sweets/chocolates)	4	3	5
Precision tools/defense	—	—	1
Average	3	3.6	3.5

Source: Estrin, Gelb, and Singh 1995.
1 = passive response only: accumulation of debt and arrears, nonpayment of suppliers, accumulation of inventories, etc.
3 = mainly production responses: closing production lines, altering product mix, laying off workers, reorganizing production toward cheaper inputs, etc.
5 = more active responses: new organization, marketing and sales development, export orientation, quality development, information systems, cost control, etc.

far more restructuring in viable firms than in nonviable ones. Conversely, passive firms are typically nonviable. Even more strikingly, almost every viable and potentially viable firm had a long-term strategy. This study also established a close relationship between viability and privatization; only one nonviable firm was privatized, but almost every viable firm was either fully privatized or partially privatized. This explains the results in table 4.7, which indicate that privatization is virtually a necessary and sufficient condition for the establishment of a long-term strategy. The table also indicates the damaging consequences of failing to privatize—in the absence of clear property rights, firms appear to be much less likely to implement long-term strategies or to restructure. However, the causality suggested by the study is complex, running from economic performance to privatization as much as from ownership to company behavior.

Table 4.7
Long-term strategy in place (percent)

	Poland	Czechoslovakia	Hungary
Yes	47	54	73
No	47	23	13
Unclear	7	23	13

Source: Estrin, Gelb, and Singh 1995.

Table 4.8
Output growth by ownership category: Poland, 1993 (percent of group)

	POE	PRE	SA	SOE
<−10%	5	12	20	16
−10%−10%	21	31	53	43
10%−25%	13	29	18	23
>25%	61	29	10	18
Total	100	100	100	100
Unweighted average (%)	66.5	20.1	9.2	9.8

Source: Belka, Estrin, et al. 1994.

Commercialization, Privatization, and de Novo Firms

Belka et al. (1995) used data from a survey of 200 Polish firms to investigate the variation in enterprise adjustment by ownership. Four categories of ownership were distinguished: (1) state-owned (SOE), (2) commercialized (SAE), (3) privatized (PRIV), and (4) de novo firms (POE). Commercialization represented the imposition of more effective state ownership, and perhaps the first step toward full privatization (see Belka et al. 1994).

The sample was not random; rather, it was stratified by ownership categories (120 state-owned, 40 privatized, 40 de novo). Hence it cannot be used to describe progress in privatization. However, since selection within each ownership category was random within the industrial sector, the sample can illustrate performance differences with respect to ownership type.

Belka et al. report that de novo firms are typically small; around one-third employ fewer than 50 persons, compared with fewer than 3 percent of state-owned and privatized firms, and only 8 percent employ more than 250 people. However, as tables 4.8 and 4.9 show, output and employment growth in the early years of the Polish upturn were concentrated in the de novo sector. Output was growing quite fast (>10 percent) in around

Table 4.9
Employment growth by ownership category: Poland, 1993 (percent of group)

	POE	PRE	SA	SOE
<−10%	16	27	28	35
−10%–10%	32	66	73	54
10%–25%	53	7	0	5
Total	100	100	100	100
Unweighted average (%)	23.3	−6.7	−6.1	−8.1

Source: Belka, Estrin, et al. 1994.

75 percent of POEs in 1993, but in less than 60 percent of privatized firms and less than around 40 percent of state-owned firms.

As one might expect, employment growth was concentrated in de novo firms; it increased by an average of 23 percent in 1993, as against declines of between 6 percent and 8 percent per year in both privatized and state-owned firms. Productivity growth was slightly higher in privatized firms—there, output growth was somewhat greater while employment declines were not significantly different across firms. Belka et al. (1994a) also report similar profit/sales ratios in privatized and commercialized state-owned firms; de novo firms were much more profitable; and losses were concentrated in the traditional state-owned sector. Similarly, investment-to-sales ratios were notably higher in de novo firms; privatized firms were intermediate between them and state-owned enterprises.

Belka et al. (1994a) present evidence on numerous other indicators of restructuring in which the behavioral lines are most clearly drawn between de novo and current or former state-owned firms. Areas of restructuring include sales, marketing, technological change, and financial structure. An important example is presented in table 4.10, which shows managers' responses concerning the relationship between actual and optimal employment levels in 1993. This table makes informative reading; even after three years of reform and a major labor shakeout leading to high unemployment, overmanning remained endemic in Polish industry. Unsurprisingly, de novo firms have almost no overmanning—they have no history of excess employment and are for the most part growing. The surprise comes from the privatized firms, where employment is reported to be too high in 50 percent of firms, almost exactly the same proportion as in state-owned firms. Indeed, a slightly higher proportion of unreconstructed state-owned firms claim employment levels to be about right than do privatized enterprises. This may indicate different managerial interpretations of optimal employment, given current levels of output, capital, and

Table 4.10
Employment relative to optimal level, by ownership type: Poland, 1993

	Ownership type			
Employment is	1	2	3	4
Too high (>20%)	0	11	5	10
Too high (10–20%)	3	9	33	15
Too high (5–10%)	14	30	20	29
About right	60	43	35	45
Too low	23	7	8	1

Source: Belka, Estrin, et al. 1994.
Note: Ownership type 1 = de novo private; 2 = privatized; 3 = commercialized; 4 = state-owned.

technology. However, interviews suggest that it actually indicates the powerful impact of stricter budget constraints on behavior throughout the state-owned sector.

In summary, while there is not much doubt about the superior economic performance of the de novo firms in the early stages of the Polish upturn, this tells us little about the relationship between ownership and restructuring, since, for the most part, de novo firms do not face the inherited problems of former state-owned companies. While there is limited evidence that privatized firms were responding slightly better to the improved economic environment in 1993, the Polish survey suggests that by then there was little to distinguish privatized, commercialized, and state-owned firms in terms of restructuring behavior. One explanation is that the primary determinant of enterprise behavior in the early years of reform was harder budget constraints, and this impacted the entire former state sector, whether privatized or not.

Restructuring and Dominant Ownership in Poland

We argued above that privatization may be too broad an indicator of ownership to discriminate between categories of firms with regard to restructuring. Earle and Estrin (1996) therefore sought to categorize the same Polish sample by dominant owner, along the lines discussed in the previous section. Dominant ownership was defined to occur when an ownership group holds more than 50 percent of the voting shares. Firms were categorized into state-owned (SO), employee-owned (EO), manager-owned (MO), outsider-owned (OO), and de novo privately owned enterprises (POE). The study found MOs to be somewhat smaller on average than EOs and OOs, and slightly larger than POEs. State-owned firms

Table 4.11
Restructuring indicators for Polish companies: means
(standard deviations)

	SO	EO	MO	OO	POE
Major investment in two years	.688	.923	.500	.800	.894
(proportion of firms)	(.465)	(.277)	(.577)	(.414)	(.315)
Total investment outlay over	.057	.127	.041	.068	.135
total income	(.052)	(.0)	(.0)	(.071)	(.085)
Sales force growth	.293	.754	−.029	.702	.888
	(.558)	(.810)	(.694)	(1.34)	(1.49)
Advertising expenditure growth	2.072	.986	2.000	3.649	.650
	(6.03)	(1.32)	(1.41)	(4.99)	(1.44)
Involuntary layoffs (1991−93)	.352	.195	.395	.192	.367
employment	(.261)	(.204)	(.145)	(.187)	(.331)

Source: World Bank survey described in Belka, Estrin, et al. 1994.

were much larger (around 800 workers, as against around 500 in EOs and
OOs, 200 in MOs, and 160 in POEs). On average, only EOs and POEs
were profitable, MOs lost around 4 percent of sales, OOs lost 7 percent,
and state-owned firms lost 9 percent.

In table 4.11, we present indicators of restructuring by ownership type
for the Polish sample. Broadly, the last two rows relate to long-term
restructuring, and the first three rows to short-term restructuring. The
findings do not entirely confirm our predictions. In terms of investment,
de novo firms are doing more than state-owned ones. Outsider-owned
firms look much less impressive than insider-controlled companies, and
employee-owned firms are investing more than manager-owned ones. On
the marketing side, insider-owned firms are typically doing more than
state-owned and de novo firms, and employee-owners concentrate on
developing the sales force while manager-owners are increasing the
amount spent on advertising. It is notable, however, that employee-
owners are much less likely to have laid off workers involuntarily in the
past three years than are manager-owners, or even the state. Surprisingly,
outsiders seem as keen to avoid layoffs as employees.

Thus, the first evidence of dominant ownership effects suggests that
while privatization does appear to impact on restructuring to a modest
extent, employee-owners appear to perform better, and outsiders worse,
than we had predicted. The explanation may lie in the way that dominant
ownership forms were selected, and in the effectiveness of control rights
for outside owners. Institutional arrangements in Poland favor insider
purchases in the liquidation legislation, so managers and workers are able

to buy their firms, provided the company generates the cash flow to repay the debts incurred in the buyout. This means that managers and workers select better firms in terms of profitability and cash generation. Managers appear to be limited by capital requirements to the purchase of smaller firms, while outsiders can obtain control only of firms in financial difficulties. It is possible, too, that their ownership rights do not confer effective control over decision making.

Enterprise Performance and Dominant Ownership in Russia

In the autumn of 1993, the World Bank undertook a study based on a large random sample of Russian firms that allowed enterprises to be categorized by dominant owner along the lines of the Polish survey, and also permitted an investigation of the range of restructuring issues. The survey contained indicators of depoliticization, such as the changing proportion of company sales to the state, the extent of price controls, and state financial aids to firms. Earle et al. (1995) analyze these variables and find some evidence for the hypothesis that, relative to state-owned firms, outsiders and POEs will be best at distancing themselves, employee-owners performing better in this regard than managerial ones.

The results of this analysis are summarized in table 4.12, which presents regressions of three indicators of state influence over firms against ownership: (1) the proportion of output each firm sells to the state; (2) whether or not the firm received any financial assistance from the government in the period 1992–94; and (3) the amount of assistance received in real rubles in 1992–94. The coefficients for nonstate owners are negative in all the regressions, indicating that private ownership is associated with depoliticization. However, the coefficients are statistically significant consistently across the equations only for de novo and employee-owned firms. OOs sell significantly less to the state but do not receive significantly different amounts of state aid. Manager-owned firms are almost identical to EOs in terms of reduced government subsidies but sell relatively more of their output to the state. Thus, once again our hypotheses are broadly confirmed, except for the role of outside owners, who are found to have less impact than predicted; in fact, their behavior often is not significantly different from continued state ownership.

The relationship between ownership and restructuring may be investigated using table 4.13, which draws together some of the findings in Earle et al. (1995). This table presents the estimates of regressions of the dynamic equations linking indicators of company performance—sales,

Table 4.12

Independent variable	Dependent variable		
	% Production sold to state	Dummy for whether firms received government financial support, 1992–1994	Amount of government assistance to firms
WO	−7.72**	−0.94***	−261***
	(2.46)	(0.29)	(110)
MO	−2.34	−0.94**	286*
	(3.52)	(0.44)	(158)
OO	−6.83*	−0.34	−205
	(3.77)	(0.41)	(166)
POE	6.90**	−1.25	365**
	(3.36)	(0.44)	(151)
N	323	3.70	353
Adj. R^2	0.023	(% correct predictions) 73.8	0.013

Source: Earle and Estrin 1996.
* Significant at 10% level.
** Significant at 5% level.
*** Significant at 1% level.

Table 4.13
Short-term and long-term restructuring in Russia, 1994

Independent variable	Dependent variables			
	Sales	% Sales to non-FSU	Capacity utilization	Employment
EO	2912	−2.71**	−3.97*	−183
	(2021)	(1.47)	(2.43)	(277)
MO	3035	1.27	−5.46	930**
	(3037)	(2.06)	(3.47)	(391)
OO	2437	3.48	−3.38	−428
	(3188)	(2.29)	(3.80)	(415)
POE	2605	0.29	5.87**	153
	(3002)	(1.28)	(3.23)	(405)
Lagged endogenous variable	2.76***	8.89***	0.87**	0.92***
	(0.08)	(1.01)	(0.04)	(0.02)
R^2	0.86	0.21	0.62	0.91

Source: Earle et al. 1995.
* Significant at 10% level.
** Significant at 5% level.
*** Significant at 1% level.

exports to the West, capacity utilization, and employment—to ownership. The presence of a lagged endogenous variable in the equations implies that ownership of the firm is correlated to adjustments in the performance variables. The table suggests that the impact of ownership on performance was, by 1993, at best very modest. The ownership variables were significant only in very rare cases, and even then the signs were not always what one would expect. Thus we found no ownership effects on changes in sales, though manager-owned firms appear to adjust employment more than all other ownership groups. All ownership types, including state-owned firms, have to some extent restructured sales to non-FSU markets, though the change has been significantly less in employee-owned firms.

Finally, higher output to capital growth is indicated for de novo firms, relative to state-owned ones, but the adjustment is significantly lower in employee-owned ones. There is no indication in these tables of the ordering of performance by ownership predicted in table 4.5.

4.6 Conclusions

Privatization is a central element in the transformation of centrally planned economies into market ones. It fulfills the twin functions of developing private ownership and the market system generally, and of motivating and enabling restructuring in the former state-owned sector. However, in transitional economies, traditional forms of privatization cannot, for the most part, be used to privatize the large number of state-owned firms, since neither private savings nor a capital market infrastructure is sufficiently developed. Several countries have used innovative policies to resolve these problems. However, though mass privatization schemes have led to large-scale changes in ownership, it remains unclear whether the ownership patterns that have emerged are actually beneficial to the transition economies.

We have investigated this issue using a series of data sets collected by the World Bank. The theoretical predictions suggested clear differences in behavior between state-owned firms, on the one hand, and privatized and de novo firms, on the other, as well as between insider- and outsider-controlled former state-owned firms. However, using the data at our disposal, such distinctions emerged only sporadically, if at all. In Poland in 1993, privatized firms did not appear to be restructuring significantly more than state-owned ones (though de novo firms were already performing much better), and employee-owned firms were undertaking at least as much restructuring, and were more depoliticized, than manager- and outsider-owned firms. Perhaps the most striking feature of the results for both Poland and Russia was not the apparent success of employee ownership, which may be a selection effect, but the failure of outsider-owned firms to restructure more than state-owned firms.

These findings are open to several interpretations. First, the data set itself is incomplete, patchy, and not necessarily capable of generalization. Hence our findings must be regarded as preliminary. Second, it is still relatively early days in the privatization process; for example, the Russian sample was collected only a few months after the privatization laws had been enacted. Effects on company performance may take years to become manifest. Third, it seems likely that in the early years of reform, harder budget constraints were at least as important in influencing company performance as ownership changes, especially in Poland. This might explain the rather modest observed advantages of privatized over state-owned firms in our data.

Finally, there are ownership selection effects, which this study suggests may bedevil attempts to assess the impact of privatization on performance in the early years of reform. For example, the Polish and Russian data suggest that the privatization programs in both countries led insiders, and especially employees, to obtain majority ownership of the best-performing companies. Their better economic condition has probably facilitated further restructuring, and probably more than counterbalances the superior incentives of outside owners to restructure. Hence the apparent deficiencies of outsider-owned firms may reflect the condition of the firms that outsiders were able to buy, rather than the fact that outside ownership is a less effective form of governance. If selection effects of this type are widespread in other countries, it will be several years before convincing tests of the relationship between ownership and company performance in transitional economies can be undertaken.

Acknowledgments

The author acknowledges with thanks numerous discussions with John Earle, without whom this chapter could never have been written. Other important contributors to the ideas presented here are Simon Commander, Alan Gelb, Cheryl Gray, Mario Nuti, and Mark Schaffer. Three anonymous referees also contributed important points. Nonetheless, they bear no responsibility for the ideas in this chapter.

5   Bank Restructuring and Enterprise Reform

Sweder van Wijnbergen

5.1   Introduction

The fact that enterprise reform and bank restructuring in Eastern Europe are two intricately intertwined problems is by now abundantly clear and well documented (see van Wijnbergen 1992 for an early statement of this problem, and World Bank 1996b for much evidence). Firms in distress stop servicing their loans, and nonperforming loans are at the root of the commercial banks' troubles. In turn, unreformed banks' failure to enforce loan contracts adequately gives firms incentives for lax loan servicing, completing the circle of causality. The problem is compounded by the fact that, in an environment of less than ideal bank supervision and weak accounting standards, banks have an incentive to hide emerging bad loan problems by capitalizing interest amortization that is due.

This problem is in fact more general—witness, for example, the analysis of banking crises in Latin America (Gavin and Hausman 1995). What makes Eastern Europe special is, first of all, the size of the problem; initially almost the entire manufacturing sector, and in many countries agriculture as well, were in state hands and the relevant corporate actors were all in varying degrees of distress. A second complication, of clear relevance for the topic of this study, is that in most CEE (Central Eastern Europe) and CIS countries, commercial banking is a relatively new activity, and the main actors are correspondingly short on experience and skills. Even in Poland and Hungary, two of the most advanced countries in the region, as late as 1987 there were no local, Western-style commercial banks. The only exception to this rule are the countries of the former Republic of Yugoslavia, where commercial banks have a long, albeit checkered, history.

The standard methods of dealing with enterprise and banking problems are not likely to work well in such circumstances in general, and are even less likely to do so in Eastern Europe. The liquidation bias built into developed Western bankruptcy laws has been documented elsewhere (see Aghion et al. 1994 for a discussion). Imperfect procedures for resolution of creditor conflicts, holdup problems in bargaining, and destructive gambles by parties that stand to lose everything make it very difficult to restructure rather than liquidate companies that end up in bankruptcy. Over 90 percent of all U.S. Chapter 11 cases end up being liquidated (Aghion et al. 1994). Of course, if a firm that has a surplus value over the liquidation value of its assets is so liquidated, welfare will decline.

These problems are likely to have especially high social costs in Eastern Europe since the Communist demise. Existing information clearly reflects the incentive structure under which the information was compiled (the Communist era); thus firms could have been loss-making because of poor management or adverse circumstances, as in the West, or because there was little incentive not to be loss-making. For this reason, there was a good chance that the destruction of surplus value through rigorous application of bankruptcy procedures would have led to even greater destruction than is taking place in the West. To this, add very imperfect bankruptcy procedures and understaffed and undertrained bankruptcy courts (if they existed at all), and it should become clear that bankruptcy, essential as it may be to enforce management discipline in the long run, is very unlikely to be an efficient tool for massive restructuring (van Wijnbergen 1992, 1997; van Wijnbergen and Boot 1995).

Similar problems exist with classical approaches to banking reform. Typically banking distress comes to the fore when nonperforming loans begin to threaten the liquidity of a bank beyond the point where central banks can or are allowed to accommodate. Managers have no incentive to ring early alarm bells because their fate will be sealed anyhow; and lax supervision means that the insolvency point is often long past by the time liquidity dries up. In contrast with historical crises in the West, bank runs have been rare or nonexistent in Eastern Europe; banking distress in the East is silent distress.

The standard approach consists of incentive reform, management change, and, importantly, wholesale removal of nonperforming loans from the books of the banks involved, with control typically transferred to a bank rehabilitation agency. Whether the latter is a special bank, as in the Czech Republic, or an agency within the central bank, as in Slovenia, its defining characteristic is that public officials unfamiliar with the companies concerned are asked to liquidate or restore to health the firms behind the nonperforming loans.

A characteristic of the standard approach is thorough confidence in the ability of the government to manage such restructuring processes. Yet a key issue that we will highlight below is not so much the incentive structure in the newly cleaned banks (cleaned of bad debts), on which much of the design of this approach is focused, as the incentives of the rehabilitation agency taking over the new loans. These programs had to be implemented by governments new to their task, with employees often not fully committed to the reform process or seriously troubled by emerging discrepancies between private and public salaries. Simply assuming that the models which work in stable countries with a long civil service tradition will work in the unsettled environment of the new public sectors in the East is obviously not right.

In some countries alternative approaches have been worked out. The Czech Republic followed a traditional approach to bank restructuring, but a distinctly nontraditional approach to enterprise reform and privatization; Poland followed a radical alternative where an integrated decentralized approach was applied to both problems at once, an approach that rested strongly on the conviction that government should be involved as little as possible. Both loan workouts and bank recovery were, after an initial recapitalization by the government, to take place largely in a decentralized manner, with an incentive structure carefully designed to avoid the problems associated with more traditional approaches. Slovenia also relied heavily on loan workouts rather than simple write-offs and, like Poland, it imposed strict budget constraints on the banks; however, unlike Poland, it entrusted a newly created government agency with most of the workout process. Hungary used a public agency, like Slovenia, but failed to enforce strict budget constraints on its banks as part of the project.

Thus a comparison of the experience in these three countries should be instructive: Poland, with a strict budget constraint approach to bank recovery and decentralized loan recovery; Slovenia, also with a strict budget constraint approach to banking reform but a centralized approach to loan recovery; and Hungary, also with a central approach to loan recovery but no strict budget constraint imposed on banks.

The issues discussed also have implications for the privatization process. One of the key problems in privatization that has emerged over the past few years is the difficulty of finding a strategic owner for companies privatized through mass privatization schemes. Such schemes are unavoidable if speed is of the essence, but unlike negotiated sales, it is difficult to find a shareholder interested in active involvement and willing to take a large enough stake to make such a role possible. Yet as Berglof (1997) has

pointed out, the very weak or nonexistent legal protection for shareholders leaves managers in control unless a strategic investor can be
found with a big enough stake to force his interests upon the manager. In
some financial architectures, banks can play this role, and even if they are
not allowed or able to do so, they can act as intermediaries by finding
someone who can. Thus restructuring through banks offers the hope not
only of faster effective privatization but also of better corprate governance mechanisms for the firms so privatized.

In this chapter we first set the stage by outlining the arguments for and
against the various approaches (section 5.2). We then discuss in particular
the novel approach, implemented mostly in Poland, but also using the
evidence from Hungary and Slovenia, to put some of the key results in
perspective and give some impression of how alternatives might have
fared (section 5.3). Section 5.4 discusses the implications for financial sector reform, and section 5.5 assesses the restructuring programs of Poland,
Slovenia, and Hungary. Section 5.6 concludes.

5.2   Who Should Be the Agent of Change?

The question of who should be the agent of change in restructuring
should obviously be preceded by asking why there should be restructuring. For some, that issue is clear. The chief of staff of former President
Salinas of Mexico made a strong case for prior restructuring for revenue
reasons (Cordoba 1994). Arguably a strong government has better tools
at its disposal to, for example, force an end to unrealistic labor contracts
than does a new private owner, in particular a foreign owner. The difference in anticipated costs would accrue to the government as a post-
restructuring price increase in excess of public restructuring costs.

However, this argument crucially rests on the assumption that the
government has the time, expertise, and resources available to implement
such programs, as was indeed done in, for example, the United Kingdom
and Mexico. But those privatization programs were much smaller than
any under consideration in Eastern Europe, and both the governments
concerned were well established, with functioning institutional structures
and reasonably adequate staffing. None of these conditions was satisfied
in the early 1990s in any country of Eastern Europe, and in most of them
is still not satisfied. Thus restructuring aimed at increasing cash value
seems ill-advised.

Another argument holds more force, and is related to the likely strong
political opposition to negative-price sales. Because of the information

disadvantages experienced by outside strategic investors, and the difficulty of getting out once an initial investment has been made, uncertainty about restructuring needs will generate an option value of staying out. This option value will depress the cash value of an unreformed enterprise below the net discounted expected revenue from it by an amount equal to the value of the staying-out option. The larger the initial commitments required as part of the sale, the greater the discount related to option value will be.

This discrepancy is likely to be larger in Eastern Europe than in the West for two reasons:

1. Accounting procedures used in the past (and still in force in the FSU countries) make it very difficult to disentangle company records.

2. Even if the accounts were transparent, they would reflect results produced under a nonprofit-oriented incentive structure.

Thus, in particular, troubled companies can be expected to raise substantially less than their social value, to the point where negative prices (subsidies) may be necessary to effect a sale. This in turn is bound to generate strong political pressure.[1]

This particular rationale for restructuring has clear implications for the way it should be done. Since information asymmetries are at the core of the argument, everything should be done to engage those who have, or have access to, inside information. Governments may have information through the line ministries that formerly controlled the enterprises, but this channel may clash with ultimate privatization plans; regionwide experience strongly suggests that line ministries are loath to prepare for privatization because that will mean an end to their control and the private benefits that accrue to the controlling functionaries. Of course, this built-in inertia has been on display elsewhere. IRI, the Italian state holding company, was explicitly set up to privatize its holdings, with a sunset provision in its statutes limiting its life to five years. That was in 1948, and IRI is still one of Italy's largest industrial groups, if not its largest.

Bringing enterprises back under public-sector control—in the most common proposal by a central agency, a "hospital for sick enterprises," typically under the aegis of an industry ministry—creates other problems. The enterprises that became large under the Communist regime did so in part because their managers successfully bargained with industry ministry officials for a disproportionally large share of centrally allocated resources. A "hospital" approach would put exactly the managers who proved to be good at this game under the Communist regime back into the same situation. It seems reasonable to expect that they would once again be good at lobbying for continuing subsidies.

Moreover—and this adds a pernicious twist—the less they adjust, the more likely they are to bargain successfully for further subsidies. The reason is that bargaining power depends on one's threat point; the more unpleasant the alternative to accommodation is to the government, the more likely the government is to be cowed into submission and continuing the subsidies. Thus, holding up the specter of mass layoffs is a powerful argument for subsidies in the bargaining process; trimming down the enterprise would reduce bargaining power commensurately.

With governments ruled out, two channels remain: managers and main creditor banks. Thus a premium rests on designing a restructuring strategy that provides incentives to these two actors to reveal their inside information and use it in the design of a new corporate structure and business plan.

A standard argument against bringing in banks is the quality issue; banks themselves are new to commercial activity, with most having had only a few years of experience by the time the programs under consideration were implemented. The counterargument is, of course, that the same objection holds for everybody else. The key issue is that it is easier to provide commercial incentives compatible with ultimate privatization to banks and/or managers than it is to provide such incentives to public officials. After all, the latter are typically confined to public-sector pay scales, and thus to them the private benefits of corporate control seem even more attractive (van Wijnbergen and Boot 1995).

There is also the issue of resistance to political pressure, but experience so far indicates that a well-structured banking system with good corporate governance mechanisms is no worse placed in relation to this factor than a government agency. Certainly the record in Slovenia, where the Bank Rehabilitation Agency, a public agency with unclear corporate governance mechanisms, turned into a very interventionist owner, is not encouraging for believers in effective government-led restructuring.

Thus the key reasons for giving serious consideration to banks as the main actors, the agents of change in the corporate restructuring process for loss-making state enterprises, are the following:

1. Through their existing credit relations, they are more likely than anybody else, except the managers, to have access to inside information about the firm's potential.

2. It is much easier to structure their incentives toward fast restructuring and privatization instead of toward delay and obstruction than it is for government agencies to do so.

For banks to actually play such a role, a series of changes in the incentive structure for both enterprises and banks is required. We shall address this in the next section.

5.3   Providing Restructuring Incentives: Renegotiating Debt Contracts

Should There Be an Efficient Framework for Debt Restructuring?

In effect, the question here is how to set up efficient postbankruptcy renegotiation procedures while bypassing formal bankruptcy procedures. Bypassing formal procedures is necessary because of the obvious inefficiency and administrative ineptitude of existing institutions in the early years after the collapse of Communism—if, indeed, they exist at all. Thus, in Poland, the law establishing the framework for the enterprise reform program that inspired much of this chapter stipulated that no party could initiate bankruptcy procedures until the procedures established in that law had run their course (see van Wijnbergen and Boot 1995). Of course, if such a provision is incorporated, it is essential to stipulate a time limit to prevent the new procedures from becoming merely a refuge from bankruptcy. Therefore the reconciliation procedures established in the Polish law had a time limit of nine months as part of the law.

In general, designing efficient restructuring procedures faces the traditional ex ante versus ex post conflict. Ex ante, such procedures should offer as little hope as possible, so as to maximize the incentive for managers to prevent such situations from arising. Ex post, however, once the stage is reached that a new capital structure is necessary to avoid socially wasteful destruction of the firm's surplus value over its liquidation value, efficient renegotiation procedures are called for. This very deep conflict between ex ante and ex post objectives complicates the design of bankruptcy procedures across the world.

For the massive restructuring needs of postcollapse Eastern Europe, the situation was much simpler. The post-Communist trauma in state-owned enterprises (SOEs) is clearly a one-off problem. The debts inherited from the past were incurred under an incentive framework and an ownership structure different from those which will obtain in the future. Restructuring them as part of a more general transition clearly sends no signal to future creditors. Thus, the argument against following the ex post rationale —that it will give the wrong signals to enterprises not yet in such dire straits—does not apply in these circumstances.

The qualification "as part of a more general transition" is of course a key restriction; simply restructuring debts but leaving everything else as before will lead to a reemergence of the situation. A clear example is provided by the Polish experience in 1990. The flirtation with hyperinflation just prior to the Big Bang of January 2, 1990, and the price jump following that reform basically wiped out all SOE loans held by the banking system; yet in 1992, 30 percent of the main banks' loan portfolios were again low grade, and the loans had been made to the same enterprises whose debts had been wiped out in the earlier inflation explosion.

Finally, the Polish experience suggests that the one-off nature of such restructurings can be reinforced by embedding the procedures in a law that has a sunset provision built in: the machinery for restructuring would lose its legal basis three years after enactment of the law.

What Does Such a Framework Look Like?

To increase commercial banks' interest in restructuring rather than liquidating the companies that are failing to service their loans adequately, banks should be given an interest in the upswing potential of the firms. The only way to do this is to convert some or all of the debt they hold into equity. In Eastern Europe, this has the added advantage that such conversions can be used to introduce effective private ownership into the process. This suggests that conversion of some of the debt into equity should be the focal point of the restructuring exercise, rather than debt write-downs and full collection of what remains. Debt-to-equity conversion offers a more promising way to achieve efficient use of the assets controlled by the enterprises than does liquidation into a thin capital market and a depressed economy.

In principle, bankruptcy proceedings allow for such restructuring as an alternative to liquidation. However, this rarely works in practice: even carefully crafted bankruptcy laws have a strong built-in bias in favor of liquidation (Aghion et al. 1994). For example, the U.S. bankruptcy code has Chapter 11 proceedings, under which incentives are created for creditors to reach a nondestructive agreement on restructuring the firm. In practice, Chapter 11 proceedings end up in liquidation anyhow; Aghion et al. (1994) claim that about 95 percent of such cases ultimately go the liquidation route.

An analysis of the incentives facing the various actors holding claims on SOEs suggests five key issues that any restructuring package must deal with in order to be workable: (1) the role of the government as most senior creditor and, at the same time, equity holder; (2) the role of creditors junior to the lead bank; (3) the role of two groups of insiders that do not feature on this list, workers and managers; (4) the role of outsiders and, potentially, the issue of fresh capital injections; and (5) the need for legal support structures and the relation to regular bankruptcy proceedings. Let us consider these issues in turn.

The Role of the Government

The dual role of the government and/or its representatives creates a series of potentially destructive problems. First of all, no bank will take the initiative if most of the benefits will accrue to the public sector—which, by virtue of its seniority, retains first claim to any benefit. Thus a key element will have to be a commitment of the government to step back from its position as a senior creditor. In the Polish project, this took two forms.

First, the government announced it would not play an active role in the conciliation proceedings (the procedures created as part of the restructuring package). The tax authorities were represented on the creditor committees created, but only as an observer. Any final deal needed the approval of those authorities in order to protect, as far as was possible, the Treasury's interest without jeopardizing a deal. To avoid last-minute problems, those observers needed to be given transparent instructions concerning the conditions under which they could refuse to approve a particular deal. Failure to approve a deal would not necessarily scuttle it, but would require it to go to a council of ministers specially created to supervise the project.

Instead of playing an active role—and this is the second point—the authorities promised to match any debt reduction agreed upon by the commercial creditors pari passu. This is clearly beneficial to the banks: the market value of their claims goes up when the government cuts back its claims, while the value of the government claims, by virtue of their seniority, is not affected by what the banks do. A promising variant, eventually not pursued in the Polish package, would offer to cut back public-sector claims even more if, as part of the restructuring process, a private owner emerges at the end. This would strengthen the privatization incentives built into the set of measures.

A second problem created by the government's dual role of senior creditor *and* equity holder is the incentive for the government as senior

creditor to protect its equity holdings. This has two destructive consequences. First, a successful restructuring exercise may, even if only as a
temporary measure, require a commercial bank to convert its debt into
equity. But no bank can reasonably be expected to do so if old equity
holders retain their claims. Clearly a debt/equity (D/E) conversion implies
a step down in seniority; empirical research in the United States on Chapter 11 restructurings suggests what common sense would suggest: D/E
conversions require prior extinction of old equity before any debt holder
is willing so to convert its claims. Thus, for the government to insist on
keeping "social capital" alive means almost certainly that the proceedings
will take a destructive, liquidation-biased turn. Any incentive for commercial creditors to convert their claims would be negated.

This is destructive because conversion of debt into equity strengthens
a creditor's interest in bringing about a revival of the firm's fortunes;
the call option characteristic of equity means that after such conversion
a creditor would share in any upswing that resulted. Thus a public announcement that the government professes its immediate willingness to
sell or simply extinguish its existing equity claims as part of a successful
reconciliation proceeding is crucial for the success of such a procedure.

The second problem is that protecting the government's equity base
means privatization is a less likely outcome of the exercise. This is obviously a loss because, arguably, the problem started with the incentive
problems created by the incestuous relations between enterprise managers
and the bureaucrats assigned to supervise them.

Junior Creditors

The existence of junior creditors creates a strong bias toward liquidation.
Chapter 11 restructurings typically fail because a small creditor files
for liquidation. Small creditors who find their claims have fallen to zero
market value in the process of restructuring have an incentive to press for
liquidation; this is not because they would do better there, but because
they would likely lose less, in comparison, than more senior creditors
would. Thus a threat of liquidation often is launched primarily to blackmail senior creditors into buying out junior creditors at above the market
value of the junior claims. The coordination problems that subsequently
arise will often trigger liquidation even if nobody really wants it. Thus the
workout scheme needs to incorporate mechanisms for resolving creditor
conflicts that will not trigger excessive liquidation proceedings.

Two measures are likely to reduce this threat, and both were introduced in the Polish reform scheme. First, for the duration of the concilia-

tion proceedings, complete protection from bankruptcy was granted by legislative means (no one could file for bankruptcy while conciliation proceedings were in process). Of course, such a blanket protection makes it important to set a firm deadline by which the process has to end. In the law establishing the Polish scheme, conciliation proceedings received a nine months' window, after which banks that failed to initiate successful negotiations would lose their claim through forced sale.

Second, majority creditors need to be able to override any attempt by minor creditors to get a free ride. Bankruptcy laws typically grant the bankruptcy judge the power to impose a solution on obstructive minorities. In the absence of a court supervisor, an alternative to such a provision must be sought if proceedings are ever to end. In the Polish package a drastic solution is introduced: any creditor or group of creditors possessing more than 50 percent of the outstanding nonequity claims in value terms can impose a solution; recourse to the courts under bankruptcy law is open only to a creditor or group of creditors owning at least 20 percent of the value of all outstanding nonequity claims.

Managers and Workers

The important role of banks as major nongovernment creditors and potential firm insiders does not rule out a role for the other insiders: managers and, to a lesser extent, workers. Any package deal will likely have to buy off the workers' opposition by granting a minority stake in the newly formed corporation to workers. This is now routinely done throughout Eastern Europe and presents no special problems as long as (1) it is indeed a minority stake and (2) the shares are explicitly tradable. Tradability would give workers the long-term horizon associated with shareholding: even if they retire from the firm, they can lay a claim to any expected future profits through the capitalization of such expectations in the value of their shares.

Managers can play a useful role in these proceedings, too, the banks' dominance notwithstanding. Conciliation proceedings start with the drawing up of a business plan under the responsibility of the main bank creditor. However, nothing stops the bank from asking the manager to draft a proposal; and while the strict time limit in the Polish package may in the end force some banks to take an equity stake even if in the longer term they do not want this, they can subsequently consider swapping this equity stake with the managers for new debt. Thus management buyouts (MBOs) can certainly be engineered under this program. In fact, one of the innovative features of this package is that MBO characteristics can be built into packages that would normally be considered too large for them.

Outsiders and Fresh Capital Injections

Of course, the Holy Grail of all enterprise restructuring in Eastern Europe is securing a foreign equity stake accompanied by a capital injection. Realism suggests that especially for loss-making enterprises, one should not set one's hopes too high. But the structure of bank-led reconciliation proceedings is uniquely suited to incorporating foreign or, for that matter, any outside interest if such can be generated.

The business plan with which the proceedings start can form the basis of negotiations with any group of future stakeholders, be they internal or external to the firm. The strong position of the main creditor bank allows the creation of almost any capital structure desired; hence these proceedings form a very good framework for negotiating outside participation. The practical problem in securing such interest is that outside offers are very unlikely to materialize unless the existing management cooperates, by reason of the information asymmetry discussed earlier. This suggests that earlier hopes (van Wijnbergen 1992) of using such outside offers to bring an element of competition into MBO-based restructuring/privatization efforts may have been overly optimistic.

Relation to Existing Bankruptcy Procedures

Unless specific provision is made to avoid it, some players in this scheme may try to sideline the whole approach by attempting to start regular bankruptcy procedures. Small creditors with junior claims may have little to lose because they come out with empty hands either way; but filing for formal bankruptcy may be highly damaging to more senior creditors. Junior creditors may thus try to blackmail senior creditors into bailing them out by threatening to initiate formal bankruptcy proceedings. Hence the suspension of the possible recourse to more standard bankruptcy procedures was an essential part of the Polish package. To avoid refuge in novel approaches only to avoid formal bankruptcy, a strict time limit on the new approaches is, of course, essential.

5.4   Implications for Financial Sector Reform

One important caveat must be attached to the approach followed in Poland: the schemes rely heavily on the proper functioning of the commercial banks. It cannot be stressed enough that fast and substantial progress in implementating effective mechanisms of bank supervision is absolutely essential for the success of the scheme. The chaos among the recently created private banks in Poland demonstrates that point dramatically.

Proper functioning of commercial banks in turn requires at least three things, which we shall discuss below.

Regulation

It is difficult to overestimate the importance of prudent regulation. Any business that starts by taking the customers' money up front instead of after delivery of services is potentially prone to fraud. Such problems may range from direct fraud (insider lending) to excessive risk-taking by managers, especially if their downside risk is partially covered by deposit insurance. Experience in Chile with unregulated privatization clearly indicates that an unregulated privatized banking system inevitably leads to a major crisis. Hence, the privatization of commercial banks should proceed cautiously if at all, as long as effective regulatory mechanisms are not in place.

An effective regulatory framework requires, first of all, implementation of loan classification and general portfolio assessment systems to provide regulators with the necessary warning signals. Such a reporting system needs to be backed up by occasional in-depth, on-site audits to check on compliance and provide a more profound assessment than mechanical indicators can yield. Such audits are also necessary to safeguard against such fraudulent practices as lending to insiders while disregarding normal standards of prudence. The latter danger is particularly acute if banks can be owned by industrial groups; for that reason many countries explicitly forbid any industrial enterprise to own a bank.

Second, rules and institutions need to be set up, and the necessary personnel recruited and trained. Who collects information, implements rules, sets capital adequacy guidelines, rules in ambiguous cases, and so on? In many cases these tasks fall to the central bank, which has to deal with the banks because of its conduct of monetary policy.

Finally, choices need to be made on the approach to regulation. In the West, emphasis is increasingly shifting from direct to indirect regulation. Direct regulation places strict limits and restrictions on the type and extent of activities banks can undertake: rules for taking on insurance business, direct transfer requirements, and so on. Indirect regulation leaves the choice to banks but tries to make certain undesirable activities more expensive—for example, by higher capital adequacy requirements for more risky portfolios.

The first approach runs the risk of erosion by technological progress and financial innovation, as banks find new and unforeseen ways of doing the things regulators are trying to proscribe. The second approach clearly suffers from information requirements and difficulties of fine-tuning. For example, many claim that the explosive growth in securitization of mortgage loans in the United States is a response to the excessive risk weights of mortgage loans under the Federal Reserve's capital adequacy rules.

Sophisticated financial innovations are yet to come in Eastern Europe, and the information requirements for good indirect regulation are difficult to meet even in the West. Accordingly, a case can be made for much more direct regulation in Eastern Europe than now prevails in the West (van Wijnbergen and Boot 1995).

Enforcement of Prudential Regulation

A regulatory framework is of little use if compliance is not enforced. This raises two issues. First, what is the proper medium-term framework for enforcement? Second, since both state-owned and private banks are currently far from compliance with almost any reasonable set of prudential rules, how should the present situation be handled?

Issues in the Design of Enforcement Mechanisms

The main problem with enforcement mechanisms is how to make them as insensitive as possible to political intervention and direct attempts at fraudulent manipulation. Many countries feel that leaving enforcement in the hands of one institution makes that institution too vulnerable to such pressures. This is especially so if that institution is also responsible for implementing the prudential regulation, since then it has the tools to circumvent the rules if pressured to do so. Moreover, supervision authorities may be tempted to cover up past supervision failures in the hope that a reversal of the problem bank's fortunes will get both the bank and the supervision authorities off the hook.

Such considerations add up to a strong argument for vesting enforcement decisions in a banking commission consisting of the finance minister, the governor of the central bank, and often securities regulators. Bribing a group of people, none of whom is fully sure whether to trust the others, is substantially more difficult than exercising undue influence on a single individual. A banking commission usually establishes supervision work programs and makes enforcement decisions, but relies on central bank staff to carry out technical work. There is little doubt that such a commission, on which several agencies are represented, is more difficult to manipulate than an institution where authority ultimately rests with one person.

Recapitalizing Banks

Bank managers cannot be made responsive to the capital value of the bank if there is no capital to begin with. Hence an essential element of banking reform is recapitalization of the banks with enough income-earning assets to leave a prudential capital base in place after making provision for bad loans. Recapitalization through a prolonged period of high spreads between lending and borrowing rates is inefficient; it takes too long and, more important, works by taxing successful firms to fund the losses of the unsuccessful. This procedure could well abort private-sector growth even before it starts. A one-off capital infusion based on public debt issue would allow a less destructive way of financing the resulting liabilities.

If, as in Poland, bank recapitalization is part of an overall banking reform-cum-enterprise restructuring plan, it is crucial that the recapitalization be carried out at the outset, on an ex ante basis, even if it then has to be based on an imperfect assessment of the true value of the loan portfolio. If it is not, all incentives for the commercial banks to collect anything at all on their claims will be destroyed: with recapitalization ex post, every dollar written off will be replaced by the government with an interest-earning asset, so the banks have no incentive to try to collect or even to take equity stakes.

Objections to such a recapitalization on account of the funding requirements and associated fiscal costs are always misplaced in the case of state-owned banks, and probably in the case of privately owned banks as well. The latter assertion is certainly correct if recapitalization goes together with the state acquiring ownership—as it should, for obvious incentive reasons. For state banks, the crucial point is that such a recapitalization is no more than a recognition of debts incurred in the past; it thus requires no budgetary allocation (although the interest on the debt instruments created of course does). The argument against keeping such debts off the books (which a failure to recapitalize sufficiently would do) is that doing so inevitably leads to unpredictable and highly inefficient ways of servicing the implicit debt. In fact, in most cases undercapitalized banks end up being funded through the inflation tax as losses are picked up by the central bank. At least when the debts are recognized and their interest costs are brought into the budget, an efficient tax structure can be set up to finance those costs rather than financing them residually through inflation tax.

Establish a Proper Incentive Structure for Commercial Banks

Establishing effective bank governance ultimately requires privatization. If rapid privatization is not advisable because of the absence of effective supervision and regulation of private banks, a difficult situation is created, as was discussed above in relation to enterprise reform. Any workable solution probably requires at least two elements. First, commercialization with the creation of strong supervisory boards will be necessary to allow close monitoring of management.

Second, since monitoring will inevitably be imperfect, managers should receive incentives that point them in the right direction. Profit-related pay is one possibility, but is too tightly linked to short-term profitability. And it is especially easy for banks to shift losses into the future through the refinancing of commercially nonviable loans. Thus profit-related pay needs to be complemented by incentives that work on a longer time scale. In the West this problem is typically solved by the issue of stock options exercisable at some much later date. In Eastern Europe such arrangements are difficult because the shares for which such options should be written either do not exist or are not publicly traded. An alternative worth considering is to provide managers with the equivalent of stock options: shares in the privatization receipts as part of their annual pay.

Gradualism in Banking Reform?

Many would argue that any reform which can be implemented should go as fast as politicians will allow the reformers to go. But, particularly in the financial sector, some caution may be called for. For a regulatory framework to be effective, it needs an institutional capacity that takes time to build. Supervisors need to be trained, accounting systems and information networks must be built up, sufficient qualified personnel must be found or trained, and so on. Much of this can be done in a relatively short time if enough foreign assistance, including on-site experts, is available, but the whole process is likely to take at least several years.

This means that the immediate extension of a tough regulatory framework to all banking activities may prove not to be feasible, and this in turn would mean that the new system would immediately lose credibility. Even more damaging would be the introduction of deposit insurance, a common feature of all Western banking systems, into an incomplete regulatory environment.

Several transition issues arise. One approach, followed in Poland and Russia, starts by extending the new regulatory framework, incentive reform, and recapitalization to a subgroup of banks. In Poland, only the nine major banks were part of the wide-ranging financial and enterprise-sector reform package implemented in August 1993.[2] It should be made clear, of course, as was done in Poland, that banks which have not gone through this reform and recapitalization process will *not* be covered by deposit insurance. This is necessary both to avoid immediate bankruptcy of the deposit insurance agency and to provide these new banks with a competitive advantage to offset the higher costs due to their regulatory compliance.

The fledgling supervision authority could focus most of its attention (and the attention of foreign advisers, the hiring of whom was also part of the Polish reform program) on this subgroup of banks initially. This would alleviate the apparent conflict between the argument that banks are the right agents for change and the supervision requirements necessary for banks to play such a role in a constructive manner.

A second issue is the unusual structure of most banking systems in Eastern Europe. Typically, there are a number of medium-to-large commercial banks created out of the former branch offices of the central bank; one big savings bank holding most household deposits and lending to other banks and/or the government; and a flurry of small, new private banks. A case can be made, at least as long as the supervision capacity in the central bank has not yet been built up, for maintaining the dominance of the savings bank in the deposit market and keeping it out of lending to enterprises. In this manner, household deposits will be less at risk, since savings bank managers are not involved in direct credit to enterprises and the associated temptation to gamble in hopes of good times (see in particular van Wijnbergen and Boot 1995 for such an argument in favor of [temporary] narrow banking).

5.5   A Preliminary Assessment of Restructuring Programs: Poland, Slovenia, and Hungary

Poland

No comprehensive study has yet been made of the program described here, but some preliminary assessments are available (see in particular Belka 1995, which draws on work by Leszek Pawlowicz of the Gdansk

Institute of Economics). (This section draws heavily on Belka and on personal communications from Prof. John Bonin.) The program initially envisaged a universe of about 2,000 loans, of which ultimately only 1,200 were covered (the "base portfolio") after applying a minimum size cutoff. Most of these 1,200 loans were small, and the majority did not go through reconciliation procedures. About half the debtors resumed payment without any change in capital structure. Of the roughly 660 claims that were adjusted, 162 were dealt with in bankruptcy courts; these were mostly smaller claims totaling less than 3 percent of the total base portfolio. About 141 claims were sold in the secondary market, in all cases at 25 percent of face value or less (Belka 1995).

About 17 percent of all cases (about 200) were accepted for a conciliation procedure. However, the small percentage is misleading because the companies selected tended to be the larger ones (or, rather, to have the larger claims outstanding). In value terms they made up almost 60 percent of all claims. Banks report that those were selected mostly on the basis of future prospects. Banks applied for debt/equity (D/E) swaps in 50 of these 200 cases, but once again these were the largest ones; the claims selected for D/E swaps made up 30 percent of the total value of all claims. Out of those 50 applications, only 28 were accepted by the Ministry of Privatization. This low number of D/E swaps is something of a disappointment, since that mechanism was designed as the main restructuring vehicle for large claims, not least because it would turn conciliation procedures into a backdoor privatization device. In all other cases, bank claims were adjusted, as were the government's claims. In most cases, the more junior creditors ended up with empty hands.

There seem to be two explanatory factors behind the low number of D/E swaps effected. The major one was active obstruction through delay and/or downright rejection by the Ministry of Privatization (which, as mentioned, approved only 28 out of 50 applications). D/E swaps would result in a transfer of control from the ministry (to which all the shares of state enterprises were transferred after corporatization) to the bank converting its debt. Apparently, Ministry of Privatization officials strongly resisted this transfer of ownership, their mandate to facilitate privatization notwithstanding.

The second factor has to do with technical provisions in the tax law that had the unanticipated side effect of discouraging both corporatization and D/E swaps. At issue was, first of all, the inability to carry over past losses into a corporatized enterprise with, as a consequence, the loss of the embedded tax credits. A second tax problem stems from the fact that under Polish law, provisions against bad loans can be deducted from tax-able profits. Conversion at face value, however, is then considered a capital gain with attendant tax consequences. In practice, the impact of this provision was softened by typically writing down the loan by, say, 50 percent and then converting it into equity, a procedure that was apparently acceptable to the tax authorities.

Overall, the net result for bank capitalization has been major and apparently permanent. At the end of 1994 the commercial banks involved had a capitalization rate of well over 20 percent, substantially exceeding the original target of 12 percent. Bad loan problems, on the rise again in the rest of the banking sector, have not reemerged in the banks covered by the restructuring.

A major success of the scheme was with the so-called white elephants, the enterprises that would presumably hold the banks hostage. Original plans to place 50 of them in a special restructuring agency were dropped and replaced by the incentive mechanisms covered in this chapter, with an "intervention fund" as backup. Only three applications have been made to the intervention fund, clearly indicating that the strong incentives built into the law against applying for public money were effective. The effectiveness of this nongovernment approach to large-scale enterprises may well be one of the most important lessons from the Polish program.

Slovenia

The Polish experience is in striking contrast to that of Slovenia, where a centralized approach to enterprise reform was chosen. As in Poland, the main commercial banks were put on a strict budget constraint; but, unlike Poland, extensive rearrangement of bank assets took place, mostly in response to the dominant position of Ljubljanska Banka (LB), a bank that originally (in 1992) made up 80 percent of the total banking system in Slovenia (measured by size of the balance sheet).

Most (60 percent) of the nonperforming loans were removed from the balance sheets of the various banks; of course, LB dominated the procedure because of its disproportionate size. The total face value of the loans so transferred amounted to almost 2 billion DM, well in excess of 10 percent of GDP at the time. Thus the problem was substantially larger than the Polish problem, at least when measured with respect to GDP.

Since then LB has been brought back to health, with a Basel-standard capital adequacy ratio of around 11 percent (end of 1995), in response to a recapitalization in 1994 and a very stringent drive to increase profitability. Rehabilitation of LB has now been achieved for all practical purposes (there are still question marks regarding some of the other smaller banks). In this respect, the Slovene experience supports the Polish one: a hard-nosed approach to the banks, coupled with up-front recapitalization, will succeed in lastingly restored solvency and profitability to the banks so treated.

The process is taking much more time, however, than it took in Poland, where recapitalization brought the banks up to 12 percent. However, an aggressive pursuit of delinquent loans in Slovenia has resulted in an almost embarrassingly high capitalization of 24 percent (late 1994) of the banks covered by the program, again measured using Basel methodology. This difference in speed and extent of bank recapitalization reflects the key difference in the experience of the two countries: the very different approach to enterprise restructuring. Banks in Slovenia lost all incentive to go after bad loans because the ownership of the loans had been taken away from them.

Moreover, Slovenia's Bank Rehabilitation Agency (BRA), a "hospital for sick enterprises" as usually envisaged in the traditional approach to bank restructuring, has been singularly unsuccessful in handling the portfolio it received. As of late 1995, less than 15 percent of the assets, measured by face value, had been disposed of. The BRA is taking on the characteristics of Italy's IRI, an interventionist state agency that sees maintaining control and interference with management, rather than privatization and restructuring, as its main duties.

Thus, on this criterion (success in restructuring nonperforming loans and transfer of control) the decentralized Polish approach seems to have been much more successful than the centralized Slovene approach.

Hungary

Hungary's bad loan problem, like Slovenia's, was substantial in relation to GDP (estimated at 11 percent of GDP at the end of 1992). Contrary to Poland, no prior improvements in the governance or technical capabilities of the major banks involved had been achieved. A major objective of bank restructuring was to make the banks more attractive to foreign investors.

Hungary, like Slovenia, followed a centralized approach to loan restructuring, with an equal lack of success. Loans classified as uncollectible were swapped for 20-year bonds and placed with a special recovery agency. The scheme dealt only with loans formally classified as uncollectible, and thus left banks with many nonperforming loans. Moreover, only the loans classified as uncollectible were transferred; if an enterprise that had such a loan also had other loans (not yet classified as uncollectible), those loans were not transferred. This complicated the recovery agency's job and gave incentives to banks once again to engage in cosmetic cover-ups through lending in order to prevent more loans from showing up as bad.

Even more revealing is Hungary's continuing failure (as of late 1995 and early 1996) to deal with the bank portfolio problem. Although Hungary spent more on recapitalizing the banks than did either Poland or Slovenia, the exercise had to be repeated, promises on its one-off nature notwithstanding. No fewer than three (actually four, but the last two were two tranches of one exercise) successive recapitalizations have taken place so far. This amply demonstrates that recapitalization without further incentive reform is an invitation for more raids on the Treasury; unconditional adjustment assistance is the worst enemy of adjustment.

5.6   Conclusions

Resolving the intertwined problems of bank insolvency and enterprise reform-cum-privatization was the key problem faced by Eastern European governments (and still faced in the FSU and some other transition economies). Traditional approaches to enterprise reform and bank restructuring have been tested and designed in circumstances rather different from those encountered in posttransition Eastern Europe. In the West, the enterprise problem is typically much smaller in terms of GDP and of claims on the budget of the unreformed enterprises. Also, banking distress will typically extend to a subsection of banks, and only rarely to the banking system as a whole. Moreover, there is a tight link between the two problems, with SOE trouble spilling over into banking insolvency, and lax control of banks over their borrowers in turn providing incentives to SOEs to let loans deteriorate.

Add to this the specific information problems encountered in Eastern Europe, where company performance to a large extent reflects practices and obligations inherited from a past when a different incentive structure prevailed, and the case for alternative approaches becomes compelling. One such approach has been tried in Poland; elements of the Polish approach are also found in other countries' plans.

In this chapter we have outlined the ideas underlying approaches that give banks the leading role in enterprise restructuring, as was done in Poland; we also have drawn on the experiences of Poland, Hungary, and Slovenia to assess the likely pitfalls and chances of success of such innovative approaches.

Our comparisons have shed light on a number of outstanding issues:

1. Banks can be much more effective as agents of change than government committees whose members' jobs depend on delaying rather than promoting effective restructuring.

2. For banks to play such a role well, their incentive structure needs reform, and matching changes in the regulatory environment are critical for the success of any such scheme. Bank managers need to be aware of the unavailability of subsidies, and should have a stake in restoring profitability to their banking operations. At the same time, excessive risk-taking needs to be controlled in the interest of depositors; hence, strict regulation of capital adequacy, rules on what sort of activities are permitted and what are not, and so on are required. This will typically require extensive technical support.

3. To make banks effective, extensive legal framework agreements need to be in place, in particular to temporarily set aside regular bankruptcy procedures.

4. Since such massive restructurings are clearly one-off events, at least if done thoroughly and properly, there need be no concern about the signal such debt renegotiations give to future managers in regard to default. Establishing the rehabilitation procedures in a law with a built-in sunset provision, as in Poland, adds force to this argument.

5. While debt/equity conversions clearly heighten the banks' interest in the firms' upside potential, they will take place only if a number of conditions are satisfied. We mention three, based on the Polish and Slovene experience:

—Seniority rules need to be respected as much as possible. In particular, old equity holders should, at the very least, lose control.

—Old equity holders should not be permitted to withhold consent, as they could in Poland, where the Privatization Ministry was reluctant to relinquish control.

—Tax aspects need to be carefully worked out to make sure that there are no hidden penalties in the current accounting and tax calculation practices.

6. Vital to establishing the proper incentives to make the scheme work is a rigorous end to government subsidies. Open-ended subsidies destroy any kind of corporate control that other creditors can exercise, since their most important threat to withhold new funds. If unlimited funds are available from the public sector, no adjustment will take place.

7. There are clear risks, particularly because the approach calls for up-front bank recapitalization. If incentives are not structured correctly, and the government is insufficiently strong in insisting that there will be no repeat performance, such approaches may turn out to be both exceedingly expensive and ultimately unsuccessful. However, it is unclear whether any other approach would fare much better in such circumstances.

6 Unemployment and Restructuring

Richard Jackman

6.1 Introduction

Since the economic reforms accompanying the fall of Communism, the countries of Central and Eastern Europe (CEE) have experienced some of the highest unemployment rates in recent history. Together with the countries of the former Soviet Union (FSU), they have also witnessed other manifestations of labor-market stress, such as acute income inequality and collapsing participation rates. While no one could deny the need for enormous adjustment in the labor markets during transition, this chapter asks whether so dreadful a performance was inevitable or whether it was in part the result of misguided policy, and considers what might best be done in the next phase.

The key features of the prereform labor market of the formerly socialist economies, compared with those of market economies, can be very briefly summarized as follows:

1. A highly distorted structure of employment both across sectors and within enterprises, reflecting production for the plan rather than for the market; obsolete technology and management practices; and inappropriate relative factor prices

2. A structure of relative wages characterized by compressed differentials bearing little relationship to the market value of workers' skills

3. Very low or nonexistent unemployment.

The transition to a market economy would thus of necessity entail (1) a very substantial reallocation of labor across industrial sectors, and by occupation and type of work within enterprises; (2) large shifts in relative pay; and (3) an adjustment to nonnegligible rates of unemployment. During the transition, there was an expectation that the speed of job loss in declining sectors might be much more rapid than the rate of new job creation in the growing sectors, as a result both of structural and institutional weaknesses (e.g., in financial markets) and of obstacles to labor mobility. These problems were expected to lead, in the short run, to excessive wage differentials, on the one hand, and to structural unemployment, on the other, as workers made redundant in the declining sectors were unable immediately to satisfy the employment requirements of the growing sectors.

Influential models along these lines were developed by Blanchard (1991) and Aghion and Blanchard (1993). The basic paradigm envisaged three stages in the transition. The initial stage would be characterized by a sharp fall in state-sector employment and a sharp rise in unemployment. In the second stage the growth of private-sector firms would draw workers from the pool of unemployed. Unemployment would decline until it reached an equilibrium level, after which, in the third stage, further growth in the private sector would depend on private firms being able to bid workers away from the residual state sector. Some economists went so far as to argue that unemployment could be regarded as an "indicator of the extent to which the restructuring process has got under way" (McAuley 1991).

This approach assumes that unemployment in the transition economies is primarily a reflection of the "transformational recession" in output, as described by Gomulka (see chapter 2). But in fact the linkages between output and employment and between employment and unemployment are not at all close. Table 6.1 shows the relationship between the fall in output, the fall in employment, and the rate of unemployment for eight CEE countries, Russia, and Ukraine. Clearly the FSU countries have large falls in output, but much smaller falls in employment and low unemployment rates, whereas Poland, which has experienced the most rapid economic recovery, still has one of the highest unemployment rates in the region. Even among the CEE countries there is no obviously discernible pattern—for example, the Czech Republic has achieved an exceptionally low unemployment rate though its output decline is close to the average for the CEE countries.

How are these differences to be explained? And what are their effects? Starting with the relationship between output and employment, section 6.2 addresses the question of why employment has fallen so much more rapidly in some countries (Hungary, Poland) than in others (Russia, Ukraine). Section 6.3 considers whether a smaller fall in employment is associated with a slower rate of restructuring. Section 6.4 outlines some

Table 6.1
Output, employment, and unemployment in Central and Eastern Europe, 1989–95 (%)

	1989–92		1992	1989–95		1995
	ΔGDP	ΔE	U	ΔGDP	ΔE	U
Albania	−42	−41	27	−25	−41	20
Bulgaria	−26	−25	16	−25	−25	11
Czech Republic	−19	−9	3	−15	−9	3
Hungary	−18	−21	12	−14	−26	10
Poland	−17	−13	14	−3	−16	15
Romania	−26	−4	8	−19	−11	9
Russia	−29	−5	5	−38	−12	8
Slovak Republic	−21	−15	11	−16	−13	13
Slovenia	−17	−16	11	−6	−17	15
Ukraine	−21	−9	0.3	−40	−16	0.6

Sources: EBRD (1995, 1996). Employment figures for Russia from ILO World Employment (1995), and *Russian Economic Trends* 5, no. 2 (1996).

features of unemployment in the transition period, focusing in particular on flows and durations. Section 6.5 examines the relationship between employment and unemployment. We look in more detail at the effects of active labor-market policies in section 6.6, and conclude in section 6.7 with a discussion of policy issues, drawing both on the experience of the transitional economies and on that of comparable economies in Western Europe.

6.2   Output and Employment

The causes of the decline in output in CEE and FSU countries are described at some length by Gomulka (chapter 2). His chapter stresses that the extent of the output decline depends primarily on initial conditions, and that the choice of policy may influence the time profile but not the overall magnitude of this decline. In this section we argue that policy can, however, affect the magnitude as well as the time profile of the fall in employment associated with the output decline.

For present purposes we start from the assumption that the decline in output in a country reflects its circumstances at the time of the reforms, in particular its exposure to trade with market economies, the size of the private sector, and the size of government in general and the arms trade in particular. Taking the fall in output as given, we ask why in some countries we observe a fall in employment somewhat greater, and in others a fall substantially smaller, than the fall in output (table 6.1).

In the first few years of the transition, the impact of the output collapse on employment depends primarily on the behavior of state-owned enterprises (SOEs), which at the outset provided virtually all employment in the economy. It is generally assumed that, in the transition, SOEs became worker- or manager-controlled—that is, insider-controlled. The apparatus of state control was effectively dismantled, but the disciplines of the capital market and the profit motive had yet to be put in place. Even where SOEs were formally privatized, effective control generally remained in the hands of insiders rather than external shareholders.

How, then, might one expect insider-controlled enterprises to react to the disruptive consequences of economic transition, in particular to a collapse in the market for the goods they produce? In contrast to private firms in market economies, it is probably most sensible to envisage SOEs as responding to shocks by separating output decisions from employment decisions. In the face of a shock, production is cut back and prices are adjusted so as to maximize revenue (or to minimize the loss of revenue) in the product market. The remaining sales revenues, together with any other income or lines of credit to which the firm has access, can be used to support the wages and employment of workers. If the firm's income falls, it can cut employment or cut wages, or some mixture of the two, given that its wage bill cannot exceed its income or borrowing capacity. The choice between cutting wages and cutting employment will, in an insider-controlled firm, be made primarily in the light of the well-being of the workers. (For a model developing this approach, see Jackman et al. 1992.)

With this approach, the link between output and employment will be affected by three factors:

1. Changes in the firm's relative price

2. Access to nonsales income or credit

3. The choice between cutting wages and cutting employment.

The first of these effects has been discussed in the context of imperfectly competitive markets (e.g., Blanchard 1991), where each firm attempts to raise its relative price to increase its sales revenue and, hence, the funds available for the wage bill. But if all firms attempt to do this, the overall effect is simply an increase in the aggregate price level with no increase in the real value of the wage bill in a representative firm. This has been termed a "decentralization externality," somewhat akin to the externality in union bargaining models where each union tries to raise its relative (real) wage by increasing its money wage, leading to inflationary wage pressure but no general increase in real wages.

While considerations of this kind can help explain how employment in particular sectors (where product demand is inelastic) can be sustained in the face of falling sales volume (e.g., fuel and electricity), they cannot explain differences across economies in the response of aggregate employment (because, by definition, not all sectors can increase their relative price).

Turning to the second factor, a key element of the reform process has been the phasing out of subsidy and the imposition of hard budget constraints on enterprises. This cash squeeze on firms has in some countries been aggravated by high nominal interest rates on bank debt as an element of the macroeconomic stabilization program. These financial developments oblige firms to cut back on labor costs over and above the loss of sales revenue. One of the most important differences between countries has been the extent to which various forms of deficit finance have been allowed to continue. Poland and Hungary have perhaps been least tolerant, as was Bulgaria in the initial stages of the transition. In Russia, elsewhere in the FSU, and Romania, much of state-owned industry continued to receive financial support. In the Czech Republic, despite the free-market rhetoric, reform has been introduced quite gradually and selective subsidy and other forms of directed support have continued. In countries where the financial regime has been "softer," enterprises have responded by slowing the speed at which they cut back employment.

Where enterprises need to cut labor costs, there remains the choice between layoffs and wage cuts. From the perspective of workers' welfare, which will be the dominant consideration in insider-controlled enterprises, the key issue is what happens to workers laid off from the enterprise. Whatever expectations may have been held at the outset, it was clear early on that the labor-market prospects of unemployed workers were very poor. The alternative sources of income for most workers would consist largely of unemployment benefits, casual informal work, or the support of their families. Of these, there has been greatest variation across countries in terms of benefits (see annex 1). A number of the CEE countries, particularly Hungary and, in the early stages, Poland, have adopted a relatively generous stance on benefits. In Russia, on the other hand, benefits have been very low. The Czech Republic has adopted a restrictive approach on benefit duration in conjunction with energetic use of active labor-market policies. The combination of a generous benefit regime with a hard budget constraint in Hungary and Poland may account for the willingness of enterprises in these countries to lay off workers rather than cut wages. In a sense, in these countries, the soft budget constraint was shifted from the enterprise to the social welfare system.

The willingness and ability of enterprises in Russia and elsewhere in the FSU to maintain employment in the face of falling output has been the subject of extensive analysis (Commander et al. 1995; Layard and Richter 1995). It reflects a tradition of enterprise responsibility for workers' welfare that has involved the provision by firms of social benefits such as housing, primary health care, and nursery education. In the absence of more than minimal provision of state unemployment or other welfare benefits, enterprises have kept workers on the payroll when there is no work for them to do and even, in some cases, when there is no money to pay wages.

Of necessity, the cost of sustaining employment in the face of falling output has been reflected in cuts in labor productivity, effort, and real wages. In Russia, for example, Layard and Richter argue that the flexibility of real wages has enabled firms to maintain employment in the face of declining demand. In Romania, to take another example, survey evidence suggests that average hours worked fell from around 2,100 a year in 1989 to 1,500 a year in 1992.

Of course, even if enterprises adopt "no layoffs" policies, there are always some voluntary separations: retirements and early retirements; in some countries, emigrants or others wanting to leave the labor force; and, above all, workers leaving to take (what they hope will be) better jobs in the growing sectors of the economy dominated by de novo private firms. There is evidence that labor-shedding in the first phase took the form mainly of these voluntary separations (natural wastage). In several of the countries, separations from state-sector firms in the first few years of the transition were no higher than the normal levels prior to the reforms (see, e.g., Beleva et al. 1995 for Bulgaria; Earle and Oprescu 1995 for Romania). However, the worsening economic climate led to a sharp fall in voluntary separations.

The general conclusion of this section is that the impact of output decline on employment depends on the extent to which government policy provides financial support for firms, on the one hand, as against the public welfare system, on the other. In the first regime, workers stay on the firm's payroll and unemployment is hidden; in the second, workers are laid off and unemployment is open. It is a presumption of much analysis that the second regime is preferable, on the grounds that open unemployment provides a pool of people from whom the private sector can recruit, and that the larger this pool, the easier it will be for the private sector to grow. However, the evidence for this proposition is questionable. Section 6.3 discusses the relationship between employment and restructuring.

6.3   Employment and Restructuring

We noted in section 6.1 that the labor markets of the former socialist economies were characterized by a highly distorted structure of employment, particularly in relation to the industrial sector. There are many more people employed in agriculture and in manufacturing industry in the CEE and FSU countries than in comparable market economies. If the structure of employment in the transitional economies is to look anything like that of market economies, there must be a substantial shift in employment from manufacturing industry and agriculture to trade and services. Given the obstacles to labor mobility, it might be expected that such restructuring of employment would be one of the major tasks of the transition.

This external restructuring across sectors is of course only part of the process. Within firms, there is a need for internal restructuring of employment in response to new technologies, business practices, and relative factor prices reflecting scarcity. Initially, privatization was seen as the essential requirement for internal restructuring, but much evidence suggests that ownership has not had a critical effect in practice, perhaps in part because of the tendency toward privatization to "insiders." In many enterprises the withdrawal of subsidy and imposition of hard budget constraints have forced a rationalization of the use of labor, as we have noted, whether or not the firm is privatized.

In this section we discuss the relationship between job destruction and job creation in light of the assumption, noted in section 6.1, that job destruction will facilitate job creation by providing a pool of unemployed workers whom expanding firms can recruit. We have discussed this issue at length elsewhere (Jackman and Pauna 1997), so it will be sufficient here to summarize our conclusions. Most important, we find no evidence in the CEE countries that a more rapid rate of job destruction in declining sectors leads to a faster rate of job creation.

The scale of the problem is revealed in table 6.2a, which shows the structure of employment by broad industrial sector in six CEE countries in 1989 and in Russia in 1990. The table also shows, for comparison, the sectoral composition of employment in various market economies or groups of economies that have similar basic economic and geographic

Table 6.2a
Structure of employment, 1989 (%)

Sector	Bulgaria	Czech Republic	Hungary	Poland	Romania	Slovak Republic	Russia	Canada	South OECD	North OECD
Agriculture	19.0	11.7	16.6	26.8	27.9	13.8	13.2	4.3	10.7	4.1
Mining	2.6	3.6	2.0	3.4	2.3	1.0	} 30.3	1.4	0.4	1.0
Manufacturing	34.9	34.0	28.6	24.5	38.1	32.1		17.0	22.0	26.3
Electricity, gas, water	0.8	1.4	2.6	1.1	1.2	1.6	12.0	1.0	0.9	1.1
Construction	7.8	7.3	7.0	7.8	7.0	11.6	7.8	6.1	8.1	6.4
Trade	9.2	11.5	11.3	8.9	5.9	11.1	7.7	23.4	19.3	17.4
Transportation	6.8	6.5	7.7	7.2	6.9	6.4	4.8	6.6	6.0	6.0
Finance	0.6	0.5	0.8	1.0	0.3	0.4	21.3	11.2	6.1	8.6
Community services	18.4	23.5	23.4	19.3	10.2	22.0	26.8*	28.9	26.5	28.7
RI	24.2	17.2	16.5	23.0	36.4	18.4		—	—	—

Sources: OECD employment is from OECD, *Labour Force Statistics* (1993). The figures for each group are weighted averages. For Eastern European countries, the main data source is *Employment Observatory—Central and Eastern Europe* no. 8 (1996); for Romania, *Statistical Yearbook*, Romanian Commission for Statistics (1995). For Russia, from Goskomstat and *Russian Economic Trends* 4, no. 1 (1995).
Notes: Russia data are for 1990. Russia is compared with Canada; all other countries are compared with South OECD.

features. The South OECD group (France, Greece, Italy, and Spain) consists of European countries with substantial small-scale agricultural sectors, while the North OECD group (Denmark, West Germany, the Netherlands, and the United Kingdom) consists of more densely populated industrialized economies. The former seems a plausible comparison group for the East European countries, while the most plausible comparator for Russia, given its enormous landmass and vast wealth of minerals and natural resources, may be Canada.

The extent of labor mobility required can be gauged by calculating the proportion of the labor force that would need to move from one sector to another for the structure of employment to resemble that of comparable market economies. For this purpose, we construct a "restructuring index," which is a measure of gross sectoral employment changes. The basic analytic concept derives from the work of Davis and Haltiwanger (1990, 1992) on job creation and job destruction, but is applied here to sectors rather than to establishments. The index is the average of the number of excess jobs in sectors where employment will need to decline, and the number of net new jobs in sectors where employment should be increasing (as a proportion of the workforce).

Clearly, an index based only on broad sectoral adjustments seriously understates the extent of economic restructuring required. The reforms can be expected to lead to enormous changes in the composition of employment within as well as across sectors. But problems of structural adjustment can be expected to be most severe in relation to broad industrial sectors. Prior to the reforms, interenterprise labor mobility was quite high in Eastern Europe and in Russia, and of the same order of magnitude as in many Western European countries (Jackman and Rutkowski 1994, table 7.1). This mobility typically took the form of people moving between jobs in similar types of enterprises. As in market economies, workers appear to have been quite ready to move between jobs in the same sector. In terms of structural adjustment in the labor market, the major problem is in moving workers from agriculture or manufacturing to the service sector.

Table 6.2a provides a measure of the extent to which the employment structure of the formerly socialist countries differs from what might have emerged had their history been different and their economies developed along market lines. In all these countries, in comparison with the OECD economies, there is obviously excess employment in agriculture, mining, and manufacturing, and a deficiency of employment in services. It is conspicuous, however, that in comparison with Northern Europe, the

Table 6.2b
Structure of employment, 1994 (%)

Sector	Bulgaria	Czech Republic	Hungary	Poland	Romania	Slovak Republic	Russia
Agriculture	22.1	7.0	8.7	26.7	n.a.	10.2	15.4
Mining	3.2	2.0	1.0	2.7	n.a.	1.6	
Manufacturing	25.3	29.7	23.7	20.3	n.a.	26.8	27.1
Electricity, gas, water	1.2	2.0	2.9	1.9	n.a.	2.3	
Construction	5.7	9.3	5.4	5.7	n.a.	8.9	9.9
Trade	11.6	15.0	15.4	14.6	n.a.	12.3	9.5
Transportation	7.3	7.6	8.4	5.7	n.a.	7.8	7.8
Finance	1.3	1.6	1.9	1.6	n.a.	1.2	5.4
Community services	22.3	25.9	32.5	20.8	n.a.	29.0	22.3
RI	23.1	14.6	13.0	21.8	n.a.	14.1	26.2

Sources: OECD employment is from OECD, *Labour Force Statistics* (1993). The figures for each group are weighted averages. For Eastern European countries, the main data source is *Employment Observatory—Central and Eastern Europe* no. 8 (1996); for Romania, *Statistical Yearbook*, Romanian Commission for Statistics (1995). For Russia, from Goskomstat and *Russian Economic Trends* 4, no. 1 (1995).

imbalance in employment structure is concentrated almost exclusively in one sector—agriculture—where the CEE (population weighted) average of around 24 percent contrasts with only 4 percent in the Northern European countries. The Southern European countries provide perhaps a less extreme contrast, and may thus constitute a more appropriate comparator group.

It is noteworthy that the extent of structural imbalance differs very greatly between countries. Compared with the structure of employment in the Southern European countries, the extent of restructuring required in Romania—36.4 percent of the workforce—was, in 1989, more than double that required in Hungary (16.5 percent) or the Czech Republic (17.2 percent). While Romania is something of an outlier, the extent of restructuring required was significantly greater in Bulgaria and (because of its abnormally large agricultural sector) in Poland than in the Czech Republic, Slovakia, or Hungary. These big differences reinforce the point made earlier of the importance of initial conditions for the severity of a country's economic adjustment problems.

Table 6.2b records the equivalent figures for the structure of employment in 1994. This table presents a rather surprising picture. While the proportion employed in manufacturing has fallen everywhere, and the proportions employed in trade and finance have risen, the proportion employed in agriculture has risen in two of the countries. And, most remarkably, despite all the upheaval, the restructuring index shows very little improvement.

As noted in Jackman and Pauna (1997), this apparent lack of progress in restructuring despite substantial job losses reflects several phenomena. First, there is a problem of "moving goalposts"—the market economies are themselves in the process of relatively rapid structural change, and the transition economies need quite a rapid pace of employment reallocation simply to avoid falling further behind. (In all cases, employment changes in market economies are taking them further from the employment structure of the transition economies.) If one calculates the gap in employment structure between the transition economies in 1994 and the comparator economies in 1989, all the transition economies show some improvement, most notably the Czech Republic and Slovakia. By this measure, however, progress in Poland and Bulgaria has been very limited, and in Romania it has been almost nonexistent.

The second reason is the peculiar role of the agricultural sector as an employer of last resort. In some countries, particularly those where employment in agriculture was initially high, the collapse of non-agricultural employment has led to a reversion to small-scale farming. There is thus a perverse tendency for those countries which had the greatest surplus employment in agriculture in 1989 to experience the slowest declines or even, in the cases of Romania and Russia, an increase in agricultural employment since 1989.

Third, a significant part of the observed change in the employment structure has not been in response to the needs of the transition, but simply reflects the uneven incidence of macroeconomic recession across industrial sectors. In Bulgaria, for example, the shares of employment in mining, in electricity, gas, and water, and in transport have risen even though the initial shares in these three sectors were already too high. One reason must be that these sectors are relatively immune to recession.

Some further evidence for this last point is given in tables 6.3a and 6.3b, which show gross changes in employment by sector between 1989 and 1992, and 1992 and 1994, respectively. Between 1989 and 1992 the rate of job destruction ranged from 25.0 percent in Bulgaria to 10.2 percent in the Czech Republic, and job creation ranged from 6.7 percent in Romania to only 0.2 percent in Bulgaria. There is an clear inverse relationship between job destruction and job creation, consistent with the dominant role of aggregate shocks rather than sectoral reallocation. It is

Table 6.3a
Change in employment, 1989–92 (millions)

Sector	Bulgaria	Czech Republic	Hungary	Poland	Romania	Slovak Republic	Russia	South OECD
Agriculture	−0.12	−0.20	−0.36	−0.72	0.39	−0.08	−0.47	−1.21
Mining	−0.01	−0.07	−0.05	−0.12	0.01	0.00		0.00
Manufacturing	−0.57	−0.26	−0.35	−0.89	−0.87	−0.18	−1.30	−0.51
Electricity, gas, water	0.00	0.01	−0.02	−0.04	0.03	0.00		−0.07
Construction	−0.20	0.02	−0.13	−0.26	−0.19	−0.07	−0.70	0.31
Trade	−0.07	0.00	0.04	0.17	0.28	−0.04	−0.17	0.41
Transportation	−0.05	0.02	−0.03	−0.25	−0.11	0.00	−0.11	0.12
Finance	0.01	0.03	0.03	0.03	0.02	0.01	0.08	0.77
Community services	−0.07	−0.01	0.04	−0.24	−0.06	0.03	0.53	1.44
Total change	−1.08	−0.48	−0.83	−2.33	−0.49	−0.34	−2.14	1.74
Job creation	0.01	0.08	0.11	0.20	0.73	0.04	0.61	3.05
(%)	0.2	1.5	2.2	1.2	6.7	1.6	0.8	5.3
Job destruction	−1.09	−0.55	−0.94	−2.53	−1.23	−0.38	−2.75	−1.79
(%)	25.0	10.2	19.1	14.9	11.2	15.2	3.8	3.1

Sources: OECD employment is from OECD, *Labour Force Statistics* (1993). The figures for each group are weighted averages. For Eastern European countries, the main data source is *Employment Observatory—Central and Eastern Europe* no. 8 (1996); for Romania, *Statistical Yearbook*, Romanian Commission for Statistics (1995). For Russia, from Goskomstat and *Russian Economic Trends* 4, no. 1 (1995).

notable that in most cases, even where the share of employment in a particular sector is rising, the absolute level of employment in that sector is falling. The changes in the structure of employment between 1989 and 1992 were thus achieved largely by differential rates of job loss rather than by labor mobility across sectors.

The period from 1992 to 1994 shows a reduced rate of job destruction in all CEE countries and a more rapid rate of job creation, but no clear correlation between the two. By this stage, however, there is evidence of significant job creation, notably in Poland and the Czech Republic (where well over half the total gross increase in employment was in the trade and financial sectors). The achievement of relatively rapid rates of employment growth (140,000 people, representing about 3 percent of the workforce) in the business service sectors, trade, and finance in the Czech Republic is particularly noteworthy, and is perhaps the clearest indication that employment growth in private services need not be held back by a more gradual pace of job loss in the state sector.

Table 6.3b
Change in employment, 1992–94 (millions)

Sector	Bulgaria	Czech Republic	Hungary	Poland	Romania	Slovak Republic	Russia
Agriculture	0.00	−0.09	−0.13	0.08	n.a.	−0.05	1.03
Mining	0.00	−0.03	−0.01	−0.07	n.a.	0.01	⎫
Manufacturing	−0.13	−0.14	−0.17	−0.31	n.a.	−0.06	⎬ −2.92
Electricity, gas, water	0.00	0.00	0.00	0.13	n.a.	0.01	⎭
Construction	−0.01	0.04	−0.02	−0.23	n.a.	−0.03	−1.51
Trade	0.04	0.11	−0.02	0.46	n.a.	0.02	0.78
Transportation	−0.01	0.00	−0.03	−0.13	n.a.	0.00	−0.35
Finance	0.01	0.03	0.00	0.04	n.a.	0.01	0.02
Community services	−0.01	0.03	0.03	.018	n.a.	0.03	−1.34
Total change	−0.12	−0.05	−0.34	0.15	n.a.	−0.06	−4.29
Job creation (%)	0.05	0.22	0.04	0.98	n.a.	0.08	1.83
	1.5	4.5	0.98	6.1		3.7	2.5
Job destruction (%)	−0.16	−0.26	−0.38	−0.74	n.a.	−0.14	−6.12
	4.9	5.3	9.3	5.0		6.5	8.6

Sources: OECD employment is from OECD, *Labour Force Statistics* (1993). The figures for each group are weighted averages. For Eastern European countries, the main data source is *Employment Observatory—Central and Eastern Europe* no. 8 (1996); for Romania, *Statistical Yearbook*, Romanian Commission for Statistics (1995). For Russia, from Goskomstat and *Russian Economic Trends* 4, no. 1 (1995).

In Russia, restructuring obviously started later, and the rate of job loss in the early stages (1992–94) is quite low compared with the CEE countries. The growth of employment in the trade and financial sectors (about 800,000 people, or 1 percent of the workforce) is around average for the CEE countries during the first stage, thus suggesting that low unemployment in Russia has not discouraged creation of new firms (although, on the other hand, the remarkably high mobility of labor in Russia does not appear to have accelerated the rate of new job creation).

In Jackman and Pauna (1997) we constructed three indices of labor-market restructuring that related to the speed of restructuring, the efficiency of restructuring, and the rate of new job creation. These indices attempted to distinguish between restructuring, defined as changes in employment leading to an employment structure more like a market economy, and divergent employment changes (such as increases in employment in sectors where employment was already excessive). The "speed" index measures the extent of actual restructuring thus defined as a proportion of the original restructuring gap, as measured by the restructuring

Table 6.4
Measures of restructuring, 1989–94

	Speed	Efficiency	New job creation (%)
Bulgaria	40.5	70.0	3.9
	(48.2)	(66.8)	
Czech Republic	44.2	90.7	28.0
	(39.6)	(87.2)	
Hungary	60.3	84.1	12.8
	(54.5)	(76.0)	
Poland	35.3	70.6	23.3
	(44.4)	(64.8)	
Romania	21.1	64.8	3.4
	(30.5)	(84.2)	
Slovakia	48.7	92.5	19.1
	(48.8)	(90.3)	
Greece*	26.3	57.0	41.9
Portugal*	70.1	85.9	89.9

Source: Jackman and Pauna 1997.
Note: Indices in parentheses exclude agriculture.
* 1989–93.

index in table 6.1. Efficiency measures restructuring changes as a proportion of all changes in employment. Both concepts are measured with
inclusion and with exclusion of agriculture. New job creation measures
the amount of restructuring achieved through new job creation rather
than through job destruction.

These indices are given in table 6.4. For the CEE countries, they show a
fairly rapid rate of change and reiterate the point that the Czech Republic
has achieved as good, and in some respects a better, rate of restructuring
than the other economies, despite its low unemployment. For further
details see Jackman and Pauna (1997).

6.4   Unemployment: Flows and Duration

The sharp fall in employment has led to a correspondingly sharp rise in
unemployment. As can be seen from table 6.1, the association between
the fall in employment and the rise in unemployment is not one-to-one,
and we shall see the reasons for this in section 6.5. This section briefly
examines some of the main characteristics of the unemployment experience of the CEE countries and of Russia.

It might be expected that in economies experiencing rapid economic
restructuring, there would be a large flow of workers both into and out of

unemployment. In reality, as already noted, enterprises have been reluctant to lay off workers, and in many of the transition economies, inflows into unemployment have been lower than those observed in market economies (Boeri 1994, chart 1). The sharp rise in unemployment has taken the form not of a large inflow but rather of a very low outflow. This phenomenon has been extensively documented in a number of papers on CEE countries by Boeri (e.g., 1994, 1996), and recent survey evidence suggests the same is true of Russia (Richter 1997).

Before looking at the evidence, it is necessary to recognize that there have been peculiar difficulties in collecting unemployment statistics in the transition economies. Most countries introduced unemployment benefit systems at an early stage (see annex 1), and these schemes have generated quite detailed data on registered unemployment. But unemployment benefits have typically been available only for a limited period (usually 6–12 months), and after the exhaustion of their benefits, many people have not continued to register as unemployed. This leads to a significant underrecording of the number of people unemployed, particularly of the number of long-term unemployed. Also, in many countries, much of the measured outflow from registered unemployment is simply the result of unemployed people who are no longer entitled to benefits not continuing to register as unemployed.

At the same time there has been widespread concern, not least in the countries themselves, about abuse of the benefit system. Clearly, it is possible that many of those registered as unemployed may have some form of casual or informal work, given that many of the East European countries have sizable agricultural sectors, and some also have thriving informal sectors. Though there is little hard evidence on this, one survey in Poland found that 46 percent of unemployed people had some form of work, albeit often only casual or part-time (World Bank 1995b). A second survey found that around 35 percent of employers were informally hiring people registered as unemployed (Mroczkowski 1996).

These problems have led (as in many OECD countries) to the use of labor force survey (LFS) statistics rather than official registrations as a measure of overall unemployment rates. In centrally planned economies, statistics tended to be collected from enterprises rather than from households, and in most of the transition countries it took a few years to institute LFSs. In consequence, LFS data were not available during the early stages of the reform. Also, survey data has, of course, less coverage and is collected less frequently (e.g., annually versus monthly) than registration statistics.

Comparing registration and LFS statistics (Commander and Tolstopia-tenko 1997) shows that in Russia and Bulgaria, official registrations significantly understate the extent of unemployment, whereas in Poland and Romania the LFS figures are below those for registered unemployment. This reflects the relative harshness of the benefit regime in Russia and Bulgaria compared to the other countries. The corollary is that in the latter countries a substantial proportion of the unemployed are not receiving unemployment benefits. For example, in Bulgaria in June 1994, only 24 percent of those reporting themselves as unemployed in the LFS were drawing unemployment benefits.

The low outflow rates from unemployment imply long durations, and LFS data confirm that the proportion of long-term unemployment in total unemployment is both high and rising (Boeri 1994, chart 2; Commander and Tolstopiatenko 1997, table 1). In 1995, two-thirds of unemployed people in Bulgaria had been unemployed for more than a year, and in Hungary, Romania, and Slovakia, the figure was close to half. While these proportions may not appear abnormally high in comparison with market economies having similar overall unemployment rates, they in fact represent a much more serious problem because in CEE countries the long-term unemployed generally have exhausted their entitlement to benefits, whereas in most market economies with high long-term unemployment, benefits are available for several years if not indefinitely.

Returning to outflow rates, Boeri (1994, 1996) and others have reported data on the outflow from registered unemployment to work. The reported outflow rates, about 2 percent per month, are very low by the standards of market economies, even during recessions. Data from matched LFS samples (Boeri 1996) suggest that something on the order of 30 percent of people unemployed at a particular time will be working a year later. This is roughly in line with the 2 percent per month outflow figure and, once again, is much lower than comparable figures for market economies.

All this evidence points clearly to the conclusion that unemployed people in the transition economies have a very low probability of finding work and that, in consequence, unemployment tends to be of long duration. How can one account for this state of affairs? The first point, as noted in section 6.3, is that a degree of labor-market slack is necessary for the efficient functioning of a market economy, and much of the economic adjustment in the early years of the transition has been characterized by general employment decline rather than by restructuring in the form of decline in one sector and growth in another.

A second, and more interesting, point is that the growing sectors do not appear to recruit from the unemployed. The Hungarian Household Panel Survey (Kollo 1993) found that most workers in private firms were recruited directly from state firms, and a majority of the unemployed who found jobs returned to state-sector employers. In fact, more people entered unemployment from the private sector than unemployed people found work in the private sector. Similar results were found in the former Czechoslovakia (Vecernik 1993), Poland (Boeri 1993), and Bulgaria (Beleva et al. 1995).

Far from unemployment being the route between the declining and the growing sectors, it has proved to be more of a depository where those who have lost out in the overall economic decline await some form of economic revival. These are often people with specific skills related to traditional manufacturing activities. While the plight of these people is clearly caused by economic restructuring, their unemployment does nothing to speed the process of that restructuring. The preference of expanding firms to recruit from those who are already employed rather than from the unemployed presumably reflects a sorting effect whereby enterprises tend to lay off less-skilled or less-enterprising workers. But it is also possible that the loss of work experience and habits may make the unemployed less attractive to potential employers, and hence reduce the pool of suitable people from which the expanding sectors recruit. We return to this issue in section 6.7.

6.5   Unemployment, Hidden Employment, and Inactivity

As employment has fallen, unemployment has tended to rise, but the rise in unemployment has not been simply a mirror image of the fall in employment. Between 1989 and 1994, in Bulgaria and in Hungary the increase in unemployment was significantly less than half the fall in employment, whereas in Poland and Romania the growth in unemployment initially (up to 1992) exceeded the decline in employment.

Arithmetically, any difference between the decline in employment and the rise in unemployment must indicate a change in the size of the labor force, which, in turn, may be the result of a change in either the working-age population or the participation rate. The employment and unemployment figures suggest that there has been a fall in the labor force in many of the transition economies, particularly in Bulgaria and Hungary. Why should such a reduction have occurred, and is it more than a statistical artifact? Table 6.5 presents a breakdown of the change in the labor force in total and by gender for the CEE countries and for Russia.

There are notable differences in demographic developments between the countries. While, overall, the working-age population of the region has remained approximately constant, there has been relatively high growth in the Czech and Slovak Republics, offset by a decline, mainly due to emigration, in Albania and Bulgaria. More important, between 1989 and 1994, economic activity rates fell by around 10 percent of the working-age population in Albania, Bulgaria, and Hungary but rose in Poland and Romania.

The causes of migration within the region are partly ethnic and partly economic. In some of the countries, ethnic minority groups have taken advantage of the greater freedoms under the new political regimes to return to their homelands. A substantial proportion of the emigrants from Bulgaria are of Turkish origin, and in Romania many of the emigrants are of Hungarian origin. At the same time, there has been emigration due to economic distress (e.g., Albanians to Italy), and people have been moving into the more prosperous countries in the region, such as the Czech Republic.

It is more difficult to explain why changes in activity rates have differed so much across the countries. It has often been noted that participation rates, particularly of women, under centralized planning were higher than in market economies, reflecting the preeminence of output targets and producer interests over the traditional social structure based on the family. Thus a general fall in female participation rates (a rise in "inactivity") throughout the region would not be unexpected or necessarily a cause for concern. However, as table 6.5 shows, there was an increase in female activity rates in Poland and Romania; and where there was a rise in inactivity, as in Bulgaria and Hungary, it was as pronounced among men as among women.

It seems more plausible to attribute the fall in activity rates to the sharp overall decline in output and employment in conjunction with the features of the unemployment benefit system described in Annex 1. As unemployed people exhaust their entitlement to benefits, they resort to social assistance, to family and friends, and to work in the informal sector, abandoning the search for formal employment. Such people no longer register as unemployed, and would be classified as "out of the labor force" on the LFS definition, though in more favorable circumstances they would be working. (This is rather similar to the explanation often advanced for the declining participation rates of unskilled men in many market economies

Table 6.5
Changes in working-age population, employment, unemployment, and inactivity, 1989–94 (%)

	Total				Men				Women			
	Working-age population	Employment	Unemployment	Inactive	Working-age population	Employment	Unemployment	Inactive	Working-age population	Employment	Unemployment	Inactive
Albania	-5.0	-22.8	7.9	9.9	-8.1	-19.8	9.1	2.6	-1.9	-25.9	6.5	17.5
Bulgaria	-3.1	-24.5	11.0	10.4	-3.8	-27.1	9.7	13.6	-2.2	-21.9	12.4	7.3
Czech R.	4.5	-5.0	3.0	6.5	3.8	-3.3	2.3	4.8	5.4	-6.6	3.5	8.5
Hungary	1.9	-20.9	9.1	13.7	1.4	-20.9	10.2	12.1	2.5	-20.9	7.9	15.5
Poland	3.1	-8.7	12.6	-0.8	3.2	-7.9	12.0	-0.9	3.0	-9.5	13.2	-0.7
Romania*	-0.9	-6.8	9.0	-3.1	-1.1	-8.5	7.0	0.4	-0.7	-4.8	11.2	-7.1
Russia*	1.2	-5.9	2.1	4.9	1.3	-5.8	2.5	4.3	1.1	-5.9	1.7	5.4
Slovak R.	5.4	-13.3	12.2	6.5	4.7	-8.8	12.1	1.4	6.1	-18.3	12.3	12.1

Source: Authors' computations based on Employment Observatory—Central and Eastern Europe no. 7 (1995) and Institute for Comparative Labor Relations Research, The Restructuring of Employment and the Formation of a Labor Market in Russia (Moscow: The Institute, 1996).
Note: All figures are percentages of working-age population in 1989.
* The figures for Romania represent changes between 1989 and 1993; figures for 1994 are not available. For Russia, all figures denote change from 1992 to 1994.

in recent years.) A number of the countries have encouraged early retirement; workers participating in such schemes, and also those on government training programs (see section 6.6), do not register as unemployed.
All these may be described as "discouraged workers," that is, people who
are not counted as unemployed since they are not actively seeking work
because of adverse labor-market conditions.

Whether or not unemployed people enter or remain on the unemployment register depends largely on whether or not they can qualify for
unemployment benefits, and this in turn depends on the rules and regulations governing the unemployment benefit system. Initially, in both Poland
and Romania, the receipt of benefits did not depend on previous work
experience, and it was alleged that many people, particularly married
women who had not previously worked, entered the labor force in order
to collect unemployment benefits. Initially, too, unemployment benefits
were available in Poland for an indefinite duration. While the conditions
for payment of benefits have been made more restrictive (the current regulations are summarized in table A1 of annex 1), it remains the case that
benefits have been more readily available and more generous in Poland
and Romania than in Russia, Bulgaria, or the Czech Republic. (We have
already noted that Poland and Romania are the only countries where the
LFS measure of unemployment is lower than the number of registered
unemployed.) The Hungarian system has the most generous replacement
ratio, up to 75 percent of previous income, but in combination with quite
tight restrictions on availability, so that some unemployed people (young
people with little work experience) can draw benefits for only three
months.

All this suggests that much measured economic inactivity is in fact
disguised unemployment or (to the extent that unemployed people have
informal-sector work) disguised underemployment. No doubt part of the
fall in female participation reflects a wish by some women to leave the
labor force, but there is no systematic tendency for female participation
rates to fall more sharply than those of men, which suggests that the discouraged worker effect is the dominant influence. An implication is that
the fall in employment is probably a much better indicator of labor market
conditions than is the unemployment rate.

6.6   Active Labor-Market Policies

With double-digit rates of recorded unemployment after just a few years
of transition, and facing large and potentially increasing expenditures on
unemployment benefits, most CEE countries have introduced, even in the

Table 6.6
Public expenditure on ALMPs (% of GDP)

	Bulgaria	Czech Republic	Hungary	Poland	Slovakia
Total	0.14	0.18	0.62	0.39	0.25
Public employment services and administration	0.09	0.10	0.15	0.01	0.11
Training and retraining	0.01	0.01	0.20	0.03	0.03
Youth measures	—	0.03	—	0.07	0.01
Subsidized jobs (private sector)	—	0.02	0.12	0.13	—
Enterprise start-ups	—	0.01	0.02	0.02	—
Public sector job creation	0.03	0.02	0.14	0.10	0.04
Jobs for disabled	—	0.01	—	0.04	0.01

Source: OECD *Employment Outlook*, 1995, table U.

early years of the reform, a wide variety of Western-type active labor-market policies (ALMPs). These have included direct job-creation measures, such as wage subsidies, public works, loans for businesses or for unemployed people to start up businesses, training and retraining, and early retirement, as well as the development of job placement services. Most of the programs have been developed with the assistance, at least in the initial stages, of Western governments and international organizations, which have tended to envisage ALMPs as having an important role to play through assisting labor mobility and helping people move from declining to growing sectors. Recent detailed reviews of ALMPs in the transition economies have been brought together by the OECD (1997) and Godfrey and Richards (1997).

However, as shown in table 6.6, public expenditure on ALMPs remains low, not only as a share of GDP (ranging in 1994 from only 0.14 percent in Bulgaria to 0.62 percent in Hungary) but also relative to passive labor-market expenditures. By way of comparison, expenditure figures in OECD countries range from 2.95 percent of GDP (Sweden) to only 0.09 percent (Japan), with most West European countries in the range of 1.0–1.5 percent (OECD 1995, annex table T). In many of the countries, expenditures on ALMPs have come from the employment funds rather than general government revenues, so that, with rapid growth in unemployment, the resources available have been drained away to pay for unemployment benefits, and spending on active policies has suffered. Benefits absorb 80 percent or more of public expenditure on the unemployed in Poland, Bulgaria, and Romania; about two-thirds in Slovakia and Hungary; and about 45 percent in the Czech Republic, by far the lowest in the region.

These proportions are in line with those of OECD countries, with only Sweden matching the Czech Republic in spending as much as 55 percent of unemployment outlays on active measures.

In Central and Eastern Europe, local labor offices generally have considerable autonomy in deciding how to spend their budget for ALMPs. Central governments typically limit themselves to general formulations of policy. This variation has permitted some analyses of the relative effectiveness of different programs (e.g., Boeri and Burda 1996, for the Czech Republic), but elsewhere it has been suggested that the absence of standardized procedures has prevented the development of monitoring systems (see Gora and Lehmann 1995, on Poland). Gora and Lehmann also argue that lack of expertise on the part of the staff in the local labor offices has reduced the effectiveness of the programs; Boeri and Burda, by contrast, find the efficiency of employment exchanges in the Czech Republic higher than in most OECD countries.

An underlying rationale of some types of ALMPs is to target the most disadvantaged categories, such as the long-term unemployed, new entrants, the elderly, the disabled, and those without benefits or other sources of income. Unemployment among the disadvantaged categories remains high, particularly among youth; incidence of long-term unemployment has reached at least 40 percent and is still increasing in all the countries, with the exception of the Czech Republic. The concentration of unemployment among these groups is characteristic of many market economies with comparable overall unemployment rates.

Detailed microeconomic assessments of the effectiveness of ALMPs in market economies have in general been disappointing. A number of examples are given in a recent survey (OECD 1993), in particular of training schemes that appear to have improved neither the employment prospects nor the wages of participants. There is equally little evidence that such temporary work brings any real improvement in the future employment prospects of participants, though most analyses of such programs have tended to focus on whether the total number of jobs is actually increased in the short run, which also is not entirely clear. Assistance with job placement, however, appears generally helpful and cost-effective in OECD countries and in the Czech Republic (Boeri and Burda 1996).

These difficulties are clearly exacerbated in many of the transition economies by low budget allocations, and consequently low participation of unemployed people in targeted programs (only a few thousand in Romania or Bulgaria, for example), as well as lack of staff expertise at the local level. For example, only the Czech Republic and Slovenia allocate significant shares of the ALMP budget, 18 percent and 22.8 percent, respectively, to jobs for new graduates and teenagers; all other countries spend less than 2 percent.

The former Czechoslovakia adopted the most comprehensive package of ALMP measures, involving a short period (six months) of unemployment benefits followed by a guaranteed temporary job or place in a training scheme, based on the Swedish employment principle. This package appears to have been effective in holding down unemployment during the early years of the transition. Following the split, the Czech and Slovak unemployment rates have diverged. The reasons for this have been explored by Ham et al. (1993), with the main finding that there are a number of special adverse factors in the Slovak Republic, and some advantageous ones in the Czech Republic. ALMPs play a helpful role in both countries.

The overall good performance of the Czech economy, with low unemployment rates and an unemployment/vacancy ratio comparable with the Western European ones, has enabled the Czech authorities to maintain, and even decrease, expenditures on both passive and active programs after the separation. The Slovaks, faced with a very different prospect—rates of unemployment among the highest in the region (45 percent long-term unemployed in 1994)—have experimented with several reforms of the ALMP system. There have been significant differences between the Czech Republic and Slovakia in the allocation of the ALMP budget. The Slovaks spend most (77.3 percent in 1994) on directly subsidizing new job creation, with funds going mainly either to existing employers or to unemployed who strive to become self-employed in socially purposeful jobs (SPJs); the Czechs have changed their emphasis from SPJs to retraining and jobs for graduates. Recent evidence (for details, see Terrell et al. 1995) suggests that in Slovakia, ALMPs have had a real impact on unemployment, particularly on outflows to jobs. ALMP participants account for 10–18 percent of outflows.

Hungary and Poland are the only countries where public expenditure on ALMPs has steadily increased during the transition. At the same time, they have experienced, probably not unrelated to these, increases in outflows to jobs (Boeri 1996), although they are still much lower than in the Czech Republic. In the early years of the reform, Hungary introduced a complex system of ALMPs. Using a cohort of unemployed, Micklewright and Nagy (1994) estimate that exits to ALMPs represent 10 percent of all recorded exits other than exhaustion and censoring. However, with more than 40 percent of the total exits, exhaustion represents by far the largest single exit state from insured unemployment. They conclude that "Huge expenditure would be needed to develop ALMPs so as to offer a guaranteed place on such programmes to the unemployed" (Micklewright and Nagy 1994).

In Poland, in spite of the increase in the budget allocated to ALMPs, its share relative to GDP (close to 0.30 percent in 1994) is still minor, and according to Gora and Lehmann (1995), it apparently has no impact on the unemployment rate. Gora and Lehmann identify the lack of central government involvement in the implementation and monitoring of the programs, together with lack of targeting and selection criteria, as main causes that contribute to the ineffectiveness of ALMPs. Significantly, training schemes do not seem to increase the chances of leaving unemployment. Other policies, such as job brokerage that provides information to facilitate job-matching, and more efficient targeting, especially toward long-term unemployed, seem to be more appropriate in Poland.

Romania and Bulgaria have yet to implement ALMPs on any significant scale, in terms either of expenditure or of participation of unemployed people. Major institutional, as well as financial, barriers have yet to be removed.

Summarizing, it appears that at this stage, ALMPs have had only a modest impact. As in market economies, they appear least effective in conditions of low demand, when there are few vacancies, and where there is poor job-matching between the skills of the unemployed and the requirements of employers. Although the transition countries have embraced a wide variety of ALMPs, implementation, conducted in general at the level of local labor offices that lack both experience and technical means, has sometimes been poor. There are likewise legitimate grounds for doubting the cost-effectiveness of training schemes for unemployed people. Not only is the evidence on the effects of such schemes in the market economies discouraging (OECD 1993), but in the context of the weak labor markets in the transitional economies, there are few job opportunities for unemployed people whether or not they are trained, and this will discourage participation. There are also acute shortages of appropriately qualified trainers.

6.7   Conclusion

The countries of Central and Eastern Europe and of the former Soviet Union have experienced very sharp falls in output. Employment has fallen and unemployment risen everywhere, but in many countries the rise in unemployment has been substantially smaller than the fall in output. The analysis of this chapter suggests that not too much should be read into this. In some countries unemployment has been kept hidden by continuing subsidies to firms, enabling them to retain workers they do not need. In other countries, workers who have become unemployed have subsequently disappeared from the statistics due to a combination of exhausted unemployment benefits and opportunities in the informal economy. Given the decline in output, underemployment of labor is inevitable, but this does not mean that all forms of underemployment are equal in terms of economic efficiency or social welfare.

We have already noted a predisposition on the part of Western economists and policy advisers to adopt a view of the transition that considers unemployment to be a necessary concomitant of restructuring, and thus encourages workers to accept the view that unemployment would accelerate, or at least facilitate, the process. The international financial institutions, in particular the World Bank and IMF, have supported the setting up of a social safety net to alleviate the hardship to individuals caused by the transition, in the belief that unemployment is a necessary element of that process. As a result, policies have been adopted (in Central and Eastern Europe but not in Russia) to subsidize unemployment rather than employment.

However, this frame of reference may not have been the appropriate starting point. Growing private firms appear to prefer to recruit persons currently holding jobs in the state sector, so that unemployment therefore does not contribute to the pool of eligible recruits. There is in any case no evidence that a crude lack of availability of labor (as distinct from shortages of particular skills) has been a constraint on economic restructuring. Rather, it is the constraints of capital, finance, entrepreneurship, and institutional infrastructure that have been binding, while labor has been the surplus factor.

The evidence surveyed in this chapter shows that different countries have responded to this problem of surplus labor in different ways. In some, particularly Russia, there has been a tendency for workers to remain employed in enterprises, even though there is no work for them to do. In others, such as Poland, most of the surplus labor takes the form of registered unemployment. In Hungary and Bulgaria, many workers have left the labor force. We have argued that these different outcomes reflect differences in policy, and in particular the unemployment benefits system. Enterprises run in part for the well-being of their workers may choose to retain everyone. Such firms will reduce employment only if the government gives them financial incentives to lay off workers.

How can one evaluate these different policies? From the standpoint of economic efficiency, one would want to start from an analysis of market imperfections. In the labor market, unemployment benefits subsidize open unemployment relative to other states, and thus give insider-managed enterprises an incentive to lay off more workers than is socially optimal. (Arguments that unemployment should be subsidized because it improves job-matching, based on the assumption that the unemployed search more efficiently than those already working, do not seem to apply to the transition economies, given that most recruitment comes from the employed rather than the unemployed.) From a pure efficiency perspective, unemployment benefits should be kept to a minimum. In their absence, one would expect wages to be low, employment high, and unemployment low, as is roughly the case in Russia. While the performance of the Russian labor market can hardly be described as successful, the policy regime has enabled it to survive far worse economic conditions, and public budgetary constraints, than any of the Central European countries.

Where economic conditions are less dire, considerations of equity and social justice have led governments to introduce West European-style benefit systems. With open unemployment rising rapidly, the policy response has been to curtail the duration of benefits so as to encourage the unemployed to search for work, and to avoid the emergence of long-term unemployment. The growth of long-term unemployment is a cost the transition economies can ill afford. With unemployment benefits in most countries lasting for at most a year, there appears to be no visible budgetary cost of long-term unemployment. But, to the extent that the long-term unemployed are not engaged in productive activity, they constitute a burden on their families and the public welfare systems. To the extent that they engage in informal work, they add to the growth of the non-taxpaying and often nonlegal shadow economy. Experience in market economies suggests that long spells of unemployment, and the associated loss of skills and work habits, can undermine a worker's morale and make his or her ultimate reintegration into the labor market more difficult.

Hence there has been considerable interest in the use of ALMPs to assist the unemployed back to work. But ALMPs do not of themselves, as we have seen, offer a solution to the unemployment problems of the transition economies. As current experience in Sweden and other market economies confirms, such policies are most effective in conditions of nearly full employment. Where full employment has been achieved, as in the Czech Republic, the buildup of long-term or structural unemployment can be avoided by Swedish-style ALMPs, as shown by the Czech experience.

The attainment of full employment in the Czech Republic has been extensively investigated. The main factors appear to be a moderately soft financial regime, an initially effective incomes policy, limiting job losses in state enterprises, and exceptionally fortunate geographic and historical circumstances offering opportunities for new firms. Though the policies of the Czech government were extraordinarily well designed, and successful in terms of labor-market outcomes, one doubts that they would of themselves have been successful in achieving full employment had they been obliged to confront the more formidable problems of some of the other countries in the region.

As the current high rates of (open and hidden) unemployment in the CEE countries start to recede, the special arguments about supporting employment during transition will fall away. As the economic background becomes more like that of Western Europe, the need will develop to avoid the policies and institutional arrangements that have led to persistent high unemployment in many market economies. The most critical concern might be with long-term unemployment. Though benefit durations are limited, in some countries social assistance schemes may be allowing many people to lapse into indefinite worklessness, while others support themselves in the (nontaxpaying) shadow economy. A gradual introduction of Swedish-style ALMPs might be helpful in preventing the entrenchment of long-term unemployment and in stemming the growth of the informal economy—for example, providing a temporary job or training after six months' unemployment for those under age twenty-five, along the lines currently being introduced in the United Kingdom,

The obstacles to reform in Russia, and elsewhere in the FSU, are much more formidable, and until the economic background is stabilized, it seems unrealistic to expect improvements in the labor market. Current policies, which encourage low wages and high employment, are still needed, and provide a suitable environment for new firms. But poor management and the lack of finance and infrastructure mean that any recovery in Russia or the FSU countries still lies a long way in the future.

Annex 1: Unemployment Benefits

Unemployment benefit systems in Central and Eastern Europe were initially designed on social insurance principles, much as in most OECD economies, with benefit entitlement depending on work experience and the benefit paid related to previous earnings (and not means-tested). Gross replacement ratios in the early years were rather generous by Western standards—for example, in Hungary and Poland, benefits are initially 70

Table A1
Unemployment Benefit Systems in Central and Eastern Europe, 1995 (main legislative rules)

	Albania	Bulgaria	Czech R.	Hungary
Qualifying conditions	employed for 12 months and lost job during the transition period; pay below certain limits	employed for 6 months in the last year and lost job; pay in job below min. wage	employed for 12 months in last 3 years; not eligible for old-age, sickness, or maternity benefit; no severance pay; no paid job	employed for 12 months in last 4 years; not eligible for old age or disability pension; no severance pay
Waiting period	7 days	7 days	7 days	none (180 days if quit job voluntarily)
Disqualification	2 refusals of job	refusal of job or retraining without just reason	refusal of suitable job (except for serious health, personal, or family reasons)	refusal of adequate job, retraining, or public work
Duration	12 months	6–12 months (depending on age and length of employment)	6 months	3–12 months (depending on age and length of employment)
Rate of benefit	flat rate of 2,200 leks for first 6 months, then reduced by 10% (min. wage = 2,620)	60% of previous gross wage (75% in case of retraining); lower limit = 90% of min. wage, upper limit = 140% of min. wage	60% of previous net wage for first 3 months, then 50% (70% throughout in case of retraining); no lower limit, upper limit = 140% of min. wage	75% of average wage of previous 4 quarters for first 23–90 days, then 60%; lower limit = 8,600 forints, upper limit = 18,000 forints for first period, then 15,000 (min. wage = 9,000)
Social assistance	Min. 2,500 leks, max. 5,000 leks, per family (depending on family income, size, and age)	100% of min. wage	Up to subsistence level per family (amount depending on family size and age)	80% of min. of old-age pension per person

Sources: *Employment Observatory—Central and Eastern Europe* no. 8 (1996); OECD, *Short-term Economic Indicators: Transition Economies* (Paris: OECD, 1995).

Poland	Romania	Russia	Slovakia
employed for 6 months in the last year with pay above 50% of min. wage; not eligible for old-age pension; pay in present job below 50% of min. wage; no agricultural land above a certain size	employed for at least 1 year (or 6 months in the last year if with temporary job); not eligible for old-age pension; pay in job below 50% of min. wage; no agricultural land above a certain size	able-bodied non-working persons who are ready and able to start work and who do not have a job or earnings for reasons independent of themselves	employed for 12 months in last 3 years; not eligible for old-age, illness, or maternity leave benefit; no severance pay, no paid job; being dismissed
none (90 days when quit job voluntarily without notice)	0–30 days	none	7 days
3 refusals of suitable job, training, intervention, or public work within 6 months	refusal of suitable job (except for serious health, personal, or family reasons)	2 refusals of suitable job offers, illegal benefit receipt, or violation of reregistration rules and conditions	refusal of suitable job (except for serious health, personal, or family reasons)
12 months (18 when employed for 25–30 years)	9 months + 18 of support allocation	12 months during 18-month period; for prepensioners, 24 months during 36 months	6–9 months (depending on age)
36% of average country wage of previous quarter (52% or 75% in special cases); no lower and upper limits	50%, 55%, 60% of net monthly wage for last 3 months (depending on length of employment); lower limit = 75%, 80%, 85% of min. wage; upper limit = 200% of min. wage; support allocation = 60% of min. wage	from 45% to 75% of the former average wage for the last 2 months, but not less than the minimum wage and not more than the average wage; for new job seekers, the minimum wage	60% of previous net monthly wage for first 3 months, then 50%; no lower limit, upper limit = 150% of min. wage
Max. 80% of min. old-age pension per person	53–73% of net min. wage per person (depending on family size)		up to subsistence level per family (amount depending on family size and age)

percent of the previous wage. However, benefits decline sharply over time, both because the benefit entitlement is reduced (e.g., from 70 percent to 50 percent after three months in Poland) and because of the effects of inflation. (Benefits are linked to a worker's previous wage and thus fixed in nominal terms.) Some countries provide a floor to the level of benefits (e.g., in Poland 33 percent of the average wage), and because of the erosion of individual benefit entitlements by inflation, many unemployed workers soon find themselves at this floor. Thus, in practice, in most Central and Eastern European countries, benefit levels relative to wages are lower than in most of Western Europe. In Russia, and elsewhere in the FSU, minimum unemployment benefits have been set equal to the minimum wage, which, in conditions of rapid inflation, has been allowed to fall to below subsistence standards.

Eligibility for benefits also tends to be more restrictive than in most market economies, particularly for school dropouts and for those leaving their jobs voluntarily. More important, as already noted, the duration for which benefits can be paid is in the range of six months to a year, and the arrangements for income support for unemployed people not receiving benefits are not systematic. Effectively, then, the benefit system in most of Central and Eastern Europe, though built on West European principles, is now significantly less generous than in most of Western Europe, though more extensive than in the United States or Japan (Boeri 1993; Scarpetta and Reutersward 1994). The main features of the benefit systems of the Eastern European countries are set out in table A1.

It might be thought that CEE countries, given their low per capita incomes and severe fiscal problems, would be unable to afford the costs of providing a comprehensive system of unemployment benefits, and might prefer to let the unemployed fend for themselves. In fact, most have given priority in the budget to setting up unemployment funds to ensure that benefits can be paid. In part this no doubt reflects a general predisposition to adopt Western practices, but it may also reflect a (possibly mistaken) view.

There would be some point to such a policy if unemployment played a productive role in economic restructuring, but we have seen that the opposite is the case. Unemployment is not the route by which workers move from the declining state sector to the private sector. Unemployed workers are less attractive recruits for private firms than workers in state firms, and a policy leading to higher unemployment may thus have restrained rather than encouraged the growth of the private sector.

7

Why China Grew

Wing Thye Woo

7.1 Introduction

China's average annual growth rate of 9.5 percent since the economic reforms started in late 1978 stands in sharp contrast to the general economic collapse in Eastern Europe and the former Soviet Union when these countries implemented economic reforms in the early 1990s. Hence, it is not surprising that it has become fashionable among some China specialists to identify and expound a new wisdom from China: that a gradual, incremental reform strategy is superior, and that state-owned enterprises (SOEs) can be adequately reformed without privatization.[1] Our aim in this chapter is to show that this new wisdom about "lessons from China" is wrong. We make our case by using standard neoclassical economic theory to identify an alternative set of factors responsible for the growth, and reviewing in detail the evidence of improvements in the SOE sector, where reform has been truly incremental in its implementation.[2]

According to the new wisdom from this group of China specialists, the deus ex machina of the incremental reform strategy is the "ex-post coherence of Chinese reforms." Specifically, China's seemingly disparate reforms have generated high growth because incremental experimentation has unleashed an unintended virtuous cycle:

After fifteen years, it is clear that there is substantial ex-post coherence to the Chinese reform process. It should also be clear that this coherence is not the result of a carefully plotted reform strategy. Indeed, during some crucial periods, the coherence of the reform process emerged in spite of, not because of, the policies of the Chinese leaders. Coherence was a characteristic of the economic environment in which the transition path unfolded, rather than of the explicit choices of policy-makers.... There are certain critical, or core, features of the command economy, and once these are eliminated or weakened, the system has a tendency to devolve into another type of system. Provided there is some political will to move the system in the direction of a market economy during this dissolution process, a positive process of transformation may be set into motion even without a clear or comprehensive commitment to a reformed market economy at the outset. (Naughton 1995, p. 309)

In accordance with this line of analysis, we will refer to the position of this group of China specialists as ex post reasoning (EPR). To the most enthusiastic proponents of EPR, the benefits of economic liberalization promised by neoclassical economic theory are either nebulous or socially undesirable, or both:

The extent of ... [China's] economic achievements challenges popular views about appropriate strategies for socialist transition and contributes to growing scepticism concerning fundamental tenets of economic theory. (Rawski 1995, pp. 1172–73)

... in the absence of more successful growth stories than that of post-1978 China, it is doubtful that a *more economically liberal regime* could have produced a significantly better overall record of growth, especially if social equity and stability are accorded any weight. (Putterman 1995, p. 1064; emphasis added)

Adherents of EPR are also distinguished by their disagreement with the dominant view among Chinese officials and Chinese economists that SOE reform in China has been a failure. EPR sees China, unlike any other nation, as having succeeded in reforming its SOE sector (i.e., a case of "Chinese exceptionalism"), even though Chinese officialdom is not aware of it. This paradoxical stance of EPR is seen in the following thesis, antithesis, and suggested synthesis.

Thesis: "This review leads to the conclusion that reform has pushed China's state-owned enterprises in the direction of 'intensive' growth based on higher productivity rather than expanded resource consumption ..., we observe a consistent picture of improved results—higher output, growing exports, rising total factor productivity, and increased innovative effort—against a background of gains in static and dynamic efficiency that reflect the growing impact of market forces" (Jefferson and Rawski 1994, p. 58).

Antithesis: "The current problems of SOEs are: excessive investments in fixed assets with very low return rates, resulting in the sinking of large amounts of capital; low sales-to-production ratio, giving rise to mounting inventories. The end result is that the state has to inject an increasing amount of working capital through the banking sector into the state enterprises" (Zhu 1996).

Suggested Synthesis: "Focusing on profitability, [state bureaucrats] see the erosion in state sector profits as a profound crisis of the state sector.

Without good measures of total factor productivity, they conclude that state sector performance is deteriorating. Foreign observers, hearing the cries of alarm from the state planners, shake their heads knowingly as they perceive still further evidence that state ownership is intrinsically inefficient. Neither party sees that the difficulties are the result of an ultimately beneficial transition to a different type of economy, and are entirely compatible with gradually improving efficiency" (Naughton 1995, p. 314).

We find both the "Chinese exceptionalism" assertion and Naughton's suggested synthesis to be implausible. We do not believe that Chinese officials are ignorant of elementary economic theory ("competition from new non-SOEs erodes SOE profits") and of the technically sophisticated literature on total factor productivity estimation. Furthermore, we attribute China's gradual reform strategy not to the logic of experimentation but to the logic of political compromise, and to the complexity of political and economic change in a country of more than one billion people. We should point out that China has achieved the greatest success in those areas (e.g., agriculture and coastal provinces) where reforms have gone the farthest. Finally, we find it analytically difficult to distinguish between Naughton's "ex post coherence of Chinese reforms" and *post hoc, ergo propter hoc*.[3]

Recent events in China have not been kind to the "Chinese exceptionalism" of Jefferson, Rawski, and Naughton. In September 1997, the Chinese Communist Party (CPC) announced at its Fifteenth Party Congress that China would privatize 369,000 of its 370,000 SOEs. This development is, in fact, a formalization and acceleration of the privatization process that had started five years earlier. At the Fourteenth Party Congress in 1992, the CPC had formally jettisoned the central plan as a mechanism for resource allocation, and in a plenum the following year, the CPC had identified "ambiguous property rights" as a key reason for the inefficiency of the SOEs.

The CPC's decision to privatize was definitely not taken lightly, and certainly not based on ignorance, as claimed by Naughton. China already had nineteen years of frustrating experience with reforming SOEs along the market socialism principles of Oskar Lange, and the straw that finally broke the camel's back was when the SOE sector ran a net loss in 1996. With the recent decision to privatize, China is joining Eastern Europe and the former Soviet Union in converging toward the private market economies of Western Europe and East Asia.

In this chapter, we argue that China's growth can be explained by a few key characteristics of its economic structure and economic policy. First,

China began the rapid growth period extremely poor, and therefore has benefited from the "advantages of relative backwardness." China has been able to import modern technology, management, and capital from abroad, for use alongside very inexpensive domestic labor, in order to produce labor-intensive manufactures. As a result, China has enjoyed one of the greatest export booms in history. Moreover, China began the reform period with a legacy of profound inefficiency in agriculture, so that there was a natural one-time boost to agricultural output and productivity in the first years of reform.

Second, China's economic policy has benefited from its economic structure: an overwhelmingly rural-based, agricultural, labor-intensive economy. Although China was, officially, a "socialist" economy, at the start of market reforms less than 20 percent of its labor force was in SOEs. Almost all the rest were in peasant villages throughout the hinterland. For political reasons, but in conformity with this basic economic structure, the Chinese government adopted a two-track approach to reforms, in which the countryside and the coastal provinces were substantially liberalized to engage in market activities, while the SOEs were kept under state control. This was expensive from the point of view of the budget, since the SOE sector required subsidies to cover losses, but was affordable, since the vast majority of the labor force was outside the state-owned sector. This situation contrasts starkly with that of Eastern Europe and the former Soviet Union, where the state sector dominated the economy at the start of market reforms.

The market sector has been substantially deregulated, and in fact has become, de facto, a laissez-faire economy. Taxation of private activity is low, and regulations governing labor markets, the environment, competition, and other areas of market activity are nonrestrictive. In fact, the nonstate enterprises, as their share of GDP has increased, pay less income taxes as a proportion of GDP: in 1985 nonstate enterprises paid income taxes equivalent to 1.1 percent of GDP; in 1994 they paid only 0.2 percent (World Bank 1996a, table 21). Although the legal infrastructure of the marketized part of the economy is underdeveloped, regulatory intrusion is also low. Labor-market participants in the nonstate sector expect little from the state in the form of social protection, and in fact receive very little. Once again, the situation differs markedly from that of Eastern Europe and the former Soviet Union, where the public's expectations were for continued guarantees of jobs, income, retirement benefits, and other social benefits, which had long been promised, if imperfectly delivered, by the government.

In China the nonstate sector has boomed while the state sector has continued to experience serious problems, not the least of which are the continuing low productivity growth of SOEs, and their large financial losses, even in boom years. Thus, the success of China's reforms should be attributed mainly to the success of the nonstate sector, and to the good fortune that problems in the state-owned sector have not destabilized the macroeconomy. China's macroeconomic situation has remained delicate for years; in fact, extreme inflationary pressures in 1988–89 most probably contributed to the political unrest that culminated in the Tiananmen Square tragedy in June 1989. Overall, however, China's monetary and banking policies have protected the real income of savers, thereby contributing to remarkably high savings rates. These high savings, in turn, have helped the government to finance its budget deficits in a noninflationary manner.

These issues are addressed in the following sections. Section 7.2 outlines the three most important components of the gradual reform program implemented after 1978, and explains the political basis for the gradualist policies. Section 7.3 identifies the main sources of growth and puts the basis of China's impressive economic performance into the context of a liberalizing, surplus-labor economy. Section 7.4 discusses the shortcomings of attempted reforms of the SOE sector. Section 7.5 reviews our analysis and indicates the key remaining challenges for economic reform in China.

7.2   The Dual-Track Method of Gradual Liberalization

The basic strategy for moving from economic planning to a market system has been the gradual liberalization of economic activities through the dual-track approach: establishing a market track parallel to the existing plan track in a particular sector or aspect of economic activity. To give a sense of the reforms, we outline this dual-track approach as it was applied to production and price deregulation, ownership diversification, and international integration.

Dual-Track Production and Pricing

The dual-track approach started at the end of 1978 with rapid and comprehensive liberalization of the agricultural sector. The agricultural communes were disbanded over a two-year period, state procurement prices for agricultural products were raised, and free markets for certain agricultural products were permitted. Farmers now enjoy great production freedom; in 1993 only 5 percent of their production was set by the state plan.

In 1984 this dual-track arrangement was extended to industrial goods, with state procurement quotas for consumer goods much lower than for producer goods. The proportion of planned production in total industrial output value was reduced from over 90 percent in 1978 to 5 percent in 1993.

Dual-Track Ownership Structure

An SOE is a nationally owned enterprise in the sense that the central government is the ultimate authority for the operations of the enterprise and the disposition of its assets, even though the SOE in most cases has been assigned to the provincial or county government for supervision and management. Nonstate enterprises are those enterprises in which the central government lacks final authority over the disposition of assets. The nonstate sector consists of community-owned (collective-owned) enterprises (COEs), cooperatives, individual-owned enterprises, private corporations, and foreign joint ventures. COEs are owned by all the residents of the city or township or village; cooperatives, by small groups of persons. The most prominent nonstate enterprises are the rural enterprises known as township and village enterprises (TVEs).[4] The nonstate sector produced 57 percent of total gross industrial output in 1993, compared with 31 percent in 1984 and 22 percent in 1978.[5]

It must be emphasized that the SOE sector has not been withering away, as might be implied by claims that China is "growing out of the plan" (e.g., Naughton 1995). The SOE sector has actually retained its relative standing in overall employment: 18 percent of the labor force in 1978 and 1993. There were 35 million more SOE workers in 1993 than in 1978.

What has happened is that the nonstate sector has drawn resources from agriculture rather than from state industry. In other words, the new nonstate sector has grown by siphoning rural employment into nonstate enterprises, especially rural and coastal TVEs. Most workers in SOEs have chosen not to shift to the nonstate enterprises because SOEs offer a more generous package of wages and social protection, largely as a result of the huge subsidies and other benefits that the state has continued to bestow on the SOE sector. SOEs provide generous pensions and heavily subsidized housing, medical coverage, child care, food, and recreational facilities. The Chinese peasants, by contrast, receive none of these benefits and consume only one-third as much as urban residents consume. The peasants, therefore, were only too glad to shift out of low-income agricultural activities to the higher-income jobs in the nonstate sector, notably in the TVEs.

Global Opening

In 1980, four southern coastal cities (Shantou, Shenzhen, Xiamen, and Zhuhai) were designated Special Economic Zones (SEZs). The SEZs were given autonomy to experiment with new institutions, mainly related to the international economy. They could approve foreign-funded enterprises (FFEs) and extend generous tax exemptions to them. The pre-1994 income tax rate for FFEs was 15 percent, compared with 55 percent for SOEs outside the SEZs, and FFEs had two years' tax holiday from the first profit-making year, then a 7.5 percent income tax rate for the following three years. SOEs operating within the SEZs not only were exempted from the central plan and had complete autonomy in hiring and firing, they could even get exemptions from various business and trade taxes. Of the 20,000 enterprises operating in Shenzhen, the biggest SEZ, in 1992, 5,000 were FFEs (Bell et al. 1993).

The resulting phenomenal growth of the SEZs spurred other regions to demand special privileges. The result is a plethora of designated cities that have various subsets of the privileges granted to the SEZs: there are now 14 open coastal cities, 20 economic and technological development districts, and 72 cities running comprehensive reform experiments. Hainan province became the fifth SEZ in 1988.

Beside setting up export platforms like SEZs to attract foreign investment, China liberalized its trade and exchange regimes. In 1978 all foreign trade was conducted through 12 state-owned foreign trade corporations (FTCs), as specified by the central plan. In line with the general liberalization of the economy, plan trade diminished in importance and the management of the FTCs was given to the provincial governments. By 1989 there were 4,000 FTCs, and enterprises were increasingly allowed to engage directly in foreign trade. In place of a trade plan, there was a licensing system to control trade. There were several reductions in export and import taxes in 1991–92 as China sought to rejoin GATT. The average tariff rate in 1993 was 36 percent (Tseng et al. 1994). On April 1, 1996, China cut tariff rates by one-third across the board, to bring the average tariff rate to 23 percent.[6]

The liberalization of the exchange system took the form of allowing enterprises to retain part of their foreign-exchange earnings, and reducing

Table 7.1
China's exports, 1987–94

	Total exports (billion yuan)	TVEs' exports as % of total exports	Total exports as % of GDP
1987	147	10.9	13
1988	177	15.3	13
1989	196	18.9	12
1990	299	16.4	17
1991	383	17.5	19
1992	468	25.4	19
1993	529	44.4	17
1994	1,042	32.6	23

Sources: TVE export data are from the Township and Village Enterprises Yearbooks 1988–95; total export and GDP data are from State Statistical Bureau, *Statistical Yearbook of China* (1994).

the number of official exchange rates (which, incidentally, had been steadily devalued). Two years after the unification of the official exchange rate in 1984, a foreign-exchange adjustment center (better known as the swap market) was established to allow certain enterprises to trade their retained foreign earnings. Participation in the swap market was widened in 1988 to include all enterprises that were permitted to retain foreign earnings, and in 1991 to all domestic residents. In 1994 the official exchange rate was unified at the existing swap rate.

The opening of the economy to foreign trade and investment has caused Chinese exports to boom, especially, in recent years, exports from the TVEs. (See table 7.1.)

The rising export:GDP ratio shows that with the opening to the outside world, export-processing has become a major component of China's industrialization strategy (the ratio was 4 percent in 1984). It is possible that the nonstate sector (TVEs plus the other types of non-SOEs) has become the major foreign-exchange earner since 1993. If so, China is replicating the phenomenon that occurred earlier in the successful East and Southeast Asia economies, whose nonstate sectors generated export-led growth by exploiting their comparative advantage in labor-intensive goods.

Gradual Reform Strategy: The Product of Political Disagreement

It is important to remember that the Chinese Communist Party (CPC) still holds power, and that China's reforms began 12 years before the collapse of Communism in Eastern Europe and the Soviet Union. This means that all decisions on economic reform, especially before the collapse of the Communist Party of the Soviet Union in 1991, could not directly contradict standard Marxist dogma, and had to be be couched in standard Marxist terminology. For example, "collective ownership (localized socialism)" was considered an inferior but still acceptable form of public ownership, while private ownership of large enterprises was taboo (albeit decreasingly so over time); and peasants could lease but not own land.

After the death of Mao Zedong in 1976, there were three competing economic agendas within the CPC: that of the Maoists, under Hua Guofeng; that of the central planners, under Chen Yun; and that of the pragmatists, under Deng Xiaoping. The Maoists were the incumbents, and the central planners and the pragmatists were the recently rehabilitated apparatchiks. The announcement of economic reform in December 1978 marked the restoration to power of the key officials purged during the 1966–76 Cultural Revolution, and the beginning of a new coalition between the central planners and the remnants of the Maoists to prevent the pragmatists from straying too far from Marxist-Leninist practices. Hence the delineation in the post-1978 period between conservative and liberal reformers.

The conservative reformers enunciate the "birdcage economy" doctrine. In the conception of its originator, Chen Yun, the central plan is the cage and the economy is the bird. The premise is that without central planning, production would be in chaos (i.e., without the cage, the bird will fly away). The amount of market activities tolerated to keep the economy working is analogous to the amount that the cage needs to be swung to create the illusion of greater space required to keep the bird happy.

The liberal reformers, on the other hand, believe that only a market economy will promote long-term economic development. The absence of consensus within the Chinese elite has persisted throughout the reform period. On the eve of the Tiananmen Square events, *The Economist* reported:

At the heart of the rivalry between Mr. Zhao [the party leader] and Mr. Li [the premier] are very different ideas about where China should be going. Mr. Zhao would like to steer China out of the current mess by freeing more prices, ... generating more competition between factories and between provinces ... [reducing] sharply the amount of industry directly owned by the state ... [and] finding ways to stop party people from interfering in the way factories are run. Mr. Li thinks China can modernize itself only if the center keeps a firmer hand on things. ("China: At It Again" [Feb. 25, 1989]: 34)

In short, "muddling through" has not been a strategy, as claimed by McMillan and Naughton (1992), so much as a result of the lack of political consensus.

In view of these basic policy differences, it is not surprising that dual-track reform emerged as the compromise solution—both conservative and liberal reformers were able to implement part of their programs. This is the basic reason why the CPC located all the SEZs in southern China, far from the important political centers, and why the 1979–96 period is marked by boom-bust reform cycles reflecting the shifting balance of power between competing factions. This factional struggle is the primary reason why the desired economic mechanism identified by the CPC went from "a planned economy with recognition of the law of exchange value" in 1978 to a "planned economy supplemented by market regulations" in 1979–84, to a "planned commodity economy" in 1985–88, and (after two more changes) to "a socialist market economy with Chinese character-istics" in 1992.[7] The 1992 statement was very significant because the word "plan" was finally dropped from official rhetoric. The phrase "socialist market economy with Chinese characteristics" is an implicit denial of the universality of socialism, and hence a rejection of the planned economies of the Soviet bloc, where state ownership of production units was the norm.

The demise of the Communist Party of the Soviet Union in 1991 en-abled the Chinese reformers to restart the economic liberalization that had been suspended by the hard-liners who dominated policy-making after the 1989 Tiananmen Square shootings. The process of marketization and internationalization of the Chinese economy actually accelerated[8] because the Soviet experience convinced the leadership of the CPC that the com-bination of "centralized control, enforced egalitarianism, international iso-lation and ideological dogmatism" was suicidal (Garver 1993, p. 26).

Official thinking on the role of SOEs has evolved, and the debate between the conservative and liberal reformers now concentrates on the operational definition of "socialism with Chinese characteristics." By late 1995 the most market-oriented of the conservative reformers were in favor of keeping the 4,000 large industrial SOEs and 10,500 medium industrial SOEs under state ownership, and privatizing the more than 65,000 small industrial SOEs; the most radical of the liberal reformers were in favor of the state's keeping ownership of only the 1,000 largest industrial SOEs. The lack of political consensus on SOE reform is the reason why there has been only incremental privatization so far.

7.3   The Nature of Chinese Economic Growth

There have been two phases to China's economic growth, and the turning point corresponds to the policy regime change toward accelerating

Table 7.2
Contribution to GDP growth rate by sector, and by ownership in the industrial sector
(percent)

	Growth in 1979–93	Growth in 1979–84	Growth in 1985–93
Primary sector	16.5	31.8	11.6
Industrial SOEs	13.8	20.3	11.7
Industrial COEs	25.0	12.8	28.9
Individual-owned industrial enterprises	5.9	0.2	7.7
Other ownership forms of industrial enterprises	6.9	0.8	8.9
Construction sector	5.7	5.2	5.9
Tertiary sector	26.2	28.9	25.3
Total	100.0	100.0	100.0

Source: The official statistics calculated real GDP growth rates for 1981–90 using 1980 prices, and for 1991 onward using 1990 prices. This is an inconsistency I eliminated by rebasing GDP on 1990 prices, that is, I calculated the growth rates for the entire 1978–93 period using 1990 prices.

reforms in the nonagriculture sectors and to the emergence of industry as the undisputed primary engine of growth. The sectoral contributions to GDP growth in the 1979–93 period, and in the subperiods 1979–84 and 1985–93 are given in table 7.2.

Agriculture was a leading growth sector in 1979–84. Its contribution to aggregate output expansion almost matched that of industry (32 and 34 percent, respectively). In 1985–93 industry accounted for 57.5 percent of the increase in output, and the tertiary sector greatly outstripped the primary in terms of contribution (25 percent versus 12 percent). The biggest contributor to GDP growth was the industrial COE sector (29 percentage points). Industrial individual-owned enterprises accounted for almost 8 percentage points of the aggregate output growth.

The growth performance of 1985–93 may be a better guide (than that of the entire period) to understanding the growth prospects of China. This is because agriculture is unlikely to become a major growth sector again.

The leading role of the industry sector in GDP growth since 1978 (even more so since 1984) places China's economic growth within the context of traditional economic development. The unusually large contribution of the tertiary sector to growth places China's experience within the context of economic transition from traditional central planning. Central planning has traditionally regarded service activities as "unproductive," and hence has restricted their growth.[9] The rapid development of the service sector after 1978 reflects this earlier underdevelopment.

The Mechanics of Growth

Woo (1996) conducted a growth accounting exercise based on the three sectors—primary (agriculture, forestry, and fishing), secondary (industry and construction), and tertiary—as defined by Chinese statistics. Each sector is assumed to be characterized by a Cobb-Douglas production function:

$$Y = \sum (\alpha_i x_i^{\beta_i} z_i^{(1-\beta_i)}) L^{\beta_i} K^{(1-\beta_i)}, \tag{7.1}$$

where

$Y = \text{GDP}$

$L = \text{total labor force}$

$K = \text{total capital stock}$

$w_i = \text{sector } i\text{'s share of GDP}$

$x_i = \text{sector } i\text{'s share of labor force}$

$z_i = \text{sector } i\text{'s share of capital stock.}$

GDP growth can be decomposed into portions that are due to capital accumulation, labor force growth, and total factor productivity (TFP) growth:

$$(dY/Y) = (dL/L) \sum w_i \beta_i + (dK/K) \sum w_i (1 - \beta_i) + \sum w_i \beta_i (dx_i/x_i)$$
$$+ \sum w_i (d\alpha_i/\alpha_i) + \sum w_i (1 - \beta_i)(dz_i/z_i), \tag{7.2}$$

where

$$\text{TFP growth} = \sum w_i \beta_i (dx_i/x_i) + \sum w_i (d\alpha_i/\alpha_i) + \sum w_i (1 - \beta_i)(dz_i/z_i).$$

TFP growth is in turn partitioned into labor reallocation effect and net TFP growth:

$$\text{labor reallocation effect} = \sum w_i \beta_i (dx_i/x_i)$$

$$\text{net TFP growth} = \sum w_i (d\alpha_i/\alpha_i) + \sum w_i (1 - \beta_i)(dz_i/z_i).$$

Net TFP growth is the residual that contains technological improvements.

Labor reallocation is singled out for attention because the bulk of the Chinese labor force consists of peasant farmers, a third of whom were living below the absolute poverty line in 1978. We have argued in Sachs and Woo (1994) that this "surplus labor" feature has made China's transition from central planning fundamentally different from the transition of Eastern Europe and the former Soviet Union (EEFSU).[10] Specifically, this means that in China the shift of labor away from agriculture toward industry and services increases aggregate output because the marginal product of labor (MPL) in the primary sector is lower than the MPLs in the secondary and service sectors.[11] In short, the marketization of a centrally planned economy means normal economic development for China but structural adjustment for an EEFSU country.

Given the unreliability of data on the sectoral distribution of capital stock, upon which the estimates of sectoral β's were based (β represents the exponent for the labor variable in the Cobb-Douglas production function), we drew upon the production function literature on China to generate a range of TFP growth rates by using different values of a common β—specifically, $\beta = 0.4$, 0.5, and 0.6. The official data on sectoral distribution of labor should be used critically. The official estimate of labor in agriculture is based on registered residency status but is an overstatement because of illegal rural migration, especially to coastal TVEs. The official estimate of the size of illegal migration is 80 million, and the World Bank's highest estimate is 150 million. The official estimate (80 million) does not include the 20 million people who migrate within their home district.[12] We assume illegal rural migration to have been 100 million since 1984, with 60 percent of the migrants ending up in industrial jobs.[13]

Taking the range of estimates into account, the official growth rates could be reasonably accounted for as shown in table 7.3.

We emphasize that the above estimates of TFP growth, labor allocation, and net TFP growth should be considered together with the range of estimates associated with them (see Woo 1996 for details).

There are two robust key findings from the detailed analysis. The first is that net TFP growth was lower in 1985–93 than in 1979–84. This suggests that a part of the TFP growth unleashed by the 1978 reforms was a *one-off recovery in efficiency* from the decade-long Cultural Revolution and from the overregulation of the economy by central planning. This one-time recovery was not limited to the agricultural sector; Perkins et al. (1993) and Woo (1996) found that it was also present in the industrial sector—which bodes ill for future Chinese growth.

The second robust result from the growth accounting exercise is that the reallocation of labor from agriculture accounted for 46 percent of TFP growth. This labor reallocation effect was higher in 1985–93. To indicate the magnitude of this effect, we may note that Denison (1974, p. 127)

Table 7.3
China's growth by sources (percentage points per annum)

	1979–84	1985–93
Official growth rate	9.3	9.7
Inconsistent use of base years	0.2	0.3
Overstatement of industrial output*	0.5 to 0.7	0.9 to 1.2
Capital accumulation	4.9	5.5
Labor force growth	1.3	1.1
Reallocation of labor from agriculture	1.1	1.3
Net TFP growth	1.1 to 1.3	0.3 to 0.6

Source: Woo 1996.
Note:
* Woo (1996) noted that the official GDP growth rates are exaggerated. The major causes of this exaggeration are the following:
1. The pervasive reporting by industrial COEs of nominal output value as real output value.
2. The incentive for officials at the local industrial bureaus to exaggerate output growth to advance their careers.
3. The procedure for reporting the base-year values of new product lines that overstates them.
4. The inconsistent use of base-year prices.
In fact, the official growth rate of the industrial sector in 1993 may have overstated the actual growth rate by 10 percentage points, which means that actual GDP growth in 1993 may have been 8.9 percent instead of the official growth rate of 13.4 percent.

estimated that labor reallocation from the farm sector accounted for only 13 percent of TFP growth in the United States in the 1948–69 period.[14] The large labor allocation effect in China reflects the existence of a large amount of labor employed in low-productivity agriculture and the success of the post-1978 Chinese reforms in creating higher-productivity jobs in the industry and service sectors.

Explaining the Growth

The high rate of capital accumulation (the biggest contributor to Chinese growth) has its basis in the liberalization of a labor-surplus economy with a high savings rate. Investment is highly profitable because the surplus labor has prevented the real wage from rising significantly, and the large pool of domestic savings has prevented the interest rate from rising. The importance of the latter is revealed in the fact that household savings are about 23 percent of disposable income in China, versus 21 percent in Japan, 18 percent in Taiwan, 16 percent in Belgium, 13 percent in West Germany, and 8 percent in the United States (World Bank 1990, table 4.9).

It should be noted that China's high household savings rate has helped to stabilize the economy as well as enabling a high rate of capital accumulation. It reduced inflation in the Chinese economy in two ways. First, the flow of savings through the banks reduced the need to print money to meet the excessive resource demand of the SOE sector. Second, since money was (until recently) the only form of financial savings in China, the high savings rate meant an increasing demand for money, which dampened inflation pressure. This inflation-dampening effect can be seen in the rise of the M2:GNP ratio from 38 percent in 1979 to 106 percent in 1992.

In addition to the "advantages of backwardness" in economic structure and the high savings rate, several other factors have contributed to China's impressive growth performance. The most important of these is China's integration into the global economy. This factor operates in four ways. First, the access to international markets for labor-intensive manufactured goods accelerated the movement of labor out of low-productivity agriculture and into high-productivity industry. Second, China could now buy modern technology (including some previously embargoed). Third, foreign direct investments increased the capital stock, transferred new technology, made global distribution networks available, and introduced domestic firms to more efficient management techniques. Fourth, the competition from international trade forced Chinese enterprises to be more efficient and innovative.[15]

The second supplementary factor is that China's reforms did not start from a situation of severe macroeconomic crisis or a severe external debt crisis requiring an austerity program. China has been developing its economy by having the TVEs employ idle agriculture labor, whereas Poland and Russia had to try to tame inflation and restructure their full-employment economies simultaneously.

A third supplementary factor is the results of the two disastrous leftist campaigns, the Great Leap Forward (1958–62) and the Cultural Revolution (1966–76). These undermined belief in Marxist dogmas, weakened the state's administrative capacity, and discredited central planning. The Great Leap Forward program of crash industrialization starved 30 million to death during 1958–61, and the Cultural Revolution effort to build the new socialist man purged 60 percent of party officials. The legacy of these two disasters enabled Deng Xiaoping, when he returned to power in 1978, to quickly transfer a significant amount of economic policy-making power (which translated into a transfer of economic and political resources) to the provinces. The central ministerial and party apparatuses were too politically exhausted and too discredited to resist his decentralization.

This ending of Beijing's stranglehold on political power has been fundamental to the continuation of economic reforms. In 1989, when the conservatives, in the immediate aftermath of the Tiananmen Square incident, sought to reimpose a Stalinist centrally planned economy, the provincial representatives were strong enough to block this recidivist tendency. Furthermore, after the collapse of the Soviet Union, it was the mobilization of this new decentralized political power by Deng Xiaoping that forced the conservative faction to accept the new vision of a socialist market economy.

A fourth supplementary factor is the fact that central planning in China was always much less intensive than in EEFSU. The Soviet central plan controlled 25 million commodities, whereas its Chinese counterpart controlled only 1,200 (Qian and Xu 1993). Furthermore, the breakdown of the national distribution system during the Cultural Revolution forced local authorities to promote small and medium industrial enterprises to meet local demand.

The existence of strong family ties between mainland and overseas Chinese is a fifth supplementary factor. The explosive growth of the SEZs in southern China has been fueled by the wholesale movement of labor-intensive industries from Hong Kong and Taiwan, which were losing their comparative edge in such industries. In comparison with alternative sites in Southeast Asia, China was closer, wages were lower, and language difficulties were nonexistent. Managers could commute daily from Hong Kong to supervise their factories in Shenzhen. Family connections greatly reduced the transaction costs of investment by providing reliable local supervisors, inside information on the enforcement of regulations, and contacts with the local authorities.

Of all the factors identified as important causes of China's achievements in 1978–95, only the high savings rate and the globalization of China's economy could be considered lessons for economic reforms elsewhere. The other factors (initial conditions and structural features) are essentially specific to China's circumstances.

China's Economic Performance in the East Asian Context

The experience of Vietnam confirms that it is China's structural conditions, rather than its gradual reform process, which mainly account for its superior growth performance vis-à-vis the EEFSU countries. During 1985–88, Vietnam implemented a gradual reform strategy that did not address serious macroeconomic imbalances. The program failed: inflation

Table 7.4
The size of the labor reallocation effect in Japan, 1905–1965

Period	Labor reallocation effect (in percentage points)
1905–19	0.63
1919–31	0.25
1931–38	0.61
1952–55	0.76
1955–61	1.46
1961–65	1.07

Source: Ohkawa and Rosovsky 1973 (p. 116).

accelerated while growth and trade performance remained unchanged. In 1989, Vietnam enacted an East European-style Big Bang, including price liberalization, a 450 percent devaluation to unify the exchange market, and sharply tightened credit policy. Collective farms were broken up and leased to families. Growth accelerated, inflation ended, agricultural productivity soared, and small, nonstate enterprises proliferated.

In contrast to Eastern Europe, the Big Bang did not cause an output decline in Vietnam. The difference lies in Vietnam's economic structure in 1988. As an overwhelmingly agricultural economy, Vietnam enjoyed the same gains as China from the flow of peasants to the nonstate, non-agricultural sector. Strong market-oriented reforms (macroeconomic stabilization and liberalization), not gradualism per se, tend to accelerate this shift.

Economic development in China, and in Vietnam since 1978, actually fits quite well with the general East Asian development pattern. Economic growth in Japan, Malaysia, Taiwan, and Thailand also has been described by a two-sector model focusing on the flow of workers from agriculture to industry. The resulting waves of labor-intensive exports in line with the product cycle theory has been poetically described as the "flying geese" pattern of industrialization.

The high labor reallocation effect in China resembles that observed in Japan in the mid-1950s, when the trend growth rate accelerated as Japan's integration into the global economy intensified. The contribution to aggregate output growth from the reallocation of labor from agriculture is shown in table 7.4.

Given the East Asian growth experience and China's large pool of low-productivity rural labor, we regard the labor-allocation effect of 1.2 percentage points to be a reliable estimate of the contribution to China's TFP growth in the medium run.

7.4   Response of the SOE Sector to Reform

Liberalization Reforms in the State Enterprise Sector

There have been three stages in the liberalization of the Chinese state industrial sector. The first was from 1979 to 1983; the second, from 1984 to 1993; and the third, from 1994 on. The first two stages were clearly inspired by market socialism, which emphasized increasing the operational autonomy of the SOEs.

The key elements of the first-stage reforms were (1) enterprises were allowed to retain part of their profits to use at their discretion; (2) a bonus system for superior individual work effort was introduced; (3) in 1983; SOEs started paying costs on their capital use through the replacement of budgetary grants by bank loans; and (4) the system of profit remittance was replaced by an income tax (*ligaishui*) in order to separate the two roles of the state: tax collector and enterprise owner.[16] The second-stage reforms increased autonomy in pricing, production, labor compensation, investment, and use of retained profits; they also introduced various contract schemes between different levels within the firm, and between the firm and the state.

None of the preceding SOE reforms fundamentally altered the ownership structure of the enterprises, though they did significantly affect the control structure. In November 1993, the Communist Party of China declared that the property rights of SOEs would be clarified in order to improve SOE performance. This was the first time that the ambiguity of property rights was officially recognized as a cause of poor SOE performance:

Large and medium-sized State-owned enterprises are the mainstay of the national economy; ... [for them] it is useful to experiment with the corporate system.... As for the small State-owned enterprises, the management of some can be contracted out or leased; others can be shifted to the partnership system in the form of stock sharing, or sold to collectives and individuals.[17]

The November 1993 development came about because the Chinese leadership concluded that the decentralized reforms of 1979–92 had not improved SOE efficiency significantly, if at all. In August 1996, Vice Premier Wu Bangguo, who has direct responsibility for SOE reform, pronounced the SOEs to be suffering from "worsening economic performance, a declining sales-to-production ratio, bulging stockpiles, and increasing losses."[18]

As we pointed out earlier, the Chinese officials' diagnosis of worsening SOE performance is not shared by the EPR fraternity—Naughton even suggested that the Chinese officials were unaware of the true picture. We will now review the performance of the SOE sector along several dimensions to show that the worries of the Chinese officials are justified.

The Evidence on TFP Growth in the SOE Sector

The evidence on improvements in production efficiency in Chinese SOEs is mixed. However, even if one believes that there has been positive TFP growth, it is hard to applaud the outcome without having to adopt a double standard. Most studies find that the TFP growth rate is much lower in the SOE sector than in the TVE sector—2.5 percent and 3.5 percent, respectively.[19]

Using different data sets, Huang and Meng (1995) found the annual TFP growth rate for SOEs to be −5 percent in 1986–90; Woo, Hai et al. (1994) found it to be zero in 1984–88; Bouin (forthcoming) found it to range from −0.7 to 0.2 percent for 1989–93; and Parker (forthcoming) found it to average 1 percent in 1985–91 and to decline over time. Parker even found direct evidence against the effectiveness of the decentralizing reforms: the center-supervised SOEs were more efficient than province-supervised SOEs, even though the former had less operational autonomy.

When Woo, Hai et al. deflated their intermediate inputs, using the intermediate input deflator constructed by Jefferson et al. (1992), they found the same result as Jefferson et al. (1992): 2.4 percent for TFP growth in the SOE sector. However, Woo, Hai et al. found that Jefferson et al.'s deflation method caused the implicit deflator for the value-added (VAD, value-added deflator) of SOEs in their sample to decline throughout the sample period, contrary to the upward movement of the Consumer Price Index (CPI). This was not a problem that was caused by Woo, Hai et al.'s sample because they found that Jefferson et al.'s VAD also declined.

Woo, Hai et al. pointed out that a sustained decline in VAD in the face of a rising CPI is internationally unprecedented. The quadrupling of oil prices at the end of 1973 and the doubling of oil prices in 1979 could not cause a sustained decline in VAD anywhere in the world. Furthermore, such a contrary trend was not seen in either Hungary or Poland during their gradual reforms in the 1970s and 1980s.

The condition for a secularly declining VAD is given by

$$\left(\frac{P_t^G - P_0^G}{P^G}\right) < \left(1 + \frac{a_t - a_0}{a_0}\right)\left(\frac{P_0^I M_0}{P_0^G Q_0}\right)\left(\frac{P_t^I - P_0^I}{P_0^I}\right),$$

where

M_i = intermediate inputs in period i, in physical units

Q_i = gross output in period i, in physical units

P_i^G = price of gross output in period i

P_i^I = price of intermediate input in period i

$a_i = M_i/Q_i$, the input-output coefficient in period i.

The hallmark of central planning is that prices of intermediate inputs (to industry) were artificially suppressed and prices of industrial goods were artificially raised in order to concentrate revenue in the industrial sector, thus making revenue collection convenient for the state. This means that $(P_0^I M_0/P_t^I M_t)$ is much smaller than unity. Since the prices of intermediate inputs had risen relative to output prices, the more efficient use of intermediate inputs rendered $[1 - (a_t - a_0)/a_0]$ less than unity. The net result is that intermediate input prices had to rise significantly more than output prices in order for a declining VAD to occur.

First, since China liberalized output prices before input prices, the downward movement of Jefferson et al.'s VAD in 1980–84 suggests that the intermediate input deflator constructed by them *overstated the rise of intermediate input prices* (P_I). Second, the flawed measurement of the real gross output of SOEs (Woo 1996; Jefferson et al. 1995) means that the official gross output price index *understated the rise in output prices* (P_M). In our opinion, these two price mismeasurements constituted the reason why Jefferson et al.'s VAD declined.[20] Since these two price mismeasurements imply that the quantity of real gross output is overstated and the quantity of real intermediate input used is understated, Woo, Hai et al. suggested that this exaggeration of the growth in real value-added is the reason for the positive TFP growth found by Jefferson et al.

Our observations do not, of course, prove that an opposite trend between VAD and CPI is impossible. It is just possible that China's economic structure (i.e., a_0 and a_t) is sufficiently different from other centrally planned economies and capitalist countries that such an opposite trend can easily occur—the Chinese exceptionalism argument. In response to the skepticism of Woo, Hai et al., Jefferson et al. (1995) argued that their measurements of P^G and P^I were correct, and Chinese exceptionalism was valid—China's production structure is sufficiently different from that of the United States that an input-price shock is more likely to produce a declining VAD.[21] However, Sachs and Woo (1997) pointed out that Jefferson et al.'s (1995) finding is not robust: it holds only for the Industrial Census data but not for the Input-Output Table data.[22]

Naughton (1994) defended Jefferson et al.'s positive TFP results by pointing out that the VAD in Groves et al. (1994, 1995a)—which found strong TFP growth in response to the decentralizing reforms—also displayed declining VADs.[23] To us, Naughton's defense could just as easily be read as an indication of the unreliability of the results in the Groves et al. papers. This is because the latter had constructed estimates of P^I based on firm survey data. Naughton felt obliged to warn the reader:

Reliance on retrospective reconstruction might bias inflation rates for intermediate inputs upward if managers idealize the pre-inflation period. This would produce a corresponding upward bias in the TFP growth rates. (Naughton 1994, p. 483)

In this context, it is notable that the Groves et al. (1994) results were stronger than Lee's (1990) results. Groves et al. found that their measures of worker incentive (bonus:total wage ratio and proportion of contract workers) were individually significant in increasing TFP, whereas Lee found that the incentive measures were statistically significant as a group but not individually. This difference in findings suggests to us that Groves et al.'s declining VAD indicates that they had overestimated the rise in intermediate input prices, and the resulting larger TFP estimates allowed Groves et al. (1994) to have stronger results than Lee.

The point is that a significant part of the TFP debate rests on the validity of Jefferson et al.'s and Groves et al.'s claim of Chinese exceptionalism. However, the more fundamental issue is that, regardless of one's reading of the estimated magnitudes of TFP growth in the SOE sector, the more important question is whether a higher TFP growth rate necessarily means that the new behavior of SOEs has increased economic efficiency (welfare). According to Bai et al. (1996), it does not, in the case of China, and this is why the Chinese public and Chinese leaders have continued to see SOE reform as a failure. Bai et al. point out that TFP growth is a good index of welfare improvement only

in the context of profit-maximizing and market-oriented firms. However, for SOEs under reform, these conditions are not satisfied (in fact, this is the very reason for SOE reform).... One of the important non-profit objectives of the managers is their excessive pursuit of output. (Bai et al. 1996)

In Bai et al.'s judgment, Kornai's (1992) observation that "SOE managers are embedded in a bureaucratic hierarchy, in which the size of the firm, or output level, is a proxy for status" still applies to China. Furthermore, in China, where the soft-budget constraint is real, it is to the managers' advantage to make their SOEs "too big to be allowed to fail." Groves et al.'s (1995b) finding on SOE managers' compensation, that "sales are significant in explaining wages over the full sample period but that profits are just insignificant," reveals the existence of incentives for Chinese managers to attach importance to the output level, as well as to profits.[24] Parker's (forthcoming) finding of overusage of capital and labor in Chinese state-owned construction companies confirms that such incentives did have an impact on firms' operations.

When both output and profits were included in the objective function of the SOE managers, Bai et al. found that "a higher productivity as measured by the TFP growth may actually lead to lower profitability and therefore, in many cases, lower economic efficiency." The mental image of some Chinese SOEs producing undesired goods more efficiently may not be a hypothetical one. Inventory investment in China averaged 7 percent of GDP in 1980–93, compared with an average of 2–3 percent in the OECD countries. Only some Eastern European countries prior to 1990 had such high inventory investment rates.

Even if one believes that SOE managers in China are out to maximize only profits, one should be reminded that enthusiastic attempts at innovations comprise only one method of maximizing an SOE's profits, and even then an uncertain one. The fact remains that it continues to be financially more rewarding for an SOE manager in China to spend time developing good relations with the state bureaucracy than to increase production efficiency. Until the 1990s, the large and medium-sized SOEs had to fulfill production quotas at below-market prices, and they received subsidized inputs in return. If the amount of subsidized inputs was high, the quota system generated a positive rent to the enterprise. Li (1994) estimated that an SOE which made positive market profits on its above-quota production in 1986–88 received a rent 2.7 times that of its market profit.[25] Bureaucratic haggling was vastly more profitable than competing in the market! Li's rent estimate may be the lower bound because it did not include the rent that an SOE received from tax-bargaining, a practice so pervasive that an average SOE paid an effective income tax rate of 33 percent instead of the legal rate of 55 percent then in force.

Taken together, Bai et al.'s argument and the two observations on inventory investment and on profit-via-lobbying suggest that there are serious systemic problems within China's SOE sector. These problems have not been adequately discussed because they have been over-shadowed by the large growth in SOE output. On the narrower issue of whether the SOE output growth has been extensive or intensive in nature, one observer's judgment is that the "dispute so far appears inconclusive, *especially given the small productivity increases under dispute*" (Walder 1995; emphasis added). In short, even if TFP growth has been positive, its contribution is minor.

The Case of the Disappearing SOE Profits

Groves et al. (1995b) found evidence that China's industrial bureaus were actively rewarding good managers, demoting bad ones, and hiring new ones under creative arrangements like auction; and that the resulting flow of managers improved these firms' labor productivity compared with the average labor productivity for these industries.[26] A recent field trip to Chongqing, one of the ten largest industrial cities and dominated by state-owned heavy industries, confirmed that the changing of managers did improve economic performance. It also found that unexpected new costs emerged over time:

Municipal officials often find that factory directors appointed to money-losing firms do well and are able to bring the firms out of losses in the first two years, then they start to take part in graft and embezzlement, bribery, and most frequently, pirating state assets. (Chen 1996)

The Chongqing experience echoed the earlier Eastern European experience that new and better-educated managers could indeed run SOEs more efficiently; however, over time, these smarter managers figured out how to use the autonomy given them to steal from the firms. Herein may lie an important reason why profitability of the state sector in China has plummeted across the board.

Since additional decision-making powers were given to SOE managers in 1985, there has been a steady increase in SOE losses. The situation stabilized in 1990–91, when the state attempted to recover some of the decision-making power devolved to the SOEs. In 1992, decentralizing efforts were accelerated on the initiative of local leaders after Deng Xiaoping called for faster economic reforms in order to avoid the fate of the Soviet Union. The unexpected result was that the faster economic growth was accompanied by larger SOE losses. About two-thirds of Chinese SOEs ran losses in 1992 although output growth in that year was

13 percent. These enterprise losses cannot be blamed on price controls because such controls affected only a small proportion of SOEs in 1992. State enterprise losses have continued to accelerate since then. In the first quarter of 1996, the enterprise sector slid into the red with a net deficit of 3.4 billion yuan.[27]

There are two competing explanations for the disappearing SOE profits. The EPR view attributes the collapse of SOE profits to the emergence of competition from the nonstate enterprises.[28] The anti-EPR view identifies overcompensation of SOE personnel as at least as important as competition from non-SOEs in reducing SOE profits.

Naughton's (1995) defense of the EPR view consisted of showing the *sectorwide* (average of SOEs and non-SOEs) rate of return to capital in different sectors of industry in 1980 and 1989. In 30 out of 38 cases, the 1989 profit rates were lower than those in 1980.

The main difficulty with Naughton's explanation is that the profit rates of SOEs in sectors of industry that experienced little entry by non-SOEs showed the same dramatic drop as those of SOEs in sectors with heavy penetration by non-SOEs. Fan and Woo (1996) compared the SOE profit rate and the proportion of output sold by SOEs in different sectors of industry in 1989 and 1992. In four of the five cases where the degree of SOE domination was unchanged, the profit rates were lower in 1992 (e.g., the profit rate of the tobacco industry dropped 82 percentage points, and that of petroleum refining dropped 13 percentage points). The 1992 profit rates were lower in six of the seven cases where the degree of SOE domination had declined by less than 5 percentage points.[29]

The emphasis put by the anti-EPR view on the appropriation of firms' profits by managers and workers is based on the pre-1990 experiences with decentralizing reforms in EEFSU, and on the above-mentioned lack of a correlation between the decline in SOE profit rates and the change in the degree of SOE domination of that sector. This anti-EPR view identifies the devolution of financial decision-making power to the SOEs as the root of the subsequent excessive compensation of SOE personnel. With the end of central planning, the key source of the industrial bureaus' information regarding the SOEs was the reports submitted by the SOEs themselves. This reduction in the monitoring ability of the state in a situation of continued soft-budget constraint meant that there was little incentive for state-enterprise managers to resist wage demands because their prospects of promotion to larger SOEs was determined in part by the increases in workers' welfare during their tenure. Furthermore, the easy availability of loans from the local banks (which faced continual pressure from the local authorities to promote local development) made it possible to increase labor compensation and capital investment at the same time.

This SOE tendency to overreward workers was officially acknowledged in 1984 when the government introduced a progressive bonus tax to control the generous dispensation of bonuses that began in 1979. An annual bonus of up to four months of basic wages was exempted from the bonus tax; a fifth month's bonus would require the SOE to pay a 100 percent bonus tax, a sixth month's bonus would be subject to a 200 percent bonus tax, a seventh month's bonus to a 300 percent bonus tax, and so on.

One of the earliest attributions of the erosion of SOE profits to the decentralizing reforms was a 1986 report by the China Economic System Reform Research Institute (*Tigaisuo*), which pointed out the emerging tendency of SOEs to overconsume and overinvest through various book-keeping subterfuges.[30] Woo, Hai et al. (1994), Woo (1994), and Fan and Woo (1996) used various samples and national data to show that the sum of direct income (wages and bonuses) and indirect income (e.g., subsidies and in-kind distribution) increased more than labor productivity growth. Minami and Hondai (1995) found that the labor share of output in the machine industry started to rise with the acceleration of decentralized reforms in 1985, and since 1988 has exceeded the estimated output elasticity. Bouin (forthcoming) calculated that the marginal product of labor of SOEs increased by 5 percent in 1989–93 while the product wage of SOE workers rose by 7 percent.

Naughton (1994) was skeptical of the excessive compensation explanation because "the SOE wage bill, including all monetary subsidies, has remained approximately unchanged at about 5% of GNP since 1978." There are two difficulties with Naughton's refutation. The first is that the correct test for the excessive compensation hypothesis is to normalize the SOE wage bill by value-added in the SOE sector and not by economy-wide GDP. The second difficulty with Naughton's refutation is that direct cash income is only a part of the total package of labor compensation. Since the main categories of direct cash compensation were subject to state regulation, the primary method of increasing workers' income was through indirect means like better housing, improved transportation, new recreational facilities, and study tours; these expenses were listed either as production costs or as investment expenditures financed from deprecia-tion funds. The ingenuity of disguising extra compensation can be quite impressive, as shown in the following account:

In some enterprises, shares, with promised interest rates higher than bank deposit rates in addition to fixed dividend payment, are simply a device to raise the level of wages and bonuses which have been regulated by the government to control inflation. (Chen 1994, p. 12)

Jefferson et al. (1994) pointed out that the estimated labor share of output in Woo, Fan et al. (1993) was less than the estimated output elasticity: 48 percent and 54 percent, respectively. This criticism would be fatal if it were not that Woo, Fan et al.'s estimated labor compensation did not include the almost-free housing, medical care, cafeteria subsides, and non-cash gifts received by workers. If the average proportion of income that workers in market economies pay for housing were taken into account in Woo, Fan et al.'s estimated labor compensation, labor share would have exceeded 54 percent of output.[31]

SOEs and Macroeconomic Instability

The financial weakness of SOEs has destabilized the macroeconomy in two ways (Fan and Woo 1996). The first is through the state budget. The financial contribution of the SOE sector has declined steadily in the reform period. SOEs paid income taxes amounting to 19.1 percent of GDP in 1978, 6.6 percent in 1985, and 1.7 percent in 1993; they remitted gross profits of 19.1 percent, 0.5 percent, and 0.1 percent respectively (World Bank 1995a, table 7.3; 1996, table 23). The consequent widening of the budget deficit contributed to faster monetary growth. The second way is through the banking system, since the bulk of SOE losses were covered not by budget subsidies but by bank loans. An even more important cause of money creation has been investment loans to the SOEs. Since the promotion of SOE managers depended significantly on the *expansion* of their enterprises, they (with the support of local authorities) have put continual pressure on local banks for investment loans, and often have received them.

The central bank's accommodation of requests for loans to cover losses and to finance investments has meant that the amount of reserve money growth directed to the SOEs has been substantially greater than the budget deficit itself, causing the "consolidated government budget deficit," including subsidized loans to the SOEs, to be over 10 percent of GDP in 1990 and 1991 (Wong et al. 1995, p. 29). Broadman (1995) reported:

While explicit and implicit fiscal (i.e., on-budget) subsidies [to SOEs] as a percent of GDP have been declining in recent years (from about 5.9 percent in 1990 to

about 3.5 percent in 1993), quasi-fiscal (i.e., financial system) subsidies ... have
been increasing (from about 3.8 percent in 1990 to about 6.0 percent in 1993). The
net result is that total subsidies to SOEs are large and remain virtually unchanged.
(pp. xii)

The Generation of Social Tensions by Embezzlement

In December 1995, the State Administration of State Property reported
that asset-stripping in the SOE sector "has been about 50 billion yuan
[annually] since the early 1980s."[32] This would mean that the cumulative
loss of SOE assets in 1983–92 was equivalent to some 24 percent of the
original value of fixed assets in the SOE sector in 1992, or some 34 percent of the net value of fixed assets in the SOE sector.

China's gradual "spontaneous privatization" process is likely to result
in a more unequal distribution of property ownership than a Czech-style
mass privatization program, though admittedly Russia's mass privatization process (particularly of valuable assets in the natural resource sectors)
did not prevent massive corruption. Perhaps even more important, the
steady stripping of state assets tends to subvert political legitimacy much
more than a transparent method of privatization.

The Emerging Response to the SOE Problem

It is notable that the original demands of the 1989 Tiananmen Square
demonstrators were for reduction of inflation and corruption. We think,
therefore, that the oft-given justifications for the absence of privatization
in China on the grounds of preserving social stability may be overlooking
the social tensions being created by the asset-stripping, corruption, and
macroeconomic instability caused by the unreformed ownership structure
of the SOEs.

There is no doubt that the Chinese leadership recognizes that the economic and political problems caused by the large SOE sector would be
alleviated by the privatization of SOEs. This is why the debate between
the conservative and the liberal reformers has progressed from "whether
privatization is necessary" to "what is the optimal amount of privatization." There are now 25 official property rights' exchanges and about 150
unofficial ones where state assets are sold to the public, though the latter
disappear temporarily whenever there seems to be a swing back to more
orthodox socialism at the center (Fan 1995).

Recent reports in 1994 indicated that full-scale sales of small and medium SOEs have occurred in several places. The best-known example was

Zhucheng city in Shandong province, which started privatizing SOEs in 1992, when two-thirds of its SOEs were losing money or just breaking even.[33] Almost 90 percent of county-supervised SOEs in Zhucheng have already been privatized. Sichuan province was steadily selling off money-losing SOEs, and Guangdong province was selling profitable SOEs as well, in order to finance local infrastructure and to clear the debts of unprofitable SOEs before putting them up for sale. Heilongjiang province had announced plans to privatize 200 SOEs after having sold 160 success-fully.[34] Finally, in September 1997, China announced that it would be undertaking massive privatization of its SOE sector. Thus China has not ignored the positive international experience with privatization of SOEs.

7.5 Conclusions

Two points about China's gradual reform program deserve reemphasis. The first is that the dual-track approach worked in China because of China's vast rural hinterland; it did not work in Jaruzelski's Poland or Gorbachev's Soviet Union. The TVEs and other nonstate enterprises were able to grow without sharp rises in marginal costs and without the need to force reductions of employment in the SOEs because of the pool of surplus agricultural workers. The second is that China's gradualism is an "easy-to-hard" reform sequence. It began with the relatively easier problems and left the hard ones until later. In contrast, the more radical approach in parts of EEFSU has tackled the hardest problems (including ownership transformation, structural reforms, and political democratization) at the beginning.

We are skeptical of the EPR assertion that the performance of industrial SOEs can be improved satisfactorily without privatization. The validity of the empirical work behind that assertion depends on the dubious idea of "Chinese exceptionalism": China's industrial production structure is very different from those of other countries. The plausibility of EPR also hinges on Naughton's claim that Chinese officials and economists, for unspeci-fied reasons, have not estimated TFP correctly. Furthermore, an adequate assessment of SOE performance has to go beyond the TFP criteria and include whether the SOE sector has undermined macroeconomic and social stability. The evidence is that the devolution of decision-making power to the SOEs has allowed their personnel to appropriate the profits and, in many cases, the assets as well. Finally, there is no better proof of the failure of the SOE reform than in the officially sanctioned privatization that is occurring in Communist China.

China's rapid growth can continue as long as the nonstate sector remains dynamic and essentially unhindered by financial losses or problems thrown up by the SOE sector. Dynamism of the nonstate sector, however, is likely to require continuing reforms, such as the extension of truly private ownership instead of collective ownership. Moreover, state enterprise reforms will have to be deepened in the future, to include privatization and structural adjustment, if losses in that sector are to be kept limited.

China's extraordinary growth performance should not distract attention from many profound problems that the nation will face in the coming years. While China's state sector is too small to drag down the nonstate sector, it still imposes large financial and resource costs on the economy. The underdeveloped legal system will be an increasing drag on the economy as the complexity of economic life increases, unless legal reform can keep pace with economic development. Property forms that have worked since the early 1980s, such as the rural collectively owned enterprises, are likely to be less effective in the future, especially as village-based life is gradually supplanted by a highly mobile, nonagricultural population. Political legitimacy will also be under serious stress. Growing income inequalities across regions will raise demands for compensatory policies from the center, which will prove hard to satisfy. At the same time, continuing corruption and misuse of state assets will further undermine public support for the existing political institutions. These political problems will be acted out against a backdrop of continuing serious pressures on the state budget, arising from low tax revenues and losses of the SOEs.

Acknowledgments

This chapter has benefited tremendously from the comments of Peter Boone, Anne Booth, Olivia Bosch, Ken Dark, Stanislaw Gomulka, Paul Hare, Yelena Kalyuzhnova, Peter Kenway, Richard Layard, Dic Lo, Chenggang Xu, Yi Zhu, and Victoria Zinde-Walsh on the talks I gave at the London School of Economics, the School of Oriental and African Studies, and the University of Reading in November 1995. This paper draws upon research being conducted collaboratively with Fan Gang and Jeffrey Sachs.

Why China Grew: The Role of Decentralization

Chenggang Xu and Juzhong Zhuang

The Chinese economic reform began in the late 1970s. Since its start the economic growth rate has been very high. This makes the Chinese reform very different from the transitions in Eastern Europe and the former Soviet Union (EEFSU). (See table 8.1.)

From the long-term perspective, the steady change of the ownership structure during the Chinese reform is perhaps more important than the current economic growth rate. This structural change means that the high growth rate has occurred while the Chinese economy was, and is, in the process of transition from a centralized economy to a market economy. Specifically, the share of the state sector in national industrial output has declined from almost four-fifths when the reform started to about one-third. Tables 8.2 and 8.3, which show these changes, are self-explanatory. However, there is one point that needs to be made: most of the collectively owned enterprises shown in the tables are township-village enterprises (TVEs), which are very different from collective cooperatives in the EEFSU. We shall discuss this in greater detail in due course.

Many economists argue that the success of China's economic reforms is due to the practice of gradualism, to competition across regions, to the growth of the nonstate sector, and to the experimental and the bottom-up approaches (see Jefferson and Rawsky 1994; McMillan and Naughton 1992; Perkins 1988, 1994; Yusuf 1994). These are fair summaries of the major features of the Chinese reform. But why China has followed such routes still needs to be explored.

China began its reform process with a relatively small and undeveloped state sector, a fact emphasized by Sachs and Woo (1994). Nevertheless, (1) all the regions that have proved more successful in this process have been those with well-developed, *regionally controlled* state-owned enterprises (SOE)[1]—regional control of SOEs was a special feature of the

Table 8.1
EEFSU: Average annual growth of GDP (%)

	1980–85	1985–90	1991	1992	1993
China	10.2	7.8	8.4	13.8	13.9
Russia	3.2	1.3	−13.1	−19.7	−12.0
Bulgaria	4.3	2.6	−13.5	−6.1	−5.4
Czech Republic	n.a.	1.8	−14.2	−7.1	−0.3
Slovakia	n.a.	1.5	−16.2	−6.3	n.a.
Hungary	1.8	0.6	−12.0	−4.8	−2.0
Poland	0.7	0.3	−7.6	1.8	4.0
Romania	3.8	−2.1	−13.4	−14.9	−4.4

Sources: World Bank, *Trends in Developing Economies* (1994) and *Trends in Developing Economies*, vol. 1, *Eastern Europe and Central Asia* (1993); *International Financial Statistical Yearbook* (1994).

Table 8.2
Share of industrial output, by ownership classification, 1980–94 (%)

	1980	1984	1990	1991	1992	1993	1994
State enterprises	76.1	69.1	54.6	52.9	48.1	43.0	34.1
Collective enterprises	23.5	29.7	35.6	35.7	38.0	38.4	40.9
Private enterprises	0.4	1.2	9.8	11.4	13.9	18.6	25.1

Source: State Statistical Bureau, *Statistical Yearbook of China* (1995).

Table 8.3
Rate of growth of industrial output by ownership, 1981–94 (year-to-year percentage)

	1981	1986	1989	1990	1991	1992	1993	1994
State enterprises	2.5	6.2	3.9	2.96	8.6	12.4	5.7	6.5
Collective enterprises	9.0	18.0	10.5	9.0	18.4	39.3	36.0	29.8
Individual/other enterprises	35.1	54.1	31.0	27.5	36.4	58.8	77.5	63.8
Total	4.3	11.7	8.5	7.8	14.8	27.5	28.0	26.1

Source: State Statistical Bureau, *Statistical Yearbook of China* (1995).

Table 8.4
Growth in selected developed and less-developed provinces, 1978–92 (at 1990 constant prices)

	1. Annual growth rate of national income (%)	2. Per capita national income (yuan)		3. Annual growth rate of per capita income (%)	4. Annual growth rate of population (%)
		1978	1992		
National	8.8	568	1,526	7.3	1.4
More regionally controlled provinces					
Jiangsu	11.5	591	2,322	10.3	1.1
Zhejiang	12.9	496	2,372	11.8	1.0
Guangdong	12.8	547	2,555	11.6	1.0
Average of above	11.7	538	2,256	10.8	1.0
More centrally controlled provinces					
Liaoning	7.1	951	2,314	6.6	0.4
Jilin	8.3	524	1,590	8.3	0.1
Heilongjiang	5.8	835	1,734	5.4	0.3
Average of above	7.1	770	2,213	6.8	0.3
Less-developed rural provinces					
Guizhou	8.3	300	742	6.7	1.5
Gansu	7.6	234	538	6.1	1.4
Qinghai	5.8	140	255	4.4	1.4
Average of above	7.4	282	658	6.2	1.4

Sources: State Statistical Bureau, *Statistical Yearbook of China* (1992–94), *Statistical Materials of China by Region* (1993), *China Population Statistics Yearbook* (1994).

Chinese industrial organization in the prereform period, which will be discussed further in this section; (2) growth rates in all the developed regions with a greater number of *centrally controlled* SOEs, an organizational structure closer to the Soviet model, are below the national average; and (3) growth rates in all the less developed (rural) regions are below the national average. (See table 8.4.) These figures suggest that institutional and organizational factors have been predominant in determining the success of the reform.

8.1 Economic Structures in Planned Economies: EEFSU and China

Although both China and EEFSU had centrally planned economies, the Chinese economy was organized differently. The centrally planned economies in EEFSU were organized on the principle of functional specialization

(Qian and Xu 1993). Every state-owned firm was under the control of a single ministry that specialized in administering one type of product or service. For example, the Automobile Ministry controlled all the firms in the automobile industry. A major feature of EEFSU economies was the extraordinarily high degree of industrial concentration. The strong interdependence between enterprises across different regions made comprehensive planning and administrative coordination between ministries at the top level of the government crucial for normal operation of the economy in the absence of markets. For example, in the late 1970s, under the Gosplan in the Soviet Union, there were 62 ministries responsible for 48,000 plan "positions"—12 million products planned and coordinated by the Gosplan (Nove 1983).

Economic structure of centralized economies can be characterized by using the M-form and U-form concept (Qian and Xu 1993).[2] An M-form organization groups complementary tasks together in one unit (e.g., division, regional government). A U-form organization groups similar tasks together in one unit (e.g., department, ministry). The organizational structure of the EEFSU had an unitary form—each ministry was functionally specialized.

It is important to note that a large proportion of the current Russian economy, particularly the state sector and the privatized former state sector, is still deeply affected by its pretransition U-form structure. Recently collected data show that in Russia, state-owned firms are still influenced mostly by ministries, then local governments, then workers, then unions; privatized firms are influenced almost equally by ministries, local governments, and workers, then by unions; new private firms are mostly influenced by local governments, and all other factors are neglibible (Earle and Ross 1996). These suggest that if the Soviet Union had not been organized in the U-form structure, the current performance of the privatized firms might be very different.

In contrast, the Chinese economy was organized into a multilayer, multiregional form (M-form). The ministries of the central government controlled only a small proportion of SOEs. Most Chinese SOEs were under the control of regional governments. Each regional government's functions were further divided along both geographical and functional specialization lines. For example, provincial governments control county governments and provincial-level SOEs in different industries; county governments control township governments and some county-level SOEs. This structure is duplicated from the center to the lowest level of the hierarchy of the Chinese economy.

We should emphasize here that the Chinese M-form is "deep" and differs profoundly from the U-form of the Soviet Union and Eastern Europe. In China, regions at the county level and above are relatively autonomous and largely self-sufficient. This can be further illustrated by comparing one EEFSU country (e.g., Hungary) with one province of China (e.g., Hainan). Hainan is much smaller than Hungary in terms of population and GDP, but before the transition, most Hungarian firms were directly under the control of ministries. In sharp contrast, most firms in Hainan are not directly controlled by either the central or the provincial government; instead, the control of the firms is distributed at different levels of administration hierarchy. One more striking illustration of the structural difference between China and the EEFSU is the fact that before the transition, the Hungarian central planning agencies, such as the Central Statistical Office, were larger than their Chinese counterparts, such as the State Statistical Bureau (let alone provincial-level statistical offices), although China is so much larger than Hungary. We shall elaborate these points in our discussion of coordination in different organizational forms.

Historically, in its first five-year plan (1954–58), the Chinese government sought to copy the Soviet model of a centrally planned system in full. In the process, the power of regional governments was weakened and central ministries were established. Planning was formulated at the center, by the State Council and ministries; the major function of local governments was to implement the central plan. In the late 1950s, however, simultaneously with the political break with the Soviet Union, Chinese planning procedures were changed in the direction of a regionally based system and more emphasis was put on local plans.

In 1958, under the Great Leap Forward and Mao's idea of decentralizing state industry through incentives to mobilize local officials, the number of central enterprises decreased from 9,300 to 1,200—a reduction of more than 80 percent. The gross industrial output of central industrial SOEs fell from 40 percent to 14 percent. All SOEs in light industry (except four special paper-manufacturing SOEs and a copper net factory), most heavy industrial SOEs, all engineering and administrative bureaus of the Railway Ministry under central-local dual control, all SOEs in telecommunication, all state farms, all food-processing SOEs, and all SOEs under the Ministry of Commerce—in total, 88 percent of industrial SOEs—were transferred from central to local authorities (Zhou 1984, p. 70). Correspondingly, the number of industrial products that came under the State Planning Committee was reduced to 215 (from more than 300 in 1957); the number of centrally allocated products fell by 75 percent, to 132; the proportion of government revenue directly raised by the central government was reduced from 40 percent to 20 percent; and 80 percent of central government revenue came from local governments (Zhou 1984, p. 71).

By the mid-1960s, regional governments were much more powerful and important than the ministries (in contrast with their counterparts in the EEFSU). During the Cultural Revolution (1966–76), the transformation of the organizational structure was pushed further. In the early 1970s, more than 98 percent of centrally controlled SOEs, including large and very large firms, were transferred to local governments. The number of SOEs under the direct control of ministries decreased from 10,533 in 1965 to 142 in 1970. Most ministries lost their power to control state firms altogether.[3] For example, all SOEs directly controlled by the Ministries of Metallurgy, Coal, the First Machinery Industry (all nondefense production of automobiles, machine tools, electrical machinery), and Commerce were transferred to local governments.

As a result, all government revenues fell under the control of the local governments, except for import duties, tariffs, and profits from a small number of centrally controlled SOEs. Correspondingly, local governments became responsible for most government expenditures, including investment. In the mid-1970s about 60 percent of fixed asset investment in the state sector nationwide was made by local governments. The product planning/allocation system was transformed into a region-based system under which the central government took care only of the residual balance of supply and demand in each region, including raw materials and heavy machinery, such as cement, coal, timber, iron and steel, automobiles (and tires).

The classic example of the Chinese government's pushing regional decentralization is what was termed the "five small industries" policy. The five small industries in question were steel and iron, machinery, fertilizer, coal-mining, and cement. The central government's policy in the early 1970s was to develop these in each region, thus making the regions relatively self-sufficient. These five, moreover, were regarded as the basis for agricultural mechanization. In the first five years of the 1970s, 8 billion yuan was allocated to regional governments for setting up county-run small industrial firms. These small firms also obtained preferential treatment in taxation and bank loans. Most of the profits of these small SOEs were reinvested. In 1970, almost all the counties in China established SOEs producing agricultural machinery; 300 counties established steel plants; more than 20 provinces established tractor factories and motor

Table 8.5
Firm size: China, EEFSU, and Italy, 1988 (employees per firm)

	Manufacturing	Food products	Wearing apparel
Czechoslovakia	2,930	1,609	6,600
Soviet Union	806	290	402
Hungary	460	925	307
Yugoslavia	311	243	402
China	145	75	80
Italy	96	71	71

Source: Qian and Xu 1993.

Table 8.6
Duplication in Chinese automobile industry

	1953–67	1968–82	1983–87
Number of general-purpose automobile firms	22	58	116
Number of special-purpose automobile firms	68	202	347
Total annual output	33.780*	203,945**	472,538

Source: Wang and Chen 1991.
* Average of 1966, 1967, 1968.
** Average of 1981, 1982, 1983.

plants. In 1975, these small regional SOEs produced 58.8 percent of China's total cement output, 69 percent of fertilizer, 37.1 percent of coal, and 6.8 percent of steel (Wang 1986, pp. 356–59).

When Chinese reform started in the late 1970s, the central government controlled less than half the output of state industry. For example, in the automobile industry, most of the 58 SOEs making automobiles were controlled by local governments (Wang and Chen 1991). Consistent with this, the number of products directly under the central plan in China was much smaller, only 791 in 1979 (Zhu 1985), and was never more than 1,000. With a much reduced workload, the number of ministries at the center could be much smaller, fewer than 30.

8.2 Economies of Scale and Duplication

In the Chinese M-form economy, regions are relatively self-contained and self-sufficient in terms of functions and production. Accordingly, the size of enterprises is generally small, and industries are less concentrated (see table 8.5). By the same token, there are many duplications of similar types of firms (see table 8.6).

This duplication assists the Chinese reform process for several reasons. First, duplication is necessary for creating a competitive environment within the state sector. Second, it facilitates technology diffusion across firms and regions. Third, it increases the reliability of supply in uncertain conditions created by the reform process itself, and thus reduces vulnerability.

Obviously, there are also costs associated with duplication, notably the loss of scale economies. The best example is the Chinese automobile industry; there were more than 100 firms producing automobiles in the 1980s. Most produced only a few thousand or even fewer vehicles per year, which is far too low in terms of efficiency. But, compared with the EEFSU, the Chinese economy has gained more than it has lost from such duplication.

8.3 Incentives

Alongside greater autonomy, Chinese local governments were given greater incentives to introduce reforms than were their counterparts in the EEFSU, prior to the transition in the latter. Regional competition in getting rich more quickly was a slogan set by the central government. When a region had a higher growth rate than others, the head of that region would enjoy greater power and be more likely to get a promotion. Moreover, the central government encouraged regional governments to try their own approaches to speed up growth. The combination of these policies has meant, in effect, a "tournament" competition among regional governments.[4]

Maskin et al. (1997) provide a theory for comparing the incentives of regional governments vis-à-vis ministers in M-form, as contrasted with U-form, organizations. They argue that an M-form may be better from the standpoint of providing managerial incentives. Since managers under any organizational form need incentives, the latter should be awarded on the basis of performance. But performance may not be perfectly correlated with managerial effort because of the uncertainty faced by firms. Thus, if the manager of a region shows a poor performance, he may try to blame the outcome on bad luck rather than on lack of effort. However, if other regions are prospering, it will be hard for the manager to defend himself in this way. Therefore, it is desirable to make the manager's reward depend also on his performance relative to that in other regions. But the question arises: Why cannot the same be done in a U-form? An intuitive reason is that comparing ministries may be more difficult than comparing regions that produce more or less the same array of goods.

Maskin et al. provide a theoretical foundation for the idea that the "variation" between the performances of two regions producing similar outputs is likely to be lower (in the appropriate statistical sense) than that between the performances of two production ministries. Applying their theory to a Chinese data set of 520 Chinese SOEs, they compare the Chinese organizational form (M-form) with a hypothetical U-form. In this U-form, all firms would be organized into hypothetical industrial ministries. (Although some industrial ministries do exist in China, most state firms are under the control of regional governments.) The exercise, they show, provides evidence to support the hypothesis that it is "easier" to compare different regions than different industries.

Furthermore, they find evidence that regional yardstick competition has indeed been heavily used. During the reform, the Chinese central government pursued an explicit policy of encouraging regions to "get rich first." Relative performance criteria are frequently incorporated into the procedures for determining government officials' promotions and bonuses. Maskin et al. show that, statistically, provincial officials are more likely to be promoted if the nationwide ranking of the economic performance of their province is improved, and vice versa. Chances of promotion are measured by the province's representation on the Communist Party Central Committee, while economic performance is measured by the per capita GDP growth rate.

Complementing the work of Maskin et al. (1997), Xu and Zhuang (1996b) study incentives of SOE managers and workers under M- and U-forms. In fact, the Chinese state sector consists of a U-form part—ministry-controlled (centrally controlled SOEs)—and an M-form part—regionally controlled SOEs. Thus, comparing the Chinese M-form economy with the hypothetical U-form economy provides controlled observations of the role of organizational forms. Xu and Zhuang provide evidence indicating that during China's reform period, incentives for managers and workers of SOEs under the M-form have been better than those under the U-form; and SOEs under the M-form have performed better than those under the U-form.

On the basis of a panel survey of 800 SOEs, they found that bonus incentive schemes introduced into SOEs have significant positive effects on regional SOEs' total factor productivity but have no effect on central SOEs. For local SOEs, the elasticity of gross output with respect to per-employee bonus is around 0.17, implying that, other things being equal, a 1 percent increase in per-employee bonus leads to a 0.17 percent increase in real gross output. For central SOEs, on the other hand, the elasticity is

Table 8.7
Estimated TFP growth rates of central and local SOEs (percent)

	All SOEs	Central SOEs	Local SOEs
Total output growth	41.48	41.39	41.61
Output elasticities: labor, 0.3881; capital, 0.0883; intermediate input, 0.5236[1]			
Annual TFP growth rate	1.33	−0.21	3.02
Contribution of TFP growth	6.83 (16.5)	−1.04 (−2.5)	16.02 (38.5)
of increased labor	2.57 (6.2)	3.22 (7.8)	1.92 (4.6)
of increased capital	3.35 (8.1)	4.91 (11.9)	1.78 (4.3)
of increased intermediate input	28.73 (69.3)	34.30 (94.7)	21.89 (52.6)
Output elasticities: labor, 0.25; capital, 0.25; intermediate input, 0.5[2]			
Annual TFP growth rate	0.57	−1.51	2.73
Contribution of TFP growth	2.89 (7.0)	−7.33 (−17.7)	14.42 (34.7)
of increased labor	1.66 (4.0)	2.07 (5.0)	1.24 (3.0)
of increased capital	9.49 (22.9)	13.90 (33.6)	5.04 (12.1)
of increased intermediate input	27.44 (66.1)	32.75 (79.1)	20.91 (50.3)
Output elasticities: labor, 0.3333; capital, 0.3333; intermediate input, 0.3333[3]			
Annual TFP growth rate	1.61	−0.35	3.59
Contribution of TFP growth	8.33 (20.1)	−1.74 (−4.2)	19.30 (46.4)
of increased labor	2.21 (5.3)	2.77 (6.7)	1.65 (4.0)
of increased capital	12.65 (30.5)	18.53 (44.8)	6.72 (16.1)
of increased intermediate input	18.29 (44.1)	21.83 (52.7)	13.94 (33.5)

Source: Xu and Zhuang 1996.
Note: Table is based on a sample survey of 162 central SOEs and 318 local SOEs. Results were estimated by using the standard growth accounting method. Figures in parentheses are shares of total growth.
1. Output elasticities were estimated by using "within" method (two-way fixed-effect model) and the sample data.
2. These elasticities were assumed.
3. These elasticities were assumed.

not significantly different from zero.[5] (See table A in the appendix for detailed estimation results.)

As a result of different incentives at both the government level and the firm level in the M- and U-form sectors of the Chinese economy, we expect that regional SOEs will be more efficient than the central SOEs. This is confirmed by table 8.7, which shows growth rates of total factor productivity for the full sample of all SOEs, the subsample of centrally controlled SOEs, and the subsample of regionally controlled SOEs, using the standard growth accounting method. By using output elasticities of labor, capital, and intermediate input estimated on the basis of the sample data, they found (see table 8.7) that the annual TFP growth rate during 1986–91 for the regional SOEs in the sample was 3.02 percent, which contributed 38.5 percent of the total growth in these SOEs; for the central SOEs this figure was negative, −0.21 percent, representing a negative contribution of 2.5 percent to the total growth in these SOEs. The annual TFP growth rate for the full sample of SOEs was 1.33 percent, contributed exclusively by local SOEs.[6] As shown in table 8.7, when alternative values of output elasticities, closer to those of firms in market economies, were used, the regional SOEs outperformed the central SOEs even more significantly.

A remark is in order. Although some of the evidence provided above is based on data from state enterprises, the focus here is broader than simply how to restructure the state sector. Indeed, regional government officials will have greater chances of promotion so long as the ranking of the region's economic performance in all sectors continues to improve (Maskin et al. 1997). Therefore, under this incentive scheme, regional governments have incentives to help the growth of all sectors, including the private one.

Since in a later section we will discuss the fact that the SOEs' financial performance has been declining over the reform period, we should like to emphasize that the M-form organization has effectively lessened the SOEs' problems. Since restructuring and privatizing SOEs is slow by nature (even when massive privatization can be done quickly, as in Russia and the Czech Republic, the restructuring of privatized firms still requires a long period of time), slowing down the deterioration of the SOEs' performance is extremely helpful to transition.

8.4   Coordination and Experiments in Transition

Another major feature associated with the Chinese M-form structure is its mechanism for coordination. Unlike the EEFSU, where the center played the critical role in coordinating the economy, regional governments in China have had considerable responsibility for economic coordination.

Such decentralization has had important benefits. First, local information is better, since local governments are geographically closer to the sites in question. Second, communication and information-processing between the center and the regions are greatly facilitated. Thus, in China a small task force can cope with making central plans and collecting aggregate statistics; in contrast, in the FSU, a large body of officials is needed (see table 8.8).

Table 8.8
Number of staff in planning and statistics agencies: China and FSU, selected years

	FSU	China
Statistical agency	41,000 (1987)	46 (1976)
	41,000 (1987)	280 (1981)
Planning agency	2,560 (1986)	50 (early 1970s)

Source: Huang 1994.

Third, regionally based coordination makes economywide coordination failure less likely in the case of external shock. In contrast to the U-form, which is fragile to shocks, the M-form structure localizes their effects. This also makes it easier to introduce institutional changes on an experimental scale, without causing disruption to the rest of the economy. Such benefits are particularly crucial when the functions of the center are disrupted. A good example is the sustainability of the Chinese economy during the Cultural Revolution. During that period, the Chinese central government almost completely lost its ability to coordinate the economy, while the economies of certain regions collapsed due to factional conflicts. However, the national economy did not collapse. Chinese national income merely declined for two years—by 7.2 percent in 1967 and 6.5 percent in 1968. The economy recovered quickly thereafter, even though the central government had not regained its coordination function. In sharp contrast, during their transition, most of the EEFSU economies suffered dramatic and persistent declines in measured output—30 percent or more, over four or more years.

Most successful Chinese reform measures were introduced as local experiments by regional governments, and only later promoted nationwide by the central government. Thus, one major feature of the Chinese reform has been identified as its success in using local experiments and in adopting the "bottom-up" approach (K. Chen et al. 1992; McMillan and Naughton 1992). In Eastern Europe and the former Soviet Union, some experimental reforms were introduced prior to 1989, but these were often unsuccessful; and even those which were locally successful, were rarely promoted nationwide. On this basis, it has been argued that regional experiment is not the correct approach to reforming a planned economy (e.g., Kornai 1992).

Qian and Xu (1993) analyzed coordination problems in different organizational forms in order to answer the question: Why is China special in using experimental approaches? They proposed several answers.

In a U-form organization, where there is a high degree of interdependence between operating units, allowing one or a few regions to experiment may be very costly or perhaps not feasible. This is because experiments generate shocks and may disturb the normal operations of the economy, regardless of the success or failure of the experiments evaluated locally. This makes the scope of regional experiments more limited and their chances of success smaller. Even when an experiment proves successful in a particular industry or region, its relevance to other industries and other regions is less significant because of heterogeneity across operating units. Given these features of the U-form hierarchy, economic reforms will more likely be carried out in an "top-down" fashion, in which decision making for changes has to be more centralized in order to minimize transition costs. In this sense, a U-form organization makes institutions more rigid and more difficult to change through local experiments.

In an M-form organization, however, the regional interdependence is relatively weak, so that even if the experiment fails, it will not significantly disturb the whole economy. Hence the regional experimental strategy of reform in an M-form organization is less costly and more feasible. With an M-form structure, large-scale regional experiments can be carried out, many regions have a chance to develop a large variety of "mutants," and the central government may be able to compare and select among a number of variants.[7] Furthermore, since adjacent regions are usually similar in terms of economic structure, a successful experiment in one region can relatively easily be extended to other regions. Under the M-form organization, therefore, reforms may proceed more efficiently with the "bottom-up" approach,[8] which provides a less costly way of learning to establish and to use market institutions in a unprecedented environment. This makes the M-form organization more flexible in the institutional evolutionary process.

Qian et al. (1996) studied coordination and experimentation under various organizational forms, particularly the M-form and the U-form. Coordination in organization is modeled as the adjustment of attributes and capacities of tasks in the face of external shocks. An M-form organization groups complementary tasks together in one unit. When there are exogenous shocks that disrupt attributes of tasks in their original plans, coordination is required to adjust attributes. We call these shocks "attribute shocks." A U-form organization groups substitutable tasks together in one unit. In the presence of only "attribute shocks," particularly when gains from specialization are small, communication is poor, or shocks are more likely, the expected payoff of the decentralized M-form is the higher. When facing both types of shocks, centralization does better, provided communication is good. Economic transition may be regarded as a process of experimenting with new institutions/laws and the subsequent promotion of successful results. Introducing a new institution involves a change in the existing attributes of those tasks aimed at increasing outputs or reducing costs. Different organizational forms exhibit different features when dealing with shocks, and therefore carry out experiments differently. In promotion, the result of a successful experiment is imitated by other units of an organization. Intuitively, the weaker interdependence between regions in an M-form hierarchy should make it easier to solve coordination problems locally. Thus the experimental approach is more appropriate for M-form organizations.

An example of experiment in the Chinese transition is land reform. The "household responsibility system" in agricultural reform was developed through the initiatives of local governments. It was local government officials in Fengyang county, Anhui province, who took the initiatives and risks in distributing land to rural households. This practice and its achievements were discovered later by the central government. Only then were similar nationwide reform measures approved.

8.5   The Role of the Township-Village Enterprise (TVE) Sector in the Success of the Chinese Reform

An important feature of the Chinese reform is the fast growth of the nonstate sector. A vital part of the nonstate sector is agriculture. From 1979 on, the "household responsibility system" gradually became the main institution in Chinese rural areas. The essence of this reform is the leasing of land to rural households, which pay rent and taxes, and enjoy the residual income and partial residual rights to the land. Thus rural households have both incentives and responsibilities to take risks and make efforts to improve the land "allocated" to them, and are held responsible for the outcome. This reform greatly improved agricultural productivity. The average annual growth rate of agriculture increased from about 2 percent in the 30 years or so preceding the late 1970s to about 7 percent in the period 1979–84. So successful was this reform measure that in 1984 the People's Commune system was officially abolished.

However, the contribution of the successful agricultural reform to growth should not be exaggerated, for the following reasons. Agricultural output accounted for about one-third of Chinese GNP in the late 1970s. Moreover, the growth rate of agriculture has remained lower than that of

Table 8.9
Agriculture in the Chinese economy, 1970–93 (%)

Year	Share of agriculture in national income	Agriculture output/rural output	Agriculture labor force/national labor force	Agriculture labor force/rural labor force
1970	40.39	n.a.	80.70	n.a.
1975	37.79	n.a.	77.07	n.a.
1980	35.97	68.86	70.37	93.63
1985	35.50	57.09	60.86	81.89
1990	34.76	46.10	58.75	79.35
1992	29.20	35.78	57.27	77.71
1993	25.39	n.a.	55.23	75.15

Source: State Statistical Bureau, *Statistical Yearbook of China* (various years).

Table 8.10
Annual growth rate of agriculture and GDP in China, 1978–94 (%)

Year	1978	1980	1985	1990	1992	1993	1994
Agriculture	4.1	−1.5	1.8	7.3	4.7	4.7	4.0
GDP	11.7	7.8	13.5	3.8	14.2	13.5	11.8

Source: State Statistical Bureau, *Statistical Yearbook of China* (1995).

aggregate GNP. Thus the influence of the improved agricultural growth rate should not be overestimated. In comparison, the growth rate of the output of TVEs has been higher than that of agriculture, and the share of their output in rural material output soon exceeded that of agriculture. The importance of the agricultural reform lies partly in its interaction with the TVE sector. First, through abolition of collective farms, rural households were given greater freedom to reallocate their labor and investment optimally between agriculture and TVEs. Second, the improved productivity in agriculture further released labor and increased savings/investment for the development of TVEs. Finally, TVEs were developed under the commune system (called commune-brigade enterprises). The abolition of the commune system shifted the focus of community governments from agriculture to TVEs, and had considerable influence in changing the governance of TVEs. (See tables 8.9 and 8.10)

In the nonstate sector, the largest and most dynamic sector is that of the TVEs. In fact, the TVE sector has been the most important engine driving the unprecedented growth of the Chinese economy since the late 1970s. Moreover, the development of the TVE is the most important

Table 8.11
The role of TVEs in Chinese rural economy, 1978–94

Year	TVE output (billion yuan)[a]	Share of TVE output in rural output (%)	TVE labor force (million)	Share of TVE labor force in rural labor force (%)
1978	49.31	n.a.	28.27	9.22
1980	65.69	23.53	29.99	9.42
1985	272.84	43.03	69.79	18.83
1990	846.16	50.91	92.68	22.06
1992	1797.54	70.81	105.81	24.17
1993	3154.07	n.a.[b]	123.45	27.89
1994	4258.85	n.a.[b]	120.18	26.91

Source: State Statistical Bureau, *Statistical Yearbook of China* (1990, 1995).
a. At current prices.
b. After 1992, rural output data are not available.

feature distinguishing the Chinese transition path from those of the EEFSU. (See table 8.11.)

A TVE is a collectively owned communal enterprise located in a township or a village. Since most TVEs are in the industrial sector, they are often treated as synonymous with rural industrial firms. All the residents of a township or a village that has established TVEs own these firms; the property rights of the TVEs can be exercised only collectively, through community representatives. If we have to make an analogy to a counterpart in the West, the closest equivalent might be a combination of municipally owned enterprises and producer cooperatives. In their comparative studies of TVEs and other institutions throughout the world, Gelb and Svejnar (1990) conclude that the institutions most similar to the Chinese TVEs are producer cooperatives, including cooperatives in Eastern Europe, Mondragon enterprises in Spain, and labor-managed firms in the former Yugoslavia. With some exceptions, such cooperatives have been relatively unsuccessful in Western countries; later we shall discuss some reasons why, in contrast, TVEs in China have succeeded so well.

The community is deeply involved in governing a TVE's operations. Regardless of the seemingly diffuse and unclear ownership structure, TVEs have been enormously successful. Their growth and performance are outstanding. This largely accounts for the difference between the growth rate for industry as a whole and that of the SOEs. By the mid-1980s, the share of the TVE sector was the second largest (after the state sector) in Chinese industry, and the gap has shrunk rapidly since 1984 (see tables 8.2 and 8.3). The TVE sector has also been much more efficient

Table 8.12
Growth and efficiency in the state and TVE sectors, 1979–91

Growth rates of	National industry	SOE industry	TVE
Output	13.3	8.4	25.3
Capital	—	7.8	16.5
Labor	—	3.0	11.9
TFP	—	4.0	12.0

Source: Weitzman and Xu 1994.
Note: TFP = total factor productivity.

Table 8.13
TVES: Number of firms, employment, growth rate, and share in total industrial output, 1978–94

Year	Number of industrial TVEs (1,000s)	Employment of industrial TVEs (million)	Annual growth rate of industrial TVEs' output (%)	Share in total industrial output (%)
1978	794	17.34	10.58	9.09
1980	758	19.42	19.24	9.88
1985	4930	41.37	90.31	18.81
1990	7220	55.72	10.61	25.29
1994	6986	69.62	36.10	42.04

Source: State Statistical Bureau, *Statistical Yearbook of China* (1995).

Table 8.14
TVEs: Share of selected industrial products produced by TVEs, 1990 (%)

Coal	Cement	Cotton cloth	Paper	Electric fans	Canned food
33.1	27.5	21.4	38.2	46.5	39.1

Source: Qian and Xu 1993.

than the state sector in terms of total factor productivity growth (see table 8.12).

The TVEs' impact on the economy extends far beyond their sector. Their activities generate much of the demand for intermediate products and capital goods produced predominantly by the state sector (e.g., steel, machine tools, automobiles). At the same time, TVEs greatly intensify the competition with SOEs in those industries where the state sector does not dominate (e.g., textiles, most light industries, conventional mechanical and electrical machinery). Such competition has improved many SOEs' efficiency, but has driven many others into large losses or even to the verge

Table 8.15
TVEs: Proportion of output of all TVEs, by originating sector, 1978–94 (%)

Year	Share of agricultural TVEs	Share of industrial TVEs	Share of construction TVEs	Share of transpor- tation TVEs	Share of other service TVEs
1978	7.31	78.14	7.06	3.81	3.67
1985	2.15	66.97	11.36	1.50	17.68
1990	1.68	71.50	11.26	7.66	7.91
1994	1.35	75.93	9.57	5.11	8.04

Source: State Statistical Bureau, *Statistical Yearbook of China* (1990, 1995).

of bankruptcy. Tables 8.13–8.15 present further data on TVEs: the growth rate, the efficiency improvement, the share of total industrial production, and the proportion of selected products produced by TVEs.

8.6   Institutional Features of TVEs

The phenomenal growth of TVEs was neither planned nor expected by the Chinese central government, as publicly acknowledged by Deng Xiaoping (Y. Chen 1989). Before 1984, TVEs were known as collectively owned commune-brigade enterprises (CBEs); these were initiated in 1958 when the People's Communes were established. During the 1970s, CBEs developed alongside the increasing power of local governments; their share in GNP increased by about 1 percent annually. In 1976, at the end of the Cultural Revolution, employment in this sector had risen to 17.9 million, with about 5 percent of gross social product, or 11.2 percent of national income (Xu 1995).[9] In 1984, after the dissolution of the People's Commune system, the CBEs were renamed township-village enterprises (TVEs).[10]

As products of often spontaneous initiatives by local people over vast areas, institutional arrangements in TVEs vary a great deal. Here we outline some of the major variations. First, there are important differences between township enterprises and village enterprises. A typical village will have a population of hundreds (at most, no more than a couple of thousand). Most residents in a village have lived there for decades, and they know one another well. Kinship links are prevalent in village politics. Typical townships, on the other hand, have a population of tens of thousands. This difference in community size means differences in closeness of ties among the residents, who are the nominal owners of the firms, in methods of monitoring them, and in ways of managing them.

In a typical case, these collective owners do not have clearly defined shares as the term is normally understood. Participation in the TVE is not a decision made by the residents voluntarily and independently. Instead, their participation is determined by the fact of residence and mandated by the community government. That is, the ownership is linked with residing in the community (township or village). Leaving/joining a community means giving up/gaining ownership of the assets of the community's firms. Residence is determined either by family ties, such as parental/ marital relationship or other kinship, or by authorized migration. Legal residence is enforced by the household registration system (similar to the *propiska*, the Russian internal passport system).

In contrast to the prereform era, unauthorized migration is not now deemed illegal. But immigrants do not enjoy nominal ownership as official (or recognized) residents of the community. In this aspect, the TVEs are different from a typical producer cooperative, where all the workers enjoy ownership equally. Immigrant laborers are becoming an underclass in all developed regions. This could well become a serious social problem, since in all the developed regions with great concentrations of TVEs, immigrant workers play an important role. On the other hand, this migrant labor provides greater wage and labor force flexibility, thereby enabling better adjustment to shocks.

Second, TVEs are organized differently in different regions. Among the most successful, there are three well-recognized models: Sunan (southern Jiangsu province, the Yangtse delta); Guangdong; and Wenzhou (in southern Zhujiang province). These three regions cover a vast area with a population of about 200 million; most workers are in nonagriculture sectors and include a large number of immigrants from other regions in China.

In Sunan, which is close to Shanghai, community governments maintain a strong influence over the TVEs. TVEs began to be developed on a large scale in Sunan in the 1970s, and since the early 1980s have employed most of the labor force. About half of the richest townships and villages in China are concentrated in this region. Its TVEs produce all types of products, including automobile parts, machine tools, radios, printing equipments, textile products, plastic products, and even jewelry. The superiority of the Sunan model was unchallenged until the late 1980s, when the Wenzhou and Guangdong models appeared.

A key feature of the Wenzhou model is the important role of private ownership. Although privately owned firms are not typical TVEs, the Wenzhou model nonetheless is frequently mentioned as a special type of

TVE. Greater Wenzhou, a region with a population, of some 300,000, did not really develop TVEs until the mid-1980s, when private firms started to grow rapidly. Now Wenzhou's economy is dominated by the private sector and the per capita GDP is among the highest in China.

The Guangdong model, which refers to the TVEs in the Zhujiang delta area (southern Guangdong), is closer to the Sunan model, but has more joint ventures with foreign capital, more direct trade with Hong Kong, and more private firms. Its enterprises are prominent in high-technology sectors, such as the pharmaceutical and electronics industries. China's largest producers of air conditioners, refrigerators, automatic rice cookers, and electric fans are TVEs in this region. One of the authors visited some TVEs there and was very impressed by their scale (8,000 employees in one firm) and modern production technologies and management. A considerable fraction of the richest townships and villages in China are located there.

Predicting the future is always dangerous, especially for a process still in transition. Nevertheless, TVEs have been operating successfully for a quarter of a century, and may well be expected to continue to play a major role in the Chinese economy. But the scale of the (more successful) TVEs is likely to expand, and their ownership structure may become more akin to capitalist firms as they start to employ an increasing proportion of migrant workers. Some successful TVEs will transmute into nationwide large corporations.

TVEs have outperformed not only the state sector in China but also producer cooperatives in the West. This is due to such factors as more flexible labor arrangements; a stronger urge to save, invest, and grow; and the informal institutional arrangements outlined in the next section.

8.7   What Has Helped the Development of the TVE Sector in China?

The M-Form Structure

Under the Chinese M-form structure, local firms, including SOEs, constitute a relatively self-contained regional economic network. This regional network fosters development of the TVEs for two reasons.[11]

First, nonspecialized regional economies and the decentralized planning system have given TVEs the opportunity to grow without significantly disturbing the existing system. There are broad ranges of products that the TVEs can produce to meet local demand, and often there are sufficient local products to be supplied to TVEs as inputs. Close links between TVEs (or their predecessors, the CBEs) and local SOEs date back to the 1970s (before the reform), when the central government was promoting small industrial SOEs at the county level, and implementing its plan for the mechanization of agriculture through regional initiatives. This facilitated technology transfer from SOEs to TVEs. The underlying philosophy was to modernize without destroying the country's (rural) base, thereby avoiding the extreme urbanization of many less developed countries.

Second, the M-form structure provides strong incentives for regional governments to support the development of TVEs (e.g., for fiscal reasons). Third, the banking system in the M-form structure gives regional branches autonomous power to lend to TVEs, as long as they maintain an overall balance between deposits and lending within their region.

Informal Institutions in TVEs

The transition from a centralized system to a market system ultimately involves the creation of formal institutions, such as legal and contractual systems and property rights, that are both complex and complementary. When informal institutions exist as substitutes for such previously nonexistent formal institutions, the transition can become much easier and smoother.

A TVE is best described as a vaguely defined cooperative, essentially a communal organization without a well-defined ownership structure (Weitzman and Xu 1994). The extraordinary success of TVEs presents a severe challenge to traditional property rights' theory: Why have vaguely defined cooperatives performed so well? Does this not contradict the basic precepts of property rights' theory?

Weitzman and Xu (1994) argue that if people were previously not cooperative-minded and there is no other way to make them work cooperatively, then ownership becomes the major device for resolving conflicts or enforcing cooperation in an economic organization. However, if informal institutions exist, like those mentioned above, or other mechanisms that do not rely on formal contracts and/or property rights, then the significance of ownership in solving conflicts in economic organizations may vary. One possible mechanism for enforcing an informal relationship is through a concern for long-term reputation.

The existence of effective informal institutions has greatly helped the TVEs. These institutions include implicit contracts, both in interfirm transactions and in internal relationships, as well as other informal financial, employment, and trading arrangements. They are popular substitutes for formal rules, contracts, and ownerships. Their function is particularly important when market imperfections are severe.

Examples of areas in which informal institutions have helped TVEs include the following. First, fund-raising: TVEs within the same community, or that have good long-term relationships, can provide mutual guarantees to assist one another in getting bank loans. In Wenzhou, a popular informal financial institution among private businesses is *zuohui* (forming an informal credit union). Members of a *hui* (credit union) know each other well, and there are no written contracts among them. They contribute financial resources periodically and allot funds to members on the basis of a revolving principle and mutually agreed priority (rather like the earlier nineteenth-century British building societies).

Second, TVEs are often integrated within industry groups. Member firms of each group are related through producing one type of final product, such as automobiles, diesel engines, or computers. These groups coordinate and stabilize long-term sales and purchase relationships between member firms, promote the reputation of the group, and help member firms in raising funds. Typically, member firms of an industry group are regional firms with different ownership structures (this is related to the M-form structure). The relationship within such a group is often informal, with no binding legal contracts. Long-term reputation is what matters.

Third, TVEs often operate without formal employment contracts, which can help provide flexibility. For example, when a TVE is hit by a temporary adverse shock to supply or demand, a common practice is to shut the firm down to reduce cost. At such times, the TVE pays only a subsistence wage to its employees, usually about one-eighth of normal. This practice is usually not specified in written employment contracts.

The effectiveness and scope of informal institutions vary with circumstances. For example, informal relationships are more important and more widespread in village enterprises than in township enterprises, because of the closer relationships involved.

8.8   Major Differences Between TVEs and SOEs

In contrast to SOEs, an important feature of TVEs is that government, whether central or regional, has no financial responsibility for them. TVEs have to finance themselves, and face hard budget constraints. Major sources of financing for TVEs include funds derived from the collective assets of the community, funds raised from individuals, and borrowing from the state bank(s). Such community collective assets differ from state assets in being subject neither to state intervention nor to state protection (e.g., by direct subsidy or cheap bank loan).

In the TVE sector there are no guaranteed posts for either managers or workers (though local resident workers have priority in keeping their jobs when there are layoffs). Insolvent TVEs must either go bankrupt or be taken over (in the latter case, typically within the same community). In the "recession period" of 1989 and 1990, hundreds of thousands of TVEs went bankrupt.

Systematic empirical evidence has been reported in support of the above claims. From panel surveys of SOEs and TVEs, Hussain and Zhuang (1996) found a strong positive correlation between fixed asset investment (measured in ratio of fixed asset investment to fixed capital stock) and enterprise profitability (measured in gross profits per unit of fixed capital stock) in TVEs, but no such correlation in SOEs; they also found a strong positive correlation between current and one-year-lagged fixed investment levels in SOEs, but no such correlation in TVEs. These results suggest that TVEs' investment was mainly driven by pursuing profits. On the contrary, for SOEs, investment levels were strongly influenced by inertia, and enterprise profitability was not a major criterion. Xu and Zhuang (1996a) found that for both profit-making and loss-making enterprises, fixed investment rose at an increasing rate each year from 1986 to 1991, despite the fact that during the same period, enterprise profitability was falling dramatically.

Hussain and Zhuang (1996) provide empirical evidence of the greater flexibility to set wage and employment levels in TVEs in relation to SOEs. They found that in TVEs, employment levels showed a strongly positive correlation to output, and a negative correlation to the wage rate; wages had a strongly positive correlation to enterprise profitability (specifically, the short-run elasticity of per-employee total wages with respect to per-employee gross profits was 0.19, implying that a 1 percent increase in per-employee gross profits is associated with a 0.19 percent increase in per-employee total wages; the long-term elasticity of wages respect to gross profit was 0.31). Moreover, they found that the TVEs' current employment level was not correlated to one-year-lagged employment. In comparison, although employment in SOEs, was found to be positively correlated to outputs and negatively correlated to the wage rate, and the wage rate was positively correlated to enterprise profitability, these correlations were significantly weaker than those for TVEs (specifically, SOEs' short-run elasticity of per-employee total wages with respect to per-employee gross profits was 0.012; and the long-run elasticity was 0.018). Moreover, the current employment level was strongly correlated to one-year-lagged employment in SOEs, and this correlation was significantly higher than those reported for firms in market economies. Xu and Zhuang (1996a) found, from the same SOE sample, that employment increased even in loss-making SOEs.

8.9   Conclusions: Major Problems in the Chinese Economic System

Despite the extraordinary success of the Chinese economic reform since 1980, due partly to the institutional reasons discussed in this chapter, such as the M-form structure and informal institutions, serious problems remain. These problems are also related to the soft budget constraints in the state sector. If these are not resolved, the Chinese reform may be checked. Here we list some of the most serious problems.

Facing tough competition, during the reform period profitability in the state sector has been declining and a large number of loss-making enterprises have emerged. From 1985 to 1990, the average profit rate in state industry fell from 22.4 percent to 12.4 percent, the percentage of loss-making SOEs increased from 9.6 percent to 27.6 percent, and the share of losses in total industrial net output rose from 1.6 percent to 10 percent (State Statistical Bureau [SSB] 1993b, pp. 66, 90; 1993a, p. 437). According to more recent official figures, in the first nine months of 1995, the SOEs experienced financial losses of 41.7 billion yuan (£3.2 billion), an increase of 18.8 percent over the same period in 1994. Moreover, triangular debt (long chains of unpaid and overdue debts between enterprises) swelled to 750 billion yuan at the end of August 1995, up from 630 billion yuan at the start of the year (*Financial Times*, Oct, 20, 1995, p. 6). A large number of SOEs are insolvent. A tentative estimate is that if the bankruptcy law were to be vigorously enforced, about 10 percent of SOEs (about 11,000) would go bankrupt.

Meanwhile, the government has subsidized SOE losses through many channels. The most common form of subsidy before the reform was direct subsidy, which used up a sizable proportion of the goverment's total revenues (see table 8.16). Since the mid-1980s, loans from the state banks have gradually replaced direct subsidies as the major instruments to bail out loss-making SOEs. That is why, in table 8.16, subsidies are declining, particularly in the early 1990s, while increasing losses were experienced by SOEs. Unfortunately, we have no data on subsidies in the form of bank loans. However, most insolvent SOEs continue to operate and to accumulate losses.

Table 8.16
Financial subsidies to loss-making SOEs, 1986–94

Year	Subsidies to loss-making enterprises (billion yuan)	Subsidy as % of government fiscal revenue	Subsidy as % of GDP
1986	32.48	14.37	3.18
1987	37.64	15.89	3.15
1988	44.65	16.99	2.99
1989	59.89	20.32	3.54
1990	57.89	17.48	3.12
1991	51.02	14.13	2.36
1992	44.50	10.76	1.67
1993	41.13	8.08	1.19
1994	36.62	7.02	0.81

Source: State Statistical Bureau, *Statistical Yearbook of China* (1995).

Theoretically, it is well known that the lack of a credible bankruptcy threat in the state sector will have deep impacts on the behavior of all the SOEs, regardless of whether they are profit-makers or loss-makers. Such impacts can take the form of overinvestment, poor responses to market signals, and so on (Kornai 1980, 1992; Dewatripont and Maskin 1995). Empirical evidence based on a sample survey provided by Xu and Zhuang (1996a) shows that the SOEs had indeed overinvested. Moreover, their investments had no correlation with their profitability. In the worst loss-making SOEs there were serious problems in management—such as poor responses to market changes, slowness in updating products, and labor hoarding—that have caused losses. Although incentive schemes for workers in regional SOEs have effectively increased profits or reduced losses, their impact has not been strong enough to offset the negative effect of the soft budget constraints.

The Chinese government has identified the enforcement of bankruptcy, particularly in the state sector, as a central issue in the current reform. Although a bankruptcy law was passed by the People's Congress in 1986, its implementation has never gone beyond the experimental stage. A 1993 official investigation of SOEs in five provinces that account for more than one-quarter of the total number of SOEs in China (and were responsible for more than one-third of the total losses in the state sector) found that since the bankruptcy law was officially implemented, 948 bankruptcy cases had come before the courts, about 80 percent of them between 1991 and 1993. Most of those bankrupt SOEs had more than 1,000 employees; the largest had 3,000.

There are many obstacles to the full implementation of the bankruptcy law. First, there are problems in financial institutions. Creditors prefer not to let SOEs go bankrupt, since if a loss-making SOE keeps running, the state may help and the losses may not be materialized. According to an estimate by four Chinese specialized banks, nearly 400 billion yuan, about 16.7 percent of China's 2,400 billion yuan in loans to the state sector, were nonperforming (Joint Enterprises Bankruptcy Investigation Group 1993). Such losses have been handled through the rescheduling of debts (47 percent), government subsidies (7 percent), renegotiation of contracts with the government (5 percent), use of previously accumulated profits (36 percent), and other means (5 percent). Once an SOE goes bankrupt, the creditors will suffer a definite loss. Indeed, according to this study, in almost all the bankruptcy cases it was the *debtors*, not the creditors, who applied for bankruptcy.

A second problem is that many profitable SOEs have served as guarantors for other SOEs in obtaining bank loans, or government agencies have served as guarantors for enterprises under their control. As a result, the bankruptcy of loss-making SOEs may trigger a chain reaction.

Finally, a formidable barrier against enforcing the bankruptcy law is the lack, in China as in Russia, of a social safety net for laid-off workers. Consequently, at present, before an enterprise declares bankruptcy, the government tries to arrange a takeover by another SOE. Until this is done, no bankruptcy application can be handled by a court. If no willing SOE is found, the proceedings may simply drag on. Political concern over unemployment caused by bankruptcy is paramount among Chinese government officials. Zhu Rongji, the deputy prime minister responsible for economic reform (the star of the Chinese economy, according to the Western media), admitted this to visiting Western economists[12] and joked, "If any of you were able to solve our bankruptcy problem without turning workers out onto the street, I would recommend you for a Nobel Prize."

Given the SOEs' economic inefficiency and/or the low quality of their products, together with competition from the nonstate sector and from imports, their former surpluses have melted away, and to an increasing extent have been replaced by losses. This has happened in China just as in other economies in transition (McKinnon 1993). Since the central government had relied on such surpluses as its revenue base, this led to a swift erosion of revenue as a percentage of GDP, no less severe in China than in the EEFSU.

Another problem is the regional decentralization of the fiscal system. This is based not on types of taxes and expenditures but on the level of

Table 8.17
Central and local government expenditures and revenues, 1980–94 (% of GNP)

	Expenditures			Revenue		
	Total	Central	Local	Total	Central	Local
1980	26.8	14.4	12.4	24.3	4.7	19.3
1985	21.6	9.8	11.8	21.8	8.3	13.5
1990	19.6	7.8	11.8	18.7	7.7	11.0
1992	18.1	7.5	10.6	17.0	6.8	10.3
1993	16.8	6.2	10.6	16.2	5.4	10.8
1994	11.8	6.5	5.1	12.9	3.9	9.0

Source: State Statistical Bureau, *Statistical Yearbook of China* (1995).
Notes: Definitions of fiscal revenue in China are not always identical to those used in Western countries, but the broad trends shown above are, we believe, reliable.
  Before 1993, revenues of each year include domestic and foreign borrowing. Expenditures before 1993 include repayment of principal and interest on domestic and foreign borrowing.

administrative control. The central government collects taxes only from centrally controlled entities. Each regional government is responsible for collecting tax revenues within its region. The regional government then turns over a proportion of that revenue to the central government. Every year the central government has to negotiate with regional governments for the division of regional tax revenues. This system has greatly weakened the central government's control over fiscal policy and revenue. Since the late 1980s, the central government's fiscal position has deteriorated, both in terms of the ratio to GDP and in terms of its share of total fiscal revenue.[13] As a result of this deterioration and the perceived need to continue subsidizing the loss-making SOEs, government expenditures on education, scientific research, interprovincial highways, railways, and other items have been held down in order to keep the overall fiscal deficit within reasonable limits. Both the expenditures and the revenue of the central government, as a percentage of GDP, have fallen by about a third since the late 1980s (see table 8.17).

  A further serious consequence of the decline of the central government's fiscal position has been a great increase in inequality across regions. By the early 1990s, regional inequality in China was claimed by some scholars to be among the worst in the world[14] (Wang 1995). This trend could be politically threatening. Recently the Chinese government has announced measures, such as reallocations of funds and tax privileges, to try to reverse it.

  Despite holding down desirable expenditures (e.g., on education), the weakness of fiscal revenues has led the government to run overall deficits

Table 8.18
Government budget balance, 1985–93 (% of GDP)

	Current budget balance					Overall surplus/deficit				
	1985	1990	1991	1992	1993	1985	1990	1991	1992	1993
Russia	n.a.	n.a.	n.a.	−21.6	−5.1	n.a.	n.a.	n.a.	−25.8	−8.3
Poland	n.a.	6.1	−4.6	−5.1	0.4	n.a.	2.5	−6.6	−7.6	−1.9
Hungary	6.5	5.1	3.9	1.6	−1.1	−1.1	0.5	−2.3	−5.6	−6.4
China	7.1	2.5	1.9	1.2	2.2	−0.5	−2.1	−2.4	−2.5	−2.1

Source: World Bank, *Trends in Developing Economies* (1992, 1994).

in recent years, albeit nowhere near as large as in many countries in EEFSU. The central government's deficit stood at 2.6 percent of GDP at the end of 1994 (see table 8.18).

The government's deficits are calculated exclusive of the losses of loss-making SOEs. Since the authorities have not been willing, for the most part, to close them, such SOEs are on a soft budget constraint. They meet both their operating losses and their new investment expenditures by borrowing from the banking system.

Meanwhile, the banking system has also been adjusting in this transition period. The first stage, around the mid-1980s, was to give the four huge commercial banks—the Industrial and Commercial Bank of China, the Agricultural Bank of China, the People's Construction Bank of China, and the Bank of China (the export/import bank)—more independence from the People's Bank of China, and some greater latitude for competition. But they, too, remained SOEs with a soft budget, which they needed for survival. As key elements in the central planning system, their asset portfolio had consisted largely of loans to SOEs. With a large proportion of such SOEs becoming loss-making, the related loans became non-performing. As noted earlier, many SOEs, without a credible bankruptcy threat, have tried to invest and grow their way out of their current problems.

Moreover, that same lack of a hard budget constraint meant that the SOEs' behavior was relatively impervious to increases in interest rates. Thus the capitalist technique of varying interest rates to (bank) borrowers in order to control credit expansion, investment booms, monetary increases, and inflation was not seen as practicable in China. Instead, the control method was quantitative credit restriction. This method, however, provides room for political pressure, favoritism, and corruption. In general, the massive SOEs have had much more political pull than the nascent cooperatives and TVEs, so that such quantitative methods reinforced the misallocation of capital and perpetuated a system in which the least efficient sector of the economy, the SOEs, did most of the investment.

For borrowers other than SOEs, the problems of obtaining credit, especially during periods of restriction, have in part been mitigated by the development of a dual-track system in banking, with a very rapid growth of rural and urban credit cooperatives, as well as other nonbank financial institutions (insurance companies, investment and trust institutions, etc.), which have been able to some extent to avoid the centrally imposed quantitative credit controls. Hence, the efficacy of quantitative controls is being eroded. Moreover, insofar as the credit controls are redirected to bite at the SOEs, this has typically led simply to a countervailing expansion of intercompany debt (unpaid bills), the notorious triangular debt.

Meanwhile, the authorities have been pressing on with reforms to the laws and constitution of both the central bank (Law of the People's Bank of China, adopted March 18, 1995) and the commercial banks (Commercial Banking Law, adopted May 10, 1995). The latter is intended to provide a basis for the (four main) commercial banks to become competitive, profit-maximizing entities. But they cannot become such while they are stuck with so many bad loans. At one stage in 1994 there was discussion as to whether a new group of banks, called state policy banks, would be established; they would not only extend longer-term "policy loans" but also might take over the deadweight of existing bad or nonperforming loans from the state commercial banks (Li and Ma 1994). Although these development banks have, in fact, been set up, their executives, not surprisingly, have refused to let them become a dumping ground for existing bad loans. In any case, removing existing bad loans from the commercial banks will not solve their problems unless they can prevent a buildup of further bad loans in future, which cannot be assured under the present system.

Although there has not been significant monetary financing of the central government in recent years, the erosion of its tax base, and the need for the central government to take over and extend the social safety net from its current (limited) provision by SOEs, makes the fiscal position fragile. Meanwhile, a combination of good prospects for growth, soft budgets for SOEs, and a hope that enterprises can grow out of their problems has led to enormously high investment ratios and an insatiable desire for bank credit, much of which is largely impervious to interest-rate adjustments. This is aided and abetted by local governments, which encourage their SOEs to invest as a way of expanding their own overall tax base, income, and power. China, which must be one of the few countries to regard its investment ratio as too large, looks for policy measures to reduce it. The Chinese government admitted that, second, more and stronger efforts are needed to continue to control the total size of fixed asset investment. Currently, the size of the social fixed asset investment is still too large and it is hard to bring down investment rate to the appropriate level around 30 percent.

8.10 Appendix

Table 8.A
Estimates of augmented production functions (dependent variable $=$ log real gross output)

	Local SOEs	Central SOEs
Constant	0.0142	0.0006
	(0.0119)	(0.0185)
Log per-employee bonus	0.1673*	0.0516
	(0.0677)	(0.0726)
Log labor input	0.3757*	0.3948*
	(0.0799)	(0.1652)
Log capital stock	0.0604*	0.1040
	(0.0193)	(0.0583)
Log intermediate input	0.3116*	0.5348*
	(0.0564)	(0.1406)
Wald test for joint significance	138.21	67.33
	(4)	(4)
Wald test for joint sig. time dummy	41.65	11.35
	(4)	(4)
2nd-order serial correlation test	−1.040	1.202
	(318)	(162)
Sargan test for instrument validity	16.04	13.37
	(11)	(11)

* Significant at 5% or below.
Notes: Standard errors in parentheses.
   The equations were estimated by the generalized moment method (GMM) developed by Arellano and Bond (1991).
   In all three equations, log per-employee bonus was treated as endogenous. Instrument set includes all lags on log per-employee bonus from $t - 2$ back, log provincial per-employee bonus/wage at t, and current values of all other explanatory Cobb-Douglas production functions.

Acknowledgment

Some material in this chapter is drawn from Goodhart and Xu (1996).

Notes

Chapter 1:   Why So Much Pain? An Overview

1. In China, agriculture was collective from 1956 to 1961 and from 1966 to 1978; in Poland it was always mainly private.

2. For systematic evidence, see A. Aslund et al. (1996).

3. See also table 3.2.

4. For details on individual countries, see EBRD (1996).

5. See Sachs and Woo (1994).

6. These again originated from local initiatives.

Chapter 3:   Inflation: Causes, Consequences, and Cures

1. See Gomulka (1994).

2. See IMF (1992).

3. These are the two standard components in the literature on transactions demand for money. See Goldfeld and Sichel (1990).

4. See Cagan (1956).

5. See IMF staff country reports and, for Russia, *Russian Economic Trends* (1992−) for parallel market exchange-rate data.

6. Other authors have drawn similar conclusions from this simple relation. See, e.g., de Melo et al. (1995); World Bank (1996); EBRD (1996); Sachs and Warner (1995); and Fischer et al. (1996).

7. Havrylyshyn (1994), p. 429.

8. See IMF et al. (1991).

9. Gaidar (1995), pp. 42−43.

10. This leader could still choose high inflation as his preferred policy, as was the case, for instance, in Ukraine.

11. See later issues of *Ukrainian Economic Trends*.

12. It was not at all clear that Kuchma would have chosen stabilization in any case. He had been prime minister in Ukraine during a period of high inflation, and in the election campaign he did not advocate stabilization or radical reform.

Chapter 4:   Privatization and Restructuring in Central and Eastern Europe

1. In terms of outsiders, it may be useful to distinguish between foreign and domestic owners, because the former can probably bring capital, technology, and managerial know-how to business more effectively than can the latter. This latter distinction is not referred to in figure 4.1.

2. This arises from our particular characterization of state ownership as an absence of governance over managers and workers. This may be accurate in the post-Communist context, but in general is clearly not correct. More generally, the self-management literature suggests that employee-owned firms will have serious problems of underinvestment, possibly more so than state-owned firms.

Chapter 5:   Banks, Restructuring, and Enterprise Reform

1. Moreover, for cash-strapped governments, the opportunity cost of funds is likely to exceed the costs of funds to, in particular, foreign firms, adding a further argument to the restructuring case for troubled companies.

2. At a later stage two specialized banks (BGZ, an agricultural bank, and PKO BP, the main savings bank) were included in the scheme.

Chapter 7:   Why China Grew

1. For example, Chen et al. (1992); Lin et al. (1994); McMillan and Naughton (1992); and Rawski (1995).

2. The case against this new wisdom from a comparative perspective has been made in Aslund et al. (1996); Sachs and Woo (1994); and Woo (1994).

3. We of course do not deny that stumbling around for solutions sometimes works, but we are inclined to believe that most times it causes needless suffering and is inferior to actions guided by economic theory. Sachs and Woo (1997) call EPR the experimentalist school and the anti-EPR view the convergence school. This is because EPR attributes China's successes to the discovery of new economic institutions, and the anti-EPR view attributes them to the convergence of China's economic institutions to standard capitalist market institutions.

4. The official statistics recognize three types of TVE registrations: township- and village-operated (*xiangban*), joint-operated (*liangban*), and individual-operated (*getihu*). Most academic discussions implicitly identify TVEs with *xiangban*, and this is why TVEs are commonly referred to as collective-owned even though *getihu* are clearly private in nature. See Sachs and Woo (1997) for discussion of the TVE phenomenon.

5. Strictly speaking, the 1984 reclassification that transferred industrial activities within agricultural production units from "agriculture" to "industry" renders comparison prior to that

year invalid. The COE share of gross industrial output went from 30 percent in 1984 to 38 percent in 1993, and the share of private corporations, individual-operated enterprises, and joint ventures, from 1 percent to 19 percent.

6. "Tariff Cuts Implemented Smoothly," *China Daily*, Sept. 2, 1996.

7. The "law of exchange value" is from the Marxian (labor-based) theory of value; and "commodity economy" refers to an economy in the early stage of economic development, where the emphasis should be on increasing production rather than on equality, so that concessions to market incentives may be necessary.

8. For example, on January 1, 1994, the currency was made convertible for most current-account transactions, and a new market-compatible tax system was introduced.

9. Most service activities are not counted in net material product, the aggregate income measure used in socialist economies.

10. This argument was made independently in Fan (1994). Agence France Presse (Dec. 7, 1993) reported Agriculture Minister Liu Jiang as saying that there were 150 million excess farm workers (out of a rural labor force of 450 million).

11. Chow (1993) found the value of MPL in 1978 to be 63 yuan in agriculture, 1,027 yuan in industry, 452 yuan in construction, 739 yuan in transportation, and 1,809 yuan in commerce. Figures are expressed in 1952 output values.

12. "Irresistible Force," *Far Eastern Economic Review* (Apr. 4, 1996).

13. This figure represents the sum of the official estimate of 80 million who moved out of their home districts and the 20 million who moved within their home districts.

14. U.S. national income grew 3.85 percent annually in 1948–69, and TFP growth was 1.75 percent; labor reallocation from the farm sector accounted for 0.23 percentage points.

15. In a study on enterprises in three coastal provinces, Perkins (1996, table 8) found that for 1980–92, TFP increased by 23 percent for nonexporting SOEs, 44 percent for exporting SOEs, 47.2 percent for nonexporting non-SOEs, and 117 percent for exporting non-SOEs.

16. The amount of remitted profit was individually negotiated periodically.

17. "Decision of the CPC Central Committee on Issues Concerning the Establishment of a Socialist Market Economic Structure," supplement to *China Daily*, Nov. 17, 1993.

18. "State Set to Pilot Industry Overhaul," *China Daily*, Aug. 22, 1996. There is a translation error in the article, which reported "production-sales ratio" when it should be "sales-production ratio."

19. See Jefferson et al. (1995) This is an update of Jefferson et al. (1992), which estimated them to be 2.4 percent and 4.6 percent, respectively. The much lower TFP growth for TVEs is the result of recognizing that the official TVE output data are exaggerated. See Woo (1996).

20. The change in output price on the left-hand side of the equation was smaller than the actual change, and the change in input price on the right-hand side was larger than the actual change.

21. This defense of a declining VAD is logically sounder than the claims in Jefferson et al. (1994) and Naughton (1994) that the declining VAD merely reflects that input prices have risen more than output prices—which is a necessary but not a sufficient condition for a declining VAD.

22. Roughly speaking, the Input-Output Table data are constructed by adjusting the Industrial Census data to make them conform with aggregate flow data. The Industrial Census data may understate actual value-added because of overstatement of costs by enterprise personnel, in order to divert capital income to themselves.

23. Naughton identified it explicitly for Groves et al. (1995a); we assume that it must be the same for Groves et al. (1994) because the same deflation method and sample were used.

24. They found indications that the importance of sales decreased over time while that of profits increased.

25. So total profits equaled the sum of market profits plus rent.

26. No correction was made for capital accumulation by the firm relative to capital accumulation by the industry.

27. "Record Loss Suffered by State Sector," *South China Morning Post International Weekly*, June 29, 1996.

28. This viewpoint was endorsed by Naughton (1995); Jefferson and Rawski (1994, pp. 52–53, 54–55); and K. Chen et al. (1992, p. 212).

29. A regression of the change in profit rate on the change in degree of domination yields an insignificant relation between the two variables: a coefficient of -31.2 with a t-statistic of -0.6 and an R^2 of 0.3.

30. This report has been published in English in Reynolds (1987). *Tigaisuo* was disbanded when Zhao Ziyang was ousted as Communist Party secretary after the 1989 Tiananmen Square demonstrations.

31. Thus we disagree with Putterman (1995) that Woo, Fan et al. (1994) had been refuted by Jefferson et al. Jefferson et al. (1994, p. 240) criticized Woo, Fan et al. for using a survey of urban residents to calculate the indirect income of SOE workers because the data included "earnings from second jobs, royalties, lecture fees, and transfer payments." This would be a valid criticism had they not thought that Woo, Fan et al. were using table 8 in Zhao (1992) when they were actually using table 9. The source of table 8 was an urban survey, and the source of table 9 was the bank records of SOE transactions. The bank records certainly would not contain information on the typical worker's income from royalties and lecture fees.

32. "State Asset Drain Must End," *China Daily*, Dec. 13, 1995. See also "State Toughens Stand to Protect Its Possessions," *China Daily*, June 2, 1995; "Asset Checks Can Stop Fiddles," *China Daily*, June 7, 1995; "Market Investigated for Losing State Assets," *China Daily*, June 2, 1995.

33. "China City Turns into a Prototype for Privatization," *Wall Street Journal*, June 10, 1995.

34. "Heilongjiang Puts 200 Firms on the Block," *China Daily*, June 7, 1996.

Chapter 8: Why China Grew: The Role of Decentralization

1. In this chapter we use the terms "regional government" and "local government" synonymously. Regional governments include governments at the levels of province, municipality, prefecture, county, township, and village.

2. M-form and U-form organizations were first discussed as organizational forms of multiproduct modern corporations (Chandler 1962; Williamson, 1975). M-form stands for multi-

divisional form, and U-form for unitary structure. In an M-form corporation, headquarters controls divisions. Each division is responsible for one brand of final product (e.g., the Oldsmobile division of General Motors) or the business in one region (e.g., a regional division of Sears). Complementary tasks for producing a brand product are under the control of the division. In contrast, in a U-form organization, the headquarters controls functional departments, such as engineering, manufacturing, and sales. Each department within the U-form performs one specialized function; these functions are often complementary, such as manufacturing and sales. Headquarters' involvement is necessary for coordinating complementary functions in the departments. The M-form firm emerged in the 1920s, and has been the predominant organizational form of large businesses ever since.

3. The relative roles and powers of the central, regional, and local authorities have fluctuated over the years (e.g., from one five-year plan to the next). For details, see Zhou (1984).

4. The central government's regional policies are not uniform, thereby making regional competition less fair. But given that competition occurs mainly among similar regions (e.g., coastal regions mainly compete with coastal regions, and interior regions with interior regions), any resulting trouble is limited. Another factor that may affect competition is the price system. The Chinese price reform of the late 1970s to the early 1980s began by introducing a dual price system, particularly for SOE outputs. Prices were set by government agents responsible for SOE outputs within the planning quota, and by the markets for outputs above this quota. But only a few hundred products were rigorously priced under this dual system. Thus, for most products either there were more or less nationwide official prices, or there were market prices. Next, once the dual price system was introduced in the early 1980s, the role of official prices declined rapidly. By the early 1990s, official prices for most products were merged with market prices (i.e., dual prices disappeared). Even where official prices still operated, the proportion of products traded under these prices became so small that the dual price system is no longer a significant factor.

5. The incentive effect of bonus payment was studied by estimating a Cobb-Douglas production function augmented to include a bonus variable,

$$q_{it} = \alpha_i + \alpha_t + \delta e_{it} + \Sigma \beta_j x_{it} + \varepsilon_{it},$$

where q_{it} is log output of the ith SOE at the tth period; e_{it} is log per-employee bonuses; x_{it} is a vector of conventional inputs including log labor, log net fixed capital, and log intermediate input; α_i is a constant representing the effects of those variables peculiar to the ith individual SOE but remaining unchanged over time (firm-specific fixed effects); α_t is a constant representing the effects of those variables peculiar to the tth time period but the same for all SOEs (time-specific fixed effects); and ε_{it} is a disturbance term capturing all other shocks to the productivity of the ith SOE, assumed to be serially uncorrelated. δ is the elasticity of output with respect to per-employee bonus. A positive δ implies that the bonus payment is effective in improving productivity.

This equation is fitted to subsamples of central and regional SOEs by using the GMM estimation method. To make sure that the causality goes from incentive pay to productivity, log per-employee bonus is instrumented by its lagged values at $t-2$ and backward, and current value of log provincial mean per-employee bonus (external information).

6. The estimated annual growth rate of TFP for all SOEs, 1.33 percent, is well within the range of the existing empirical estimates in the literature. For a survey on TFP growth in Chinese state industry in general, see Jefferson and Rawski (1994).

7. An important component of China's reform is the establishment of Special Economic Zones with the explicit purpose of experimentation.

8. However, the bottom-up approach has its own limitations (e.g., in the reforms of the tax system and the financial system, which we shall discuss later).

9. GDP statistics are not available before 1978. In general, gross social product is about double GDP, and national income is about 10 percent lower than GDP.

10. For more detailed discussions of the historical background and institutional features of TVEs, see Xu (1995) and Byrd and Lin (1990).

11. An econometric study of several hundred local regions in China finds that the size of the state sector is positively correlated with the growth of the TVE sector in the early stage of the reform (Wei and Lian 1994).

12. One of the authors was at this meeting in Diaoyutai State Guesthouse, Beijing, in August 1994.

13. The ratios of central revenues to local revenues and to GNP reached a low at the end of the 1970s as a consequence of the Cultural Revolution. They then rose again until the mid-1980s, since when they have again been declining.

14. Regional inequality may be compared using the following metric:

$$Vw = \sqrt{\frac{\sum_{i}^{N}(X_i - \bar{X})^2 \frac{P_i}{P}}{\bar{X}}},$$

where

$X_i = $ GNP per capita of region i

$\bar{X} = $ national GNP per capita

$P_i = $ population of region i

$P = $ total population.

Using this metric, Wang calculated the Vw of China in 1991 to be 46.3, when using data from all 30 provinces, as in note 6, and 33.6 when excluding the three main cities, Beijing, Shanghai, and Tianjin. These figures may be compared with the 1969 figure of 39 for Brazil, a country with well-known problems of regional inequality. Typical values for regional inequality in the 1950s for Western countries were: United States, 21.8; United Kingdom, 7.4; Canada, 19.9; Italy, 36.3; the Netherlands, 12.3; France, 28.9; Australia, 5.8. All the data are taken from Wang (1995).

References

Aghion, P., and Blanchard, O. (1993). "On the Speed of Transition in Central Europe." Working Paper no. 6., London: EBRD.

Aghion, P., Hart, O., and Moore, J. (1994). "Improving Bankruptcy Procedures." Discussion Paper no. 142. Cambridge, MA: Harvard Law School.

Aizenman, J. (1989). "The Competitive Externalities and the Optimal Seigniorage." Working Paper no. 2937. Cambridge, Mass.: NBER.

Alesina, A., and Drazen, A. (1991). "Why Are Stabilizations Delayed?" *American Economic Review* 81(5): 1170–1188.

Arellano, M., and Bond, S. (1991). "Some Tests of Specification for Panel Data: Monte Carlo Evidence and an Application to Employment Equations." *Review of Economic Statistics* 58: 277–297.

Arrow, K. J. (1962). "The Economic Implications of Learning by Doing." *Review of Economic Studies* 29: 155–173.

Aslund, A. (1995). *How Russia Became a Market Economy*. Washington, DC.: Brookings Institution.

Aslund, A., Boone, P., and Johnson, S. (1996). "How to Stabilise: Lessons from Post-Communist Countries." *Brookings Papers on Economic Activity* 81(1): 217–314.

Bai, C., Li, D., and Wang, Y. (1996). "Why Can Productivity Analysis Be Misleading for Gauging State Enterprise Performance?" Boston College, Economics Department. (Mimeo).

Balcerowicz, L. (1995). *Capitalism, Socialism, Transformation*. Budapest: Central European University Press.

Barbone, L., Marchetti, D., Jr., and Paternostro, S. (1996). "Ownership Transformation and Economic Performance. An Analysis of Poland's Industrial Performance in the Early 1990s." Washington, DC: World Bank. (Mimeo).

Barbone, L., and Zalduendo, J. (1996). "EU Accession and Economic Growth: The Challenge for Central and Eastern European Countries." Washington, DC: World Bank. (Mimeo).

Barr, N. (1994). *Labour Markets and Social Policy in Central and Eastern Europe*. Washington, DC: World Bank.

Barro, R., and Sala-i-Martin, X. (1995). *Economic Growth*. New York: McGraw-Hill.

Beleva, I., Jackman, R., and Nenova, M. (1995). "The Labour Market in Bulgaria." In S. Commander and F. Coricelli (eds.), *Unemployment, Restructuring and the Labour Market in East Europe and Russia*. Washington, DC: World Bank.

Belka, M. (1995). "Financial Restructuring of Banks and Enterprises in Poland: A Timely and Proper Instrument of Sanitizing Enterprise Finance." (Mimeo).

Belka, M., Estrin, S., Schaffer, M., and Singh, I. (1994a). "Enterprise Adjustment in Poland: Evidence from a Survey of 200 Firms." Centre for Economic Performance Working Paper no. 658. London School of Economics.

Belka, M., Schaffer, M., Estrin, S., and Singh, I. (1994b). "Evidence from a Survey of State-Owned, Privatized and Emerging Private Firms." Washington, DC: World Bank. (Mimeo).

Bell, M., Khor, H., and Kochhar, K. (1993). "China at the Threshold of a Market Economy." Occasional Paper no. 107. Washington, DC: IMF.

Berg, A. (1995). "Supply and Demand Factors in Output Decline in Central and Eastern Europe." In R. Holzmann, J. Gacs, and G. Winckler (eds.), *Output Decline in Eastern Europe*. Dordrecht; Boston: Kluwer Academic Publishers.

Berg, A., and Blanchard, O. (1994). "Stabilization and Transition: Poland, 1990–1991." In O. J. Blanchard, A. Froot, and J. Sachs (eds.), *The Transition in Eastern Europe*. Vol. 1. Chicago: University of Chicago Press/NBER.

Berglof, E. (1997). "Boardrooms: Reforming Corporate Governance in Europe." *Economic Policy*, vol. 24. (Apr): 91–123. Centre for Economic Policy Research.

Bhaduri, A., and Laski, K. (1992). "The Relevance of Michal Kalecki Today." Vienna: Institute for Comparative Economic Studies. (Mimeo).

Blanchard, O. (1991). "Notes on the Speed of Transition, Unemployment and Growth in Poland." (Mimeo).

Blanchard, O. (1997). *The Economics of Post-Communist Transition*. Oxford: Clarendon Press.

Blanchard, O., et al. (1991). *Reform in Eastern Europe*. Cambridge, MA: MIT Press.

Blasi, J., Kroumova, M., and Kruse, D. (1997). *Kremlin Capitalism*. Ithaca, NY: Cornell University Press.

Boardman, A., and Vining, A. (1989). "Ownership and Performance in Competitive Environments." *Journal of Law and Economics* 31(1): 1–33.

Boeri, T. (1993). "Labour Market Flows and the Persistence of Unemployment in Central and Eastern Europe." Paper presented at OECD Workshop on "The Persistence of Unemployment in Central and Eastern European Countries." Paris.

Boeri, T. (1994). "'Transitional' Unemployment." *Economics of Transition* 2(1): 1–25.

Boeri, T. (1996). "Unemployment Outflows and the Scope of Active Labour Market Policies in Central and Eastern Europe." In *Lessons from Labour Market Policies in the Transition Countries*. Paris: OECD.

Boeri, T., and Burda, M. (1996). "Active Labour Market Policies, Job Matching and the Czech Miracle." *European Economic Review* 40 (3–5): 795–803.

Bofinger, P. (1994). "Macroeconomic Transformation in Eastern Europe: The Role of Monetary Policy Reconsidered." In H. Herr, S. Tober, and A. Westphal (eds.), *Macroeconomic Problems of Transformation*. Aldershot, Hants, England; Brookfield Vt. USA: Edward Elgar.

Borensztein, E., Demekas, D., and Ostry, J. (1993). "An Empirical Analysis of the Output Declines in Three Eastern European Countries." *IMF Staff Papers* 40(1): 1–31.

Bos, D. (1990). *Privatisation: A Theoretical Treatment*. Oxford: Clarendon Press.

Bouin, O. (forthcoming). "Financial Discipline and State Enterprise Reform in China in the 1990s." In O. Bouin, F. Coricelli, and F. Lemoine (eds.), *Different Paths to a Market Economy: China and European Economies in Transition*. Paris: OECD.

Boycko, M., Schleifer, A., and Vishny, R. (1995). *Privatizing Russia*. Cambridge, MA: MIT Press.

Brada, J. (1996). "Privatization Is Transition—Or Is It?" *Journal of Economic Perspectives* 10(2): 45–66.

Broadman, H. (1995). "Meeting the Challenge of Chinese Enterprise Reform." Discussion Paper no. 283. Washington, DC: World Bank.

Brown, A., Ickes, B., and Ryterman, R. (1993). "The Myth of Monopoly." Policy Research Paper. Washington, DC: World Bank.

Bruno, M., and Easterly, W. (1995). "Inflation Crises and Long Run Growth." Working Paper no. 5209. Washington, DC: NBER.

Byrd, W., and Lin, Q. (1990). *China's Rural Industry: Structure, Development and Reform*. Oxford: Oxford University Press.

Cagan, P. (1956). "The Monetary Dynamics of Hyperinflation." In M. Friedman (ed.), *Studies in the Quantity Theory of Money*. Chicago: University of Chicago Press.

Calvo, G., and Coricelli, F. (1992). "Output Collapse in Eastern Europe: The Role of Credit." Working Paper 92/64. Washington, DC: IMF.

Calvo, G., and Coricelli, F. (1993). "Output Collapse in Eastern Europe." *IMF Staff Papers* 40(1): 32–52.

Canning, A., and Hare, P. (1994). "The Privatization Process—Economic and Political Aspects of the Hungarian approach." In S. Estrin (ed.), *Privatization in Central and Eastern Europe*. Harlow, Essex: Longman.

Chandler, A. (1962). *Strategy and Structure*. Cambridge, Mass.: MIT Press.

Charemza, W. (1993). "East European Transformation: The Supply Side." In K. Z. Poznanski (ed.), *Stabilization and Privatization in Poland*. Boston: Kluwer Academic Publishers.

Chen, A. (1994). "Chinese Industrial Structure in Transition: The Emergence of Stock-offering Firms." *Comparative Economic Studies* 36(4): 1–19.

Chen, A. (1996). "An Inertial Reform of China's State-Owned Enterprises: The Case of Chongqing." Terre Haute: Indiana State University. Economics Department. (Mimeo).

Chen, K., Jefferson, G., and Singh, I. (1992). "Lessons from China's Economic Reform." *Journal of Comparative Economics* 16(2): 201–225.

Chen, Y. (1989). "Tongyi sixiang jiji tiaozheng, cujin xiangzhen qiye chixu xietiao jiankang fazhan." (Unifying thoughts in policies to promote TVEs' growth in a sustained, balanced, and healthy way) *Zhongguo xiangzhen qiye* (Chinese Township-Village Enterprise) 9:1–8.

Chow, G. (1993). "Capital Formation and Economic Growth in China." *Quarterly Journal of Economics* 108(3): 809–842.

Claessens, S., and Djanjov, S. (1997). "Politicians and Firms." Washington, DC: World Bank. (Mimeo).

Commander, S., and Coricelli, F. (eds.) (1995). *Unemployment, Restructuring and the Labour Market in East Europe and Russia.* Washington, DC: World Bank.

Commander, S., McHale, J., and Yemtsov, R. (1995). "Russia." S. Commander and F. Coricelli (eds.), *Unemployment, Restructuring and the Labour Market in East Europe and Russia.* Washington, DC: World Bank.

Commander, S., and Tolstopiatenko, A. (1997). "Unemployment, Restructuring and the Pace of Transition." In S. Zecchini (ed.), *Lessons from the Economic Transition: Central and Eastern Europe in the 1990s.* Dordrecht; Boston: Kluwer Academic Publishers and Paris: OECD.

Cordoba, J. (1994). "Ten Lessons from Mexico's Economic Reform." (Mimeo).

Country Economic Memorandums. Washington, DC: World Bank.

CS First Boston. (1995). *A Guide to Russia Debt Markets.* London: CS First Boston.

Czyzewski, A., Orlowski, W., and Zienkowski, L. (1995). "A Comparative Study of Causes of Output Decline in Transition Economies: Preliminary Results for Poland." Warsaw: Research Centre for Economic and Statistical Studies of the Central Statistical Office and the Academy of Sciences. (Mimeo).

Davis, S., and Haltiwanger, J. (1990). "Gross Job Creation and Destruction: Microeconomic Evidence and Macroeconomic Implications." *NBER Macroeconomics Annual* 5: 123–168.

Davis, S., and Haltiwanger, J. (1992). "Gross Job Creation, Gross Job Destruction, and Employment Reallocation." *Quarterly Journal of Economics* 107(3): 819–863.

de Melo, M., Denizer, C., and Gelb, A. (1996). *From Plan to Market: Patterns of Transition.* Washington, DC: World Bank.

de Melo, M., and Gelb, A. (1996). "Transition to Date: A Comparative Overview." Washington, DC: World Bank. (Mimeo).

Denison, E. (1974). *Accounting for United States Economic Growth 1929–1969.* Washington, DC: Brookings Institution.

Dewatripont, M., and Maskin, E. (1995). "Credit and Efficiency in Centralized and Decentralized Economies." *Review of Economic Studies* (October).

Earle, J., and Estrin, S. (1996), "Employee Ownership in Transition." In R. Frydman, C. Gray, and A. Rapaczynski (eds.), *Corporate Governance in Central Europe and Russia.* Budapest: Central European University Press.

Earle, J., and Ross, R. (1996). "Ownership Transformation, Economic Behavior, and Political Attitudes in Russia." Studies in Public Policy 269. Glasgow: University of Strathclyde, Centre for the Study of Public Policy.

Earle, J., Estrin, S., and Leschenko, L. (1995). "Ownership Structures, Patterns of Control and Enterprise Behaviour in Russia." CISME Discussion Paper no. 20. London Business School.

Earle, J. S., and Oprescu, G. (1995). "Employment and Wage Determination, Unemployment and Labour Policies in Romania." In S. Commander and F. Coricelli (eds.), *Unemployment, Restructuring and the Labour Market*. Washington, DC: World Bank.

Ebrill, L., Chopra A., Christofides C., Mylonas, P., Otker, I., and Schwartz, G. (1994). "Poland: The Path to a Market Economy." *IMF Occasional Papers* no. 113 Washington DC.

EBRD. (1994, 1995, 1996). *Transition Report*. London: EBRD.

Economic Commission for Europe. (1995). *Economic Survey of Europe in 1994–95*. Geneva: United Nations.

Economic Trends. (various countries). Washington, DC: IMF.

Ellman, M. (1989). *Socialist Planning*. 2nd ed. Cambridge: Cambridge University Press.

Estrin, S. (1984). *Self Management*. Cambridge: Cambridge University Press.

Estrin, S. (ed.). (1994). *Privatization in Central and Eastern Europe*. London: Longman.

Estrin, S., and Cave, M. (1993). *Competition Policy in Central and Eastern Europe*. London: Francis Pinter.

Estrin, S., Gelb, A., and Singh, I. (1995). "Shocks and Adjustments by Firms in Transition: A Comparative Study." *Journal of Comparative Economics* 21(1): 131–153.

Estrin, S., and Perotin, V. (1991). "Does Ownership Always Matter." *International Journal of Industrial Organisation*. 9(1): 55–72.

Estrin, S., and Stone, R. (1996). "A Taxonomy of Mass Privatizations." *Transition* 7: 8–10.

Fan, G. (1994). "Incremental Changes and Dual Track Transition: Understanding the Case of China." *Economic Policy* 19 (supp.) (Dec.): 99–122.

Fan, G. (1995). "China's Incremental Reform: Progress, Problems and Turning Points." Paper presented at CEPR/CEPII/OECD conference "Different Approaches to Market Reforms: A Comparison Between China and the CEECs." Budapest.

Fan, G., and Woo, W. T. (1996). "State Enterprise Reform as a Source of Macroeconomic Instability." *Asian Economic Journal* (Nov.)

Fischer, S., Sahay, R., Vegh, C. (1996). "Stabilisation and Growth in Transition Economies." *Journal of Economic Perspectives* 10(2): 45–66.

Fischer, S., Sahay, R., and Vegh, C. (1997). "From Transition to Market: Evidence and Growth Prospects." in S. Zecchini (ed.), *Lessons from the Economic Transition: Central and Eastern Europe in the 1990s*, Boston; Kluwer Academic Press and Paris: OECD.

Frydman, R., Gray, C., and Rapaczynski, A. (eds.). (1996). *Corporate Governance in Central Europe and Russia*. London: Central European University Press.

Frydman, R., and Rapaczynski, A. (1994). *Privatization in Eastern Europe. Is the State Withering Away?* Budapest: Central European University Press.

Frydman, R., Rapaczynski, A., and Earle, J. (1993). *The Privatization Process in Central Europe*. Prague: Central European University Press.

Gaidar, Y. (1995). In Gaidar, Y., and Pöhl, K. O., *Russian Reform/International Money. The Lionel Robbins Lectures.* Cambridge, Mass.: MIT Press.

Garver, J. (1993). "The Chinese Communist Party and the Collapse of Soviet Communism." *The China Quarterly* 0(133): 1–26.

Gavin, M., and Hausmann, R. (1995). "The Roots of Banking Crises: The Macroeconomic Context." Working Paper Series, Inter-American Development Bank.

Gavin M. et al. (1996). "Managing Fiscal Policy in Latin America and the Caribbean." Working Paper Series, Inter-American Development Bank.

Godfrey, M., and Richards, P. (eds.) (1997). *Employment Policies and Programmes in Central and Eastern Europe,* ILO, Geneva.

Goldfeld, S., and Sichel, D. (1990). In B. Friedman and F. Hahn (eds.), *Handbook of Monetary Economics.* New York: Elsevier Science Publishers.

Goldman, M. (1994). *Lost Opportunity: Why Economic Reforms in Russia Have Not Worked.* New York: W.W. Norton.

Gomulka, S. (1970). "Extensions of the Golden Rule of Research of Phelps." *Review of Economic Studies* 37(1): 73–93.

Gomulka, S. (1971). "Inventive Activity, Diffusion, and the Stages of Economic Growth." Aarhus University's Institute of Economics, Monograph Series.

Gomulka, S. (1990). *The Theory of Technological Change and Economic Growth.* London: Routledge.

Gomulka, S. (1991). "The Causes of Recession Following Stabilization." *Comparative Economic Studies* 33(2): 71–89.

Gomulka, S. (1992). "Polish Economic Reform, 1990–91: Principles, Policies, and Outcomes." *Cambridge Journal of Economics* 16(3): 355–372.

Gomulka, S. (1994). "Economic and Political Constraints during Transition." *Europe-Asia Studies* 46(1): 89–106.

Gomulka, S. (1995). "The IMF-Supported Programs of Poland and Russia, 1990–94: Principles, Errors, and Results." *Journal of Comparative Economics* 20(3): 316–346.

Gomulka, S., and Lane, J. (1997). "Recession Dynamics Following an External Price Shock in a Transition Economy." *Journal of Structural Changes and Economic Dynamics* 29(1997): 155–173.

Goodhart, C., and Xu, C. (1996). "The Rise of China as an Economic Power." *National Institute Economic Review* (Feb.) 0(155): 56–80.

Gora, M., and Lehmann, H. (1995). "Labour Market Policies in Poland: An Assessment." Paper presented to OECD technical workshop "What Can We Learn from the Experience of Transition Countries with Labour Market Policies?" Vienna, Nov. 30–Dec. 2.

Granville, B., and Shapiro, J. (1996). "Less Inflation, Less Poverty. First Results for Russia." Discussion Paper no. 68. London: Royal Institute of International Affairs.

Gray, C., Frydman, R., and Rapaczynski, A. (1995). *Corporate Governance in Transitional Economies.* Washington, DC: World Bank.

Gregory, P., and Stuart, P. (1988). *Soviet Economic Structure and Development*. New York: Harper & Row.

Groves, T., Hong, Y., McMillan, J., and Naughton, B. (1994). "Autonomy and Incentives in Chinese State Enterprises." *Quarterly Journal of Economics* 109(1): 185–209.

Groves, T., Hong, Y., McMillan, J., and Naughton, B. (1995a). "Productivity Growth in Chinese State-Run Industry." In Fureng Dong, Cyril Lin, and Barry Naughton (eds.), *Reform of China's State-Owned Enterprises*. London: Macmillan.

Groves, T., Hong, Y., McMillan, J., and Naughton, B. (1995b). "China's Evolving Managerial Labor Market." *Journal of Political Economy* 103(4): 873–892.

Ham, J., Svejnar, J., and Terrell, K. (1993). "The Czech and Slovak Labour Markets During the Transition." In S. Commander and F. Coricelli (eds.), *Unemployment, Restructuring and the Labour Market*. Washington, DC: World Bank.

Handelman, S. (1994). *Comrade Criminal: The Theft of the Second Russian Revolution*. London: Michael Joseph.

Havrylyshyn, O. (1994). "Implications for Economies in Transition: Ukraine" In J. Williamson (ed.), *The Political Economy of Policy Reform*. Washington, DC: Institute for International Economics.

Holzmann, R., Gacs, J., and Winckler, G. (eds.). (1995). *Output Decline in Eastern Europe*. Boston: Kluwer Academic Publishers.

Hørder, J. (1996). "Institutions and Inflation." Economics Department, London School of Economics. (Mimeo).

Howes, S. (1993). "Income Inequality in Urban China in the 1980's: Level, Trends and Determinants." Working paper EF/3. Suntory-Toyota International Centre for Economics and Related Disciplines, London School of Economics.

Huang, Y. (1994). "Information, Bureaucracy and Economic Reforms in China and in the Former Soviet Union." *World Politics* 47 (Oct.): 102–134.

Huang, Y., and Xin Meng. (1995). "China's Industrial Growth and Efficiency: A Comparison Between the State and the TVE Sectors." Canberra: Research School of Pacific Studies, Australian National University. (Manuscript).

Hussain, A., Lanjouw, P., and Stern, N. (1994). "Income Inequalities in China: Evidence from Household Survey Data." *World Development* 22(12): 1947–57.

Hussain, A., and Zhuang, J. (1996). "Determination of Wages, Employment and Investment in Chinese SOEs and TVEs." STICERD, London School of Economics.

International Monetary Fund. (1992). *Economic Review, Russian Federation*. Washington, DC: IMF.

International Monetary Fund. (various years). *International Financial Statistics*. Washington, DC: IMF.

International Monetary Fund. The World Bank, OECD, European Bank for Reconstruction and Development. (1991). *A Study of the Soviet Economy*. Washington, D.C.: IMF, The World Bank, OECD, EBRD.

Izak, V. (1996). "Causes of Output Decline: Czech Republic." Prague: Czech National Bank. (Mimeo).

Jackman, R., Layard, R., and Scott, A. (1992). "Unemployment in Eastern Europe." Paper presented to NBER Conference. Cambridge, MA, February.

Jackman, R., and Pauna, C. (1997). "Labour Market Policy and the Reallocation of Labour Across Sectors." In S. Zecchini (ed.), *Lessons from the Economic Transition: Central and Eastern Europe in the 1990s*. Boston: Kluwer Academic Publishers and Paris: OECD.

Jackman, R., and Rutkowski, M. (1994). "Labour Markets: Wages and Employment." In N. Barr (ed.), *Labour Markets and Social Policy in Central and Eastern Europe: The Transition and Beyond*. Oxford: Oxford University Press/World Bank.

Jefferson, G., and Rawski, T. (1994). "Enterprise Reform in Chinese Industry." *Journal of Economic Perspectives* 8(2): 47–70.

Jefferson, G., Rawski, T., and Zheng, Y. (1992). "Growth, Efficiency, and Convergence in China's State and Collective Industry." *Economic Development and Cultural Change* 40(2): 239–266.

Jefferson, G., Rawski, T., and Zheng, Y. (1994). "Productivity Change in Chinese Industry: A Comment." *China Economic Review* 5(2): 235–241.

Jefferson, G., Rawski, T., and Zheng, Y. (1995). "Chinese Industrial Productivity: Trends, Measurement Issues, and Recent Developments." Working Paper no. 297. Economics Department, University of Pittsburgh.

Joint Enterprise Bankruptcy Investigation Group. (1993). "Problems in Enforcing Bankruptcy Law in the State Sector." Mimeo, University of Beijing.

Jones, C. (1995). "Time Series Tests of Endogenous Growth Models." *Quarterly Journal of Economics*. 110(2) (May): 495–525.

Koen, V. (1996). "Russian Macroeconomic Data: Existence, Access, Interpretation." Paris: OECD. (Mimeo).

Kollo, J. (1993). "Unemployment and Unemployment Related Expenditures." Budapest: Blue Ribbon Commission.

Kollo, J. (1996). "Three States in Hungary's Labour Market Transition." In S. Commander (ed.), *Enterprise Restructuring and Unemployment in Models of Transition*.

Kornai, J. (1980). *Economics of Shortage*. Amsterdam: North Holland.

Kornai, J. (1992). *The Socialist System*. Princeton: Princeton University Press.

Kornai, J. (1994). "Transformational Recession: The Main Causes." *Journal of Comparative Economics* 19(1) 39–63. Also chapter 7 in Kornai, *Highways and Byways*. Cambridge, MA: MIT Press, 1993; 1995.

Kornai, J. (1997). "Adjustment Without Recession: A Case Study of Hungarian Stabilization." in S. Zecchini (ed.) *Lessons from the Economic Transition: Central and Eastern Europe in the 1990s*. Boston: Kluwer Academic Press and Paris: OECD.

Layard, R., and Richter, A. (1995). "How Much Unemployment Is Needed for Restructuring? The Russian Experience." *Economics of Transition* 3(1): 39–58.

Lee, K. (1990). "The Chinese Model of the Socialist Enterprise: An Assessment of Its Organisation and Performance." *Journal of Comparative Economics* 14(2): 384–400.

Li, D. (1994). "The Behavior of Chinese State Enterprises Under the Dual Influence of the Government and the Market." Ann Arbor: University of Michigan. (Manuscript).

Li, X., and Ma, Y. (1994). "Fiscal Decentralisation, Financial Reform and Macro-economic Control in China: The Implications for European Monetary Union." Discussion Paper Series no. 28. Glasgow: International Centre for Macroeconomic Modelling, University of Strathclyde.

Lin, J., Cai, F., and Li, Z. (1994). "China's Economic Reforms: Pointers for Other Economies in Transition." Policy Research Working Paper no. 1310. Washington, DC: World Bank.

Lipton, D., and Sachs, J. (1990). "Creating a Market Economy in Eastern Europe: The Case of Poland." *Brookings Papers on Economic Activity*, 0(1): 75–133.

Lucas, R. (1988). "On the Mechanics of Economic Development." *Journal of Monetary Economics* 22(1): 3–42.

Maskin, E., Qian, Y., and Xu, C. (1997). "Incentives, Scale Economies, and Organizational Form." Discussion Paper No. 371 Centre for Economic Performance, London School of Economics.

McAuley, A. (1991). "The Economic Transition in Eastern Europe: Employment, Income Distribution and the Social Safety Net." *Oxford Review of Economic Policy* 7(4): 93–105.

McKinnon, R. (1993). "Financial Growth and Macroeconomic Stability in China, 1978–92: Implications for Russia and Eastern Europe." Paper presented at the Conference on Transition of the Communist Countries in Pacific Asia. San Francisco, May 6–8.

McMillan, J., and Naughton, B. (1992). "How to Reform a Planned Economy: Lessons from China." *Oxford Review of Economic Policy* 8(1): 130–143.

Meyer, K. (1995). "The Determinants of Direct Foreign Investment in Transition Economies in Central and Eastern Europe." Ph.D. dissertation, London Business School.

Micklewright, J., and Nagy, G. (1994). "Flows to and from Insured Unemployment in Hungary." Paper prepared for ILO project "Employment Policies for Transition in Hungary." (Mimeo).

Minami, R., and Hondai, S. (1995). "An Evaluation of the Enterprise Reform in China: Income Share of Labor and Profitability in the Machine Industry." *Hitotsubashi Journal of Economics* 36(2): 125–143.

Mroczkowski, T. (1996). "Informal Employment in the Transition Economy of Poland." Washington, DC: Department of International Business.

National Bank of Hungary. *Annual Report of the National Bank of Hungary*. Budapest: National Bank of Hungary.

Naughton, B. (1994). "What Is Distinctive About China's Economic Transition? State Enterprise Reform and Overall System Transformation." *Journal of Comparative Economics* 18(3): 470–490.

Naughton, B. (1995). *Growing out of the Plan: Chinese Economic Reform, 1978–1993*. Cambridge: Cambridge University Press.

Nove, A. (1983). *The Economics of Feasible Socialism*. London: George Allen & Unwin.

Nuti, D. (1995). "Mass Privatization: Costs and Benefits of Instant Capitalism." In R. Daviddi (ed.), *Property Rights and Privatization in the Transition to a Market Economy*. Maastricht: European Institute of Public Administration.

OECD (1993). *Employment Outlook*. Paris: OECD.

OECD (1997). *Lessons from Labour Market Policies in the Transition Economies*. Paris: OECD.

Ohkawa, K., and Rosovsky, H. (1973). *Japanese Economic Growth: Trend Acceleration in the Twentieth Century*. Stanford: Stanford University Press.

Parker, E. (forthcoming). "The Effect of Scale on the Response to Reform by Chinese State-Owned Construction Units." *Journal of Development Economics*.

Pawlowicz, L. (ed.) (1994). *The Financial Restructuring of Companies and Banks in Poland and Sweden*. Gdansk: Gdansk Institute for Market Economics.

People's Daily, (1995). Overseas ed., Oct. 20.

Perkins, D. (1988). "Reforming China's Economic System." *Journal of Economic Literature*. 26(2): 601–645.

Perkins, D. (1994). "Completing China's Move to the Market." *Journal of Economic Perspectives*. 8(2): 23–46.

Perkins, F. (1996). "Productivity Performance and Priorities for the Reform of China's State-Owned Enterprises." *Journal of Development Studies* 32(3): 414–444.

Perkins, F., Yuxing, Z., and Yong, C. (1993). "The Impact of Economic Reform on Productivity Growth in Chinese Industry: A Case of Xiamen Special Economic Zone." *Asian Economic Journal* 7(2): 107–146.

Phelps, E. (1966). "Models of Technical Progress and the Golden Rule of Research." *Review of Economic Studies* 33(2) No. 94: 133–145.

Pinto, B., Belka, M., and Krajewski, S. (1993). "Transforming State Enterprises in Poland." Working Paper Series no. 1101. Washington, DC: World Bank. Also in *Brookings Papers on Economic Activity*, 0(1): 213–261.

Pohl, G., Anderson, R., Claessens, S., and Djankov, S. (1997). "Privatisation and Restructuring in Central and Eastern Europe: Evidence and Policy Options." World Bank Technical Paper no. 368. Washington, DC: World Bank.

Pohl, G., Djankov S., and Anderson, R. (1996). "Restructuring Large Industrial Firms." World Bank Technical Paper No. 332, Washington, DC: World Bank.

Putterman, L. (1993). *Continuity and Change in China's Rural Development: Collective and Reform Eras in Perspective*. Oxford: Oxford University Press.

Putterman, L. (1995). "The Role of Ownership and Property Rights in China's Economic Transition." *The China Quarterly* no. 144. (Dec.): 1047–1064.

Qian, Y., Roland, G., and Xu, C. (1996). "Coordination Changes in M-Form and U-Form Organizations." Stanford University, ECARE, and London School of Economics. (Mimeo).

Qian, Y., and Xu, C. (1993). "Why China's Economic Reforms Differ: The M-Form Hierarchy and Entry/Expansion of the Non-State Sector." *Economics of Transition* 1(2): 135–170.

Rajewski, Z. (1993). "Gross Domestic Product." In L. Zienkowski (ed.), *Polish Economy in 1990–92: Experience and Conclusions*. Warsaw: Research Center for Economic and Statistical Studies of the Central Statistical Office and the Polish Academy of Sciences.

Rawski, T. (1995). "Implications of China's Reform Experience." *The China Quarterly* no. 144 (Dec.): 1150–1173.

Reynolds, B. (ed.). (1987). *Reform in China: Challenges and Choices*. New York: M. E. Sharpe.

Richter, A. (1997). "New Survey Evidence on Russian Households." Centre for Economic Performance, London School of Economics. (Mimeo).

Richter, A., and Schaffer, M. (1996). "The Performance of *de Novo* Private Firms in Russian Manufacturing." Discussion Paper no. 96/10. CERT, Edinburgh: Heriot-Watt University.

Roberts, B. (1995). "Welfare Changes During Economic Transition: The Effect of Ending Shortages in Russia." University of Miami. (Mimeo).

Rodrik, D. (1992). "Making Sense of the Soviet Trade Shock in Eastern Europe: A Framework and Some Estimates." In M. Glejer, G. Calvo, F. Cornelli, and A. Gelb (eds.), *Eastern Europe in Transition: From Recession to Growth?* Washington, DC: World Bank.

Romer, P. (1986). "Increasing Returns and Long-Run Growth." *Journal of Political Economy* 94(5): 1002–1037.

Rosati, D. (1994). "Output Decline During Transition from Plan to Market: A Reconsideration." *Economics of Transition* 2(4): 419–441.

Rosati, D. (1995). "The Impact of the Soviet Trade Shock on Central and Eastern European Economies." In R. Holzmann, J. Gacs, and G. Winckler (eds.), *Output Decline in Eastern Europe*. Bonston: Kluwer Academic Publishers.

Rostowskï, J. (1997). "Comparing Two Great Depressions: 1929–33 and 1989–93." in S. Zecchini (ed), *Lessons from the Economic Transition*. Boston: Kluwer Academic Press and and Paris: OECD.

Russian Economic Trends. (1992–1997) London: Whurr Publishers.

Sachs, J. (1994). "Russia's Struggle with Stabilization: Conceptual Issues and Evidence." In M. Bruno and B. Pleskovic (eds.), *Proceedings of the World Bank Annual Conference on Development Economics 1994*. Washington, DC: World Bank.

Sachs, J., and Warner, A. (1995). "Economic Reforms and the Process of Global Integration." *Brookings Papers on Economic Activity* 80(1): 1–95.

Sachs, J., and Warner, A. (1996). "Achieving Rapid Growth in Transition Economies of Central Europe." Cambridge, MA: Harvard Institute for International Development. (Mimeo).

Sachs, J., and Woo, W. T. (1994). "Structural Factors in the Economic Reforms of China, Eastern Europe and the Former Soviet Union." *Economic Policy*, 9(18) (Apr.): 101–145.

Sachs, J., and Woo, W. T. (1997). "Understanding China's Economic Performance." NBER Working Paper.

Sargent, T. (1983). "The Ends of Four Big Inflations." In R. E. Hall (ed.), *Inflation*. Chicago: University of Chicago Press.

Scarpetta, S., and Reutersward, A. (1994). "Unemployment Benefit Systems and Active Labour Market Policies in Central and Eastern Europe: An Overview." In T. Boeri (ed.), *Unemployment in Transition Countries: Transient or Persistent?* Paris: OECD.

Schaffer, M. (1992). "The Polish State-Owned Enterprise Sector and the Recession in 1990." *Comparative Economic Studies* 34(1): 58–85.

Schaffer, M. (1994). "'Comment' on A. Berg and O. J. Blanchard, *Stabilization and Transition: Poland 1990–1991*." In O. J. Blanchard, K. A. Froot, and J. D. Sachs (eds.), *The Transition in Eastern Europe*. Vol. 1. Chicago: NBER/University of Chicago Press.

Schaffer, M. (1996). "Worker Participation in Socialist and Transitional Economies." In U. Pagano and R. Rowthorn (eds.), *Democracy and Efficiency in Economic Enterprise*. London: Routledge.

Schaffer, M., and Richter, A. (1995). "Growth, Investment and Newly Established Firms in Russian Manuacturing." Paper presented at Conference on Economic Policy and Restructuring in Russia, June 1995.

State Statistical Bureau. (1985). *Almanac of Population*. Beijing: China Statistical Press.

State Statistical Bureau. (1986–95). *Statistical Yearbook of China* (Chinese ed.). Beijing: China Statistical Press.

State Statistical Bureau (1993). *Statistical Materials of China by Region*. Beijing: China Statistical Press.

Takla, L. (1994). "The Relationship Between Privatization and the Reform of the Banking Sector: The Case of the Czech Republic and Slovakia." In S. Estrin (ed.), *Privatisation in Central and Eastern Europe*. London: Longman.

Terrell, K., Lubyova, M., and Strapec, M. (1995). "An Overview of Labour Market Policies in the Slovak Republic." Paper presented to OECD technical workshop "What Can We Learn from the Experience of Transition Countries with Labour Market Policies?" Vienna, Nov. 30–Dec. 2.

Triesman, D. (1995). "The Politics of Soft Credit in Post-Soviet Russia." *Europe-Asia Studies* 47(6): 949–976.

Tseng, W., Khor, H., Kochhar, K., Mihaljek, D., and Burton, D. (1994). "Economic Reform in China: A New Phase." Occasional Paper no. 114. Washington, DC: IMF.

Ukrainian Economic Trends. (various years). Brussels: European Commission, Tacis Services.

United Nations. (1994). *Human Development Report*. Oxford: Oxford University Press.

Vercenik, J. (1993). "Czechoslovakia and the Czech Republic in 1990–93." Prague: Institute of Sociology, Academy of Sciences. (Mimeo).

Vickers, J., and Yarrow, G. (1988). *Privatization: An Economic Analysis*. Boston: MIT Press.

Walder, A. (1995). "China's Transitional Economy: Interpreting Its Significance." *The China Quarterly* no. 144 (Dec.): 963–979.

Wang, H. (1986). *Economic History of New China's Industry*. Beijing: Economic Management Press.

Wang, H., and Chen, X. (eds.). (1991). *Chanye zuzhi ji youxiao jingzheng—zhongguo chanye zuzhi de chubu yanjiou* (Industrial Organization and Effective Competition—A Preliminary Study of Chinese Industrial Organization). Beijing: China Economy Press.

Wang, S. (1995). "Regional Disparities and Central Government Intervention." Journal of Social Science (July), Hong Kong.

Wei, S., and Lian, P. (1994). "Love and Hate: State and Non-state Firms in Transition Economies." Cambridge, MA: Harvard University. (Mimeo).

Weitzman, M., and Xu, C. (1994). "Chinese Township-Village Enterprises as Vaguely Defined Cooperatives." *Journal of Comparative Economics* 18(2): 121–145.

Wijnbergen, S. van. (1992). "Economic Aspects of Enterprise Reform in Eastern Europe." In R. O'Brien. (ed.), *Finance in the International Economy*. Oxford: Oxford University Press.

Wijnbergen, S. van. (1994). *Eastern Europe After the First Five Years*. Amsterdam: Amsterdam University Press.

Wijnbergen, S. van. (1997). "On the Role of Banks in Enterprise Restructuring: The Polish Example." *Journal of Comparative Economics* 24(1) 44–64.

Wijnbergen, S. van, and Boot, A. (1995). "Financial Sector Design, Regulation and Deposit Insurance in Eastern Europe." In J. Rostowski (ed.), *Banking Reform in Central Europe and the Former Soviet Union*. Budapest: Central European University Press.

Williamson, J. (1995). "Output Decline in Eastern Europe: Summing-up the Debate." In R. Holzmann, J. Gacs, and G. Winckler (eds.), *Output Decline in Eastern Europe*. Boston: Kluwer Academic Publishers.

Williamson, O. (1975). *Markets and Hierarchies*. New York: Free Press.

Winiecki, J. (1991). "The Inevitability of a Fall in Output in the Early Stages of Transition to the Market: Theoretical Underpinnings." *Soviet Studies* 43(4): 669–676.

Woo, W. T. (1994). "The Art of Reforming Centrally-Planned Economies: Comparing China, Poland and Russia." *Journal of Comparative Economics* 18(3) (June): 276–308.

Woo, W. T. (1996). "Chinese Economic Growth: Sources and Prospects." Working Paper no. 96–08. Economics Department, Davis: University of California.

Woo, W. T., Fan, G., Hai, W., and Jin, Y. (1993). "The Efficiency and Macroeconomic Consequences of Chinese Enterprise Reform." *China Economic Review* 4(2): 153–168.

Woo, W. T., Fan, G., Hai, W., and Jin, Y. (1994). "Reply to Comment by Jefferson, Rawski and Zheng." *China Economic Review* 5(2): 243–248.

Woo, W. T., Hai, W., Jin, Y., and Fan, G. (1994). "How Successful Have Chinese Enterprise Reforms Been? Pitfalls in Opposite Biases and Focus." *Journal of Comparative Economics* 18(3) (June): 410–437.

Wong, C., Heady, C., and Woo, W. T. (1995). *Economic Reform and Fiscal Management in China*. Oxford: Oxford University Press.

World Bank. (1990). *China: Macroeconomic Stability and Industrial Growth Under Decentralized Socialism*. Washington, DC: World Bank.

World Bank. (1993). *Global Economic Prospects and the Developing Countries*. Washington, DC: World Bank.

World Bank. (1993, 1994). *Trends in Developing Economies*. Washington, DC: World Bank.

World Bank. (1994). *Socio-economic Time-Series Access and Retrieval System*. Washington, DC: World Bank.

World Bank. (1995a). *China: Macroeconomic Stability in a Decentralised Economy*. Washington, DC: World Bank.

World Bank. (1995b). *Workers in an Integrating World*. Washington, DC: World Bank.

World Bank. (1995c). *World Bank Atlas*. Washington, DC: World Bank.

World Bank. (1996a). *The Chinese Economy: Fighting Inflation, Deepening Reforms*. Washington, DC: World Bank.

World Bank. (1996b). *World Development Report*. New York: Oxford University Press.

World Bank. (1996c). *From Plan to Market*. Washington, DC: World Bank.

World Bank and Goskomstat. (1995). *Russian Federation: Report on the National Accounts*. Washington, DC and Moscow: World Bank and Goskomstat.

Xu, C. (1995). *A Different Transition Path: Ownership, Performance, and Influence of Chinese Rural Industrial Enterprises*. New York: Garland.

Xu, C., and Zhuang, J. (1996a). "Why Did Chinese State-Owned Enterprises Make More Losses After Implementing Bonus Schemes?" London School of Economics, (Mimeo).

Xu, C., and Zhuang, J. (1996b). "A Comparison of Central and Regional State-Owned Enterprises in China." London School of Economics. (Mimeo).

Yusuf, S. (1994). "China's Macroeconomic Performance and Management During Transition." *Journal of Economic Perspectives* 8(2): 71–92.

Zecchini, S. (ed.). (1997). *Lessons from the Economic Transition: Central and Eastern Europe in the 1990s*. Boston: Kluwer Academic Publishers and Paris: OECD.

Zhao, R. (1992). "Some Special Phenomena in Income Distribution During China's Transition Period." Economic Research (Jingji Yanju) 1: 53–63.

Zhou, T.-H. (ed.). (1984). *Dangdai zhongguo de jingji tizhi gaige* (Economic System Reform of Contemporary China). Beijing: China Social Science Press.

Zhu, R. (1996). "Guo you qiye sheng hua gaige ke burong huan" (No Time Shall Be Lost in Further Reforming State-Owned Enterprises). Speech at the fourth session of the Eighth People's Congress. *People's Daily* (overseas ed.), Mar. 11.

Zhu, R. (ed.). (1985). *Dangdai zhongguo de jingji guanli* (The Economic Management of Contemporary China). Beijing: China Social Science Press.

Zukowski, R. (1996). "From Transformational Crisis to Transformational Recovery: Factors of Output Growth in Poland's Industry Between 1992 and 1993." Warsaw: Economic Institute of the Polish Academy. (Mimeo).

Index

Note: page numbers in italics refer to figures or tables where these are separated from their textual reference.

Accounting data, 103
Active labor market policies, 142–146
Aghion, P., 100, 106, 124
Agriculture
  China, 3, 6, 25, 163, 196–197
  communes disbanded, 157–158
  credit, 55
  employment, 129, 132, 133, 158–159,
    165–166
  labor migration to industry, 139, 158–159,
    169
  land reform, 196
  Poland, 3, 34
  subsidies eliminated, 26
  underemployment, 25
Aizenman, J., 59, 69
AK model of growth, 38–39
Albania
  employment, 125, 141
  growth, 52
  inflation levels, 46, 52
  liberalization index, 44
  mass privatization, 79
  output, 50, 125
  private sector GDP, 82
  seigniorage, 53
  stabilization program, 60
  unemployment, 125
  unemployment benefits, 150
Alesina, A., 59, 69
Anti–ex post reasoning view, 176, 214n3
Armenia
  growth, 52
  inflation levels, 46, 52

liberalization index, 44
mass privatization, 79
output, 50
private sector GDP, 82
Arms industry collapse, 15. See also Defense
  expenditure
Asia, Central, 17, 18
Asia, East, 41, 168–169
Aslund, A., 51
Attribute shocks, 195–196
Austerity, 31
Automobile industry, China, 189, 190
Azerbaijan
  growth, 52
  inflation levels, 46, 52
  liberalization index, 44
  output, 50
  private sector GDP, 82

Bai, C., 173, 174–175
Balcerowicz, L., 14, 56, 61
Baltic Republics, GDP, 16, 17, 18. See also
  individual countries
Banking. See also Commercial banks; Savings
  banks
  as agent of change, 102, 104–105, 120
  China, 178, 210–211
  credit, 4
  debt, 9
  fraud, 111
  recapitalized, 113–115
  reform, 9–10, 100–101, 114–119
  Slovenia, 100, 101, 104, 117–118
Banking commission, 112–113

Bank Rehabilitation Agency, 100, 104, 118
Bankruptcy
  Poland, 105, 108–109
  proceedings, 106
  protection from, 108–109
  restructuring, 105
  state-owned enterprises, 105–106, 206,
    207–208
  township-village enterprises, 200, 205
  Western legislation, 100
Belarus
  GDP, 17, 18, 82
  growth, 52
  inflation levels, 46, 52
  liberalization index, 44
  mass privatization, 79
  output, 50
  private sector GDP, 82
  seigniorage, 53
Belka, M., 90, 115–116
Berg, A., 29
Berglof, E., 101
Bhaduri, A., 31
Blanchard, O., 26, 29, 124
Boeri, T., 137
Bofinger, P., 29, 30–31
Bonuses, 170, 177, 191–192, 217n5
Boone, P., 51
Boot, A., 105, 112
Bouin, O., 171, 177
Bruno, M., 50
Budgetary policies, 68–70
Budget deficit, 2, 32
Bulgaria
  active labor market policies, 143, 146
  employment changes, 134, 135
    gender, 141
    output, 125
    sector, 130, 132, 133
  GDP, 27, 28, 82
  growth, 52
  inflation levels, 46, 52
  labor market restructuring, 136
  liberalization index, 44
  mass privatization, 79
  NMP/GDP, 27
  output, 50, 125
  private sector GDP, 82
  stabilization program, 60
  unemployment, 125
  unemployment benefits, 150
  welfare benefits, 138
Business training, 33

Calvo, G., 29, 49–50
Canada, employment by sector, 130, 131
Capital accumulation, 37–39, 166, 167
Capitalism, 1, 4–5, 9
Capital restrictions, 94
Central planning
  employment, 24
  functional specialization, 185–186
  Hungary, 29–30, 187
  M-form, 186–187, 189–191, 193
  output, 75
  Poland, 29–30
  U-form, 186, 190, 191, 195
  unemployment, 123
Charezma, W., 30
Chechnya scandals, 56
Chen, X., 189
Chen Yun, 161
Chile, bank fraud, 111
China. See also Township-village enterprises;
    state-owned enterprises
  agriculture, 3, 6, 25, 163, 196–197
  automobile industry, 189, 190
  banking, 178, 210–211
  capital accumulation, 166, 167
  capitalism, 1
  coastal cities, 159
  coordination, 193–194
  credit unions, 204
  Cultural Revolution, 7, 161, 167, 168, 188,
    194
  decentralization, 6–7, 167–168, 187, 208–
    209
  dual-track reform, 156, 157–158, 162
  economic problems, 206–212
  employment by sector, 14
  exceptionalism, 155, 173, 180
  exchange rates, 159–160
  exports, 160
  ex post reasoning, 154–155, 171, 176, 180,
    214n3
  family ties, 168, 200–201
  foreign trade, 7, 159–160
  GDP, 13, 14, 163
  global economy, 167
  gradualism, 5–7, 10, 153, 155, 157–162,
    180, 183
  Great Leap Forward, 7, 167, 187
  growth rate, 2, 13, 153–154, 155–156,
    166, 185
  Hainan province, 187
  industry, 163
  inflation, 2, 4

investment, 167, 212
labor costs, 156
local government, 188, 190–193, 194,
   211–212
loss-making industry, 206, 208
M-form economy, 186–187, 189–191, 193
macroeconomic instability, 178–179
market sector deregulated, 156
migration, 165, 201
nonstate sector, 156, 157, 158, 196
output, 1
ownership, 158–159, 183, 184
peasantry, 156, 158–159
politics, 157, 160–162
poverty, 164
price liberalization, 25
regional inequality, 209, 218n14
savings, 157, 167
Special Economic Zones, 159, 162, 168,
   217n7
swap market, 160
tax revenues, 209
Tiananmen Square demonstration, 157,
   161, 162, 168, 179
total factor productivity, 10–11
unemployment, 2
China Economic System Reform Research
   Institute, 177
CIS, monetary policy, 59
Commercial banks, 99
  incentive structure, 114, 120
  regulation, 110, 111–112
  restructuring companies, 106
Commercialization, 90, 114, 120
Commune-brigade enterprises, 200
Communes disbanded, 157–158
Communism, 1, 13–14, 161
Communist Party
  Europe, Eastern, 75
  Soviet Union, 161, 162
Communist Party of China, 155, 160–161,
   162, 170
Community-owned enterprises, 158
Conflict of interest, privatization, 74–75
Consumer preference shift, 30
Consumer price index, 171, 172
Contracts system, 32
Coordination
  M-form, 193–194, 195–196
  politics, 69–70
Coricelli, F., 29, 49–50
Corporate governance, 33

Corruption
  credit restriction, 210
  embezzlement, 179
  managers, 175
  privatization, 179, 181
  in reform, 56
  rent-seeking, 44, 45, 76
Council for Mutual Economic Assistance,
   14, 20, 21
Creative destruction, 14, 24
Credit
  agriculture, 55
  banks, 4
  corruption, 210
  industry, 55
  inflation, 44
  loose policies, 62, 70
  and politics, 52–57
  Russia, 54, 55, 69
  Ukraine, 54, 69
Credit crunch, 29
Creditors, 107–109, 110
Credit unions, 204
Croatia
  inflation levels, 46, 52
  liberalization index, 44
  output, 50
  private sector GDP, 82
Cultural Revolution, 7, 161, 167, 168, 188,
   194
Currency board, 45, 62–63, 65
Currency devaluation, 35
Czechoslovakia
  GDP, 27, 28
  liberalization index, 44
  NMP/GDP, 27
  privatization, 78, 80
Czech Republic
  active labor market policies, 143, 145
  banking reform, 9–10, 101
  employment changes, 14, 125, 134, 135,
     148–149
    gender, 141
    sector, 130, 132
  exchange rate, 36
  GDP, 16, 17, 18
  gender/employment, 141
  growth, 2, 52
  inflation, 2, 46, 52
  insider ownership, 82, 83
  labor market restructuring, 136
  liberalization index, 44

Czech Republic (cont.)
  mass privatization, 79, 80
  output, 50, 124
  private sector GDP, 82
  seigniorage, 56
  unemployment, 2, 124, 125, 145
  unemployment benefits, 127, 150

Data problems, 16, 103, 137
Davis, S., 131
Debt
  banks threatened, 9
  foreign, 32, 35
  and inflation, 106
  triangular, 206, 211
Debt restructuring, 35, 105–106
Debt/equity swaps, 106, 116, 120
Decentralization, China, 6–7, 167–168, 187, 208–209
Defense expenditure, 3, 15, 18
Deficit finance, 127
Demographic factors, employment, 140, 141
Deng Xiaoping, 161, 167, 168, 175, 200
Denison, E., 165
De novo firms, 80, 90–92, 96
Depoliticization, transition process, 86–87
Deposit insurance, 115
Deregulation, market sector, 156
Devaluation of currency, 35
Domestic money, 47, 48
Drazen, A., 59, 69
Dual-track reform, 156, 157–158, 162
Duplication, 189–190

Earle, J., 80, 82, 83, 92, 94, 186
Easterly, W., 50
Economic policies, stabilization, 60–61
Economies of scale, 189–190
The Economist, 161
Elites, 44, 45, 76
Embezzlement, 179. See also Corruption
Emigration, 140
Employee-management conciliation, 109–110
Employee ownership, 76, 81, 82, 83, 88, 93, 97
Employment
  agriculture, 129, 132, 133, 158–159, 165–166
  central planning, 24
  changes, 14, 125, 134, 135
  demographic factors, 140, 141

gender, 141, 142
market/transition economies, 133
mobility, 139, 158–159, 169
optimal, 91–92
output, 125
and ownership, 91, 92
participation rate, 139–140
restructuring, 129–136
by sector, 14, 129–131, 132
state-owned enterprises, 126, 158
structural imbalance, 132–133
township-village enterprises, 199, 205–206
and unemployment, 139–140
Employment contracts, 204
Employment creation. See Job creation
Employment cuts, 126, 127–28
EPR. See Ex post reasoning
Estonia
  currency board, 62–63
  futures contracts, 63
  GDP, 27, 28, 82
  growth, 52
  inflation levels, 46, 52
  liberalization index, 44
  lowest GDP, 28
  mass privatization, 79
  NMP/GDP, 27
  output, 50
  private sector GDP, 82
  seigniorage, 53
Estrin, S., 76, 77, 80, 82, 83, 88, 92
Europe, Eastern
  bankruptcy, 100
  economic structures, 185–186
  inflation, 4
  privatization, 74–76
  reform process, 1–5
Europe, West, investment/GDP ratios, 41
Exceptionalism, Chinese, 155, 173, 180
Exchange rate policy, 32–33, 36, 159–160
Exchange value, 215n7
Exports, China, 160
Ex post reasoning, China's growth, 154–155, 171, 176, 180, 214n3

Fan, G., 176, 177, 178, 179
Financial sector, 32, 57. See also Banking
Financial Times, 206
Firm size, 189
Foreign assistance, 45, 58, 67–68
Foreign debt, 32, 35
Foreign direct investment, 82, 110, 167

Foreign ownership, 77
Foreign trade, 7, 30, 35–36, 159–160
Fraud, 111
FSU. *See* Soviet Union (former)
Functional specialization, 185–186
Futures contracts, 63

Gaidar, Y., 55, 62
GDP
  change, *2*
  China, 13, *14*, *163*
  data, 16–18
  and investment, 41
  Russia, 8, 13, *14*
  sectoral composition, 19–20, *82*
Gelb, A., 198
Gender/employment, *141*, 142
Georgia
  growth, *52*
  inflation levels, *46*, *52*
  liberalization index, *44*
  mass privatization, *79*
  output, *50*
  private sector GDP, *82*
Globalization, China, 167
Goldman, M., 48
Gomulka, S., 24, 26, 58
Goods, wanted/unwanted, 26, *27–28*
Gradualism
  banking reform, 114–115
  China, 5–7, 10, 153, 155, 157–162, 180,
    183
Granville, B., 58
Great Leap Forward, 7, 167, 187
Greece, labor market restructuring, *136*
Groves, T., 173, 174, 175
Growth
  AK model, 38–39
  capital accumulation, 37–39, 166, 167
  China, 2, 13, 153–154, 155–156, *166*, 185
  and inflation, 2, 51–52
  investment, 38–39, 40
  long-term, 36–39, 40–41
  R&D, 39
  by sector, 164–166
  technology transfer, 36–37
Growth theory, Solow-Swan, 36–37
Guangdong model, township-village enter-
    prises, 202

Hai, W., 171, 177
Hainan province, 187

Haltiwanger, J., 131
Handelman, S., 56
Havrylyshyn, Oleh, 54
Hørder, J., 59, 69
Hondai, S., 177
Household expenditure, 24
Household responsibility system, 196
Hua Guofeng, 161
Huang, Y., 171
Human capital, 41
Hungarian Household Panel Survey, 139
Hungary
  active labor market policies, *143*, 145–146
  bank reform, 101, 118–119
  central planning, 29–30, 187
  employment changes, *134*, *135*
    gender, *141*
    output, *125*
    sector, *130*, *132*
  foreign direct investment, *82*
  GDP, 16, *17*, *18*, *27*, *28*, *82*
  gender/employment, *141*
  growth, *2*, *46*, *52*
  inflation, *2*, *46*, *52*
  insider ownership, *82*, *83*
  labor market restructuring, *136*
  liberalization index, *44*
  NMP/GDP, *27*
  output, *50*, *125*
  private sector GDP, *82*
  recovery, 31–32
  sale of former state-owned assets, 77
  seigniorage, *53*
  unemployment, *2*, *125*
  unemployment benefits, *127*, *128*, *150*, *152*
Hussain, A., 205

IMF, monetary programs, 58, 68
Immigrant laborers, 201
Incentives
  commercial banking, 114, 120
  local government reforms, 191–193
  managers, 190
Income. *See* Wages
Income tax, 170, 178
Industry
  China, *163*
  credit, 55
  dual-track production, 158
  employment, 129–131
  labor from agriculture, 139, 158–159, 169
Industry groups, 204

Inflation
  China, 2, 4
  continuing, 70–71
  credit, 44
  and debt, 106
  economic rationale, 49–52
  Europe, Eastern, 4
  falling, 57–60, 167
  foreign assistance, 58
  and growth, 2, 51–52
  monetary policy, 58–59
  output, 50, 51
  political breakdown, 43
  price liberalization, 3–4, 8–9, 43–44
  Soviet Union (former), 2, 46, 52, 106
  Ukraine, 46, 52, 65–66
  unemployment, 2
  unemployment benefits, 152
Inflation tax, 57
Informal sector, 140
Information asymmetries, 103
Input supplies, 30
Insider ownership, 77, 81, 82, 83, 87–88,
    126
Institutions, township-village enterprises,
    200–202, 203–204
Interest rates, 29
Investment
  China, 167, 212
  falls, 18, 19
  foreign direct, 82, 110, 167
  and GDP, 41
  growth, 38–39, 40
  and profitability, 205
  restructuring, 87
Italy, state holding company, 103

Jackman, R., 129, 131, 133, 135, 136
Japan, labor reallocation, 169
Jefferson, G., 154, 171, 172, 173, 178
Job creation, 75, 129, 133
Job destruction, 129, 133
Job placement, 144
Johnson, S., 51

Kazakhstan
  GDP, 27, 28, 82
  growth, 52
  inflation levels, 46, 52
  liberalization index, 44
  mass privatization, 79
  NMP/GDP, 27

output, 50
  private sector GDP, 82
  seigniorage, 53
  stabilization program, 61
Kinship links, 200–201
Kornai, J., 15, 29–30, 174
Kyrgyzstan
  growth, 52
  inflation levels, 46, 52
  liberalization index, 44
  mass privatization, 79
  output, 50
  private sector GDP, 82
  seigniorage, 53
  stabilization program, 60–61

Labor
  costs, 87, 127, 156
  surplus, 165
  flexibility, 204, 205–206
  mobility, 11, 131, 158–159, 169
Labor force participation, women, 140
Labor force survey, 137–138
Labor market
  active labor market policies, 142–146
  nonstate sector, 156
  restructuring, 135–136
  wage inequality, 123
Land reform, 196
Lane, J., 26
Lange, Oskar, 155
Laski, K., 31
Latin America
  bank fraud, 111
  banking, 99
  seigniorage, 52
  stabilization and economic policy, 41, 61
Latvia
  GDP, 27, 28
  growth, 52
  inflation levels, 46, 52
  liberalization index, 44
  mass privatization, 79
  NMP/GDP, 27
  output, 50
  seigniorage, 53
Lee, K., 173
Li, D., 174
Liberalization index, 44
Liberalization of prices. See Price
    liberalization
Liquidation, 106

Lithuania
GDP, 27, 28
growth, 52
inflation levels, 46, 52
liberalization index, 44
mass privatization, 79
NMP/GDP, 27
output, 50
seigniorage, 53
Living standards, 18
Ljubljanska Banka, Slovenia, 117–118
Loan recovery, 101
Loans, 111, 176–177
Local government, 188, 190–193, 194, 211–212
Loss-makers, 103–104, 110, 206, 208

M-form organization, 216–217n2
centralized economies, 186–187, 189–191, 193
coordination, 193–194, 195–196
township-village enterprises, 202–203
Macedonia
growth, 52
inflation levels, 46, 52
liberalization index, 44
output, 50
private sector GDP, 82
Macroeconomics
instability, 178–179
stabilization, 14, 15
unemployment, 3–4
Management and employee buyouts, 77, 109
Managerial ownership, 81, 85, 88
Managers
capital restrictions, 94
conflict of interest, 74
corruption, 175
incentives, 190
nonprofit objectives, 173–174
self-seeking, 87
Manufacturing sector, employment, 129
Mao Zedong, 161
Marginal product of labor, 165
Market economies
employment, 133
unemployment, 23–24, 123
Market sector, deregulation, 156
Market socialism, 155, 162, 170
Maskin, E., 190, 191, 193
Mass privatization, 73–74, 78, 79, 101–102

McMillan, J., 161
Meng, X., 171
Micklewright, J., 145, 146
Migration, China, 165, 201
Military expenditure. See Defense expenditure
Minami, R., 177
Ministries, state-owned industries, 186
Moldova
growth, 52
inflation levels, 46, 52
liberalization index, 44
mass privatization, 79
output, 50
seigniorage, 53
Monetary policy, 48, 58–59
Mongolia
foreign borrowing, 68
growth, 52
inflation levels, 46, 52
liberalization index, 44
output, 50

Nagy, G., 145, 146
National accounting, 21–22
Naughton, B., 154, 155, 161, 171, 173, 176, 177
Negative-price sales, 102–103
Net material product, 27
Nomenklatura, 76. See also Elites
Nonstate sector, 156, 157, 158, 196

OECD
active labor market policies, 143
employment changes, 134
sector, 130, 131
Output falls
central planning, 75
contributing factors, 13–14
credit crunch, 29
data, 16–17
and inflation, 50, 51
nonstate sector, 158
ownership, 90
political reform, 1, 8, 13
price liberalization, 20–21, 23
township-village enterprises, 200
and unemployment, 124–129
Outsider ownership, 87–88, 93
Overseas Chinese, 168
Ownership
China, 158–159, 183, 184

Ownership (cont.)
  Communism, 161
  dominance, 92–96
  dual-track, 158–159
  employee, 76, 81, 82, 83, 88, 93, 97
  employment, 91, 92
  foreign, 77
  management, 81, 85, 88
  output growth, 90
  outsider/insider, 77, 81, 82, 83, 87–88, 93,
    126
  and performance, 85–86
  private, 80, 201–202
  privatization, 9, 73, 80–84, 90, 101
  public, 73
  restructuring, 90–94, 95
  state, 75, 80

Parker, E., 171, 174
Pauna, C., 129, 133, 135, 136
Peasantry, China, 156, 158–159
People's Bank of China, 210, 211
Performance, 84–88
Pohl, G., 15, 33
Poison pill policies, 45, 61–65
Poland
  active labor market policies, 143, 145–146
  agriculture, 3, 34
  banks, 10, 101, 110, 113, 115–117
  bankruptcy, 105, 108–109
  central planning, 29–30
  credit crunch, 29
  debt reduction, 35, 106
  economic recovery, 18, 19, 20–22
  employment changes 134, 135
    gender, 140, 141
    ownership, 91, 92
    output, 125
    sector, 130, 132
  exchange rate, 36
  foreign trade, 35–36
  GDP, 16, 17, 18, 27, 28
  gender/employment, 140, 141
  growth, 2, 52
  inflation levels, 2, 46, 52, 106
  labor market restructuring, 136
  liberalization index, 44
  management and employee buyouts, 77
  mass privatization, 79, 80
  national accounting, 21–22
  NMP/GDP, 27
  output, 1, 20–21, 33, 50, 125

  ownership, 33, 82, 83, 90–94
  private sector, 33–34
  recovery, 31–32
  seigniorage, 53, 56
  transformation model, 15, 20–22, 32–36
  unemployment, 2, 125, 137, 147
  unemployment benefits, 127, 128, 149, 151,
    152
  urban sector, 34–35
Politics
  China, 157, 160–162
  coordination, 69–70
  credit process, 52–57
  inflation, 43
  stabilization, 60, 69–70
Portugal, labor market restructuring, 136
Poverty, 45, 58, 164
Price liberalization
  aggregate effects, 22–24
  changes, 15
  inflation, 3–4, 8–9, 43–44
  output falls, 20–21, 23
  price rises, 43–44, 46–48
  recession, 25
  speed, 2–3
  structural effects, 24–25
Prices
  controlled, 3, 21
  dual-track, 157–158
  relative, 126–127
  rising, 43–44, 46–48
Principal-agent theory, 73
Private ownership, 80, 201–202
Private sector, 7, 33–34, 82, 128–129, 139
Privatization, 73–74, 76–80. See also Mass
    privatization
  conflict of interest, 74–75
  corruption, 179, 181
  Europe, Eastern, 74–76
  methods, 73–74, 76–80
    auction system, 76, 77
    public tender, 76–77
    restitution, 77–78
    voucher system, 78
  and ownership, 9, 73, 80–84, 90, 101
  performance, 73, 84–88
  Poland, 32–36
  Russia, 84
  speed of, 4–5, 32
  state-owned enterprises, 155, 179–180
Production, 73, 157–158
Products, supply-side/demand-side, 40

Profitability, 75, 88–89, 170, 175–178, 205
Profit maximizing, 30–31, 87, 174
Property rights, 86–87, 155, 170
Prudential regulation, 112–113
Public ownership, 73
Public sector control, 103–104
Public spending, 39
Public tender, privatization, 76–77

Qian, Y., 186, 194, 195

R&D, growth, 39
Rawski, T., 154
Recapitalization, banks, 113–115
Recession
  price liberalization, 25
  restructuring policies, 40, 51–52
  transformational, 15–16, 19, 22, 29–30,
  124
Reform
  as creative destruction, 14, 24
  Europe, Eastern, 1–5
  gradual, 160–62
Regions
  competition, 190, 191
  inequality, 209, 218n14
  state-owned enterprises, 183, 185, 192–
  193
Regulation, banks, 110, 111–112
Rent seeking, 44, 45, 76
Restitution to former owners, 77–78
Restructuring
  bankruptcy, 105
  commercial banks, 106
  debt, 105–106
  employment, 129–136
  investment, 87
  ownership, 90–94, 95
  performance, 85
  privatization, 9
  recession, 40, 51–52
  by sector, 89
  state-owned enterprises, 107
  unemployment, 10
  viability, 88–89
Restructuring index, 131
Retirement, early, 142
Revenues, and welfare benefits, 44–45
Romania
  active labor market policies, 143, 146
  employment changes, 134, 135
    gender, 140, 141

output, 125
  sector, 130, 132
  GDP, 17, 18, 27, 28
  gender/employment, 140, 141
  growth, 52
  inflation levels, 46, 52
  insider ownership, 77, 82, 83
  labor market restructuring, 136
  liberalization index, 44
  mass privatization, 79
  NMP/GDP, 27
  output, 50, 125
  seigniorage, 53
  stabilization program, 60
  unemployment, 125
  unemployment benefits, 151
Ross, R., 186
Ruble credits, 59
Russia
  active labor market policies, 143
  corruption, 56
  credit, 54, 55, 69
  dominant ownership, 94–96
  employment changes, 134, 135
    gender, 141
    output, 125
    sector, 14, 130, 132
  exchange rate, 36
  GDP, 8, 14, 16, 17, 18, 27, 28
  gender/employment, 141
  growth, 2
  inflation, 2, 4, 46, 52
  insider ownership, 82, 83
  liberalization index, 44
  mass privatization, 79, 80
  NMP/GDP, 27
  output, 50, 125
  price liberalization, 3
  privatization, 84
  restructuring, 95
  seigniorage, 53, 54, 56, 57
  unemployment, 2, 125
  unemployment benefits, 127, 138, 148, 151
  wages, 128
  World Bank survey, 82–83, 88, 94–96
Russian Central Bank, 54, 56, 59
Rutkowski, M., 131

Sachs, J., 58, 67, 164, 173, 183
Savings, 38, 39, 48, 157, 167
Savings banks, 115
Scale economies, 189–190

Schaffer, M., 29
Schumpeter, Joseph, 14, 24
Sectors
  employment, *14*, 129–131, *132*
  GDP, 19–20, *82*
  growth accounting, 164–166
  labor mobility within, 11, 131, 158–159,
    169
  restructuring, 89
Seigniorage, 49, 52, *53*, 54, 56, 57–58
Serbia, stabilization, 66–67
Service sector, 163
Shadow economy, 149
Shapiro, J., 58
Slovak Republic
  active labor market policies, *143*, 145
  employment changes, *134*, *135*
    gender, *141*
    output, *125*
    sector, *130*, *132*
  gender/employment, *141*
  growth, *52*
  inflation levels, *46*, *52*
  labor market restructuring, *136*
  liberalization index, *44*
  mass privatization, 79, 80
  output, *50*, *125*
  unemployment, *125*, 145
  unemployment benefits, *151*
Slovenia
  banking, 100, 101, 104, 117–118
  Bank Rehabilitation Agency, 118
  employment, *125*
  growth, *52*
  inflation levels, *46*, *52*
  liberalization index, *44*
  mass privatization, 79
  output, *50*, *125*
  unemployment, *125*
Social capital, 108
Social insurance, 149
Social justice, 148
Social support. *See* Welfare benefits
Solidarity trade union, 56
Soviet Union (former). *See also* individual
    countries
  adjustment, 3
  collapse of, 14
  Communist Party, 161, 162
  coordination, 194
  economic structures, 185–186

Special Economic Zones, 159, 162, 168,
    217n7
Stabilization
  economic policies, 41, 60–61
  political coordination, 60, 69–70
  Serbia, 66–67
  Ukraine, 65–66
Standard of living, 18
State
  ownership, 75, 80
  power, 1, 6
  purchases, 29
  restructuring and revenue, 102
State-owned assets, 77, 78
State-owned enterprises, 158
  bankruptcy, 105–106, 206, 207–208
  China/Eastern Europe compared, 7
  employment, 126, 158
  macroeconomic instability, 178–179
  Ministry controlled, 186
  nonprofit objectives, 173–174
  performance and restructuring, 85
  and private firms, 80
  privatization, 155, 179–180
  profits/losses, 175–178
  reform, 107–108, 153, 154, 170–171
  regional control, 183, 185, 192–193
  restructuring, 107
  subsidy, 127, 206, *207*
  taxation, 174, 178
  total factor productivity growth, 155, 171–
    175, 191–193
  and township-village enterprises, 204–206
  wages, 177–178, 216n31
  welfare benefits, 158–159
Structural adjustment, 44
Structural unemployment, 24, 124
Subsidies
  eliminated, 26, 30, 120, 127
  GDP, 178–179
  state-owned enterprises, 127, 206, *207*
Sunan model, township-village enterprises,
    201
Supply-side shocks, 24
Svejnar, J., 198
Swap market, 160

Tajikistan, inflation, *46*
Tariff rates, 159
Taxes
  bargaining, 174

bonuses, 177
collection, 3, 4
reductions, 26
revenue, 209
state-owned enterprises, 174, 178
Technology transfer, 36–37, 203
Tiananmen Square demonstration, 157, 161, 162, 168, 179
Total factor productivity
China, 10–11
data, 165
state-owned enterprises, 155, 171–175, 191–193
Total factor productivity growth, 11, 165, 171–175
Township-village enterprises, 6–7, 158, 183
and agriculture, 196–197
bankruptcy, 200, 205
employment, 199, 205–206
institutions, 200–202, 203–204
M-form structure, 202–203
models, 201–202
output, 200
registration, 214n4
and state-owned enterprises, 204–206
and transition, 197–200
wages, 205–206
Trade unions, 56
Training for business, 33
Training schemes, unemployed, 146
Trans-Caucasian Republics, GDP, 16
Transformational recession, 15–16, 19, 22, 29–30, 124
Transformation models, 15, 20–22, 32–36
Transition economies, 16, 86–87, 133. See also Individual countries
Triangular debt, 206, 211
Triesman, D., 56
Turkmenistan
inflation, 46
seigniorage, 53
Two-product economy, 26

U-form organization, 216–217n2
centralized economies, 186, 190, 191, 195
Ukraine
corruption, 56
credit, 54, 69
employment, 125
foreign borrowing, 68
GDP, 16, 17, 18, 27, 28
growth, 52

inflation, 46, 52, 65–66
liberalization index, 44
mass privatization, 79
NMP/GDP, 27
output, 50, 125
seigniorage, 53
stabilization, 60, 65–66
unemployment, 125
Underemployment, 25, 142, 147
Unemployed people, 137–138, 140, 142, 146
Unemployment, 136–138
acceptance of, 32
central planning, 123
data, 137
disguised, 142, 147
duration, 138–139, 148
and employment, 139–140
inflation, 2
market economies, 23–24
open, 128–129
and output, 124–129
price liberalization, 3–4
restructuring, 10
structural, 24, 124
young people, 145
Unemployment benefits
abuse of, 137
cross-country differences, 127–128, 142, 147–148, 149–152
eligibility, 142, 152
inflation, 152
limitations, 140
USSR. See Soviet Union (former)
Uzbekistan
growth, 52
inflation levels, 46, 52
liberalization index, 44
output, 50
seigniorage, 53

Value-added deflator, state-owned enterprises, 171–172, 173, 215n21
Viability, restructuring, 88–89
Vietnam, 13, 25, 168–169
Voucher system, privatization, 78, 80

Wages, 123, 126, 127–128, 177–178, 205–206, 216n31
Wang, H., 189
Warsaw Pact, collapse, 14
Weitzman, M., 203

Welfare benefits, 44–45, 55, 127, 138, 156,
      158–159. *See also* Unemployment
      benefits
Welfare state, 32
Wenzhou model, township-village enter-
      prises, 201–202
Wijnbergen, S. van, 99, 105, 112
Williamson, J., 30
Women's participation in labor force, 140,
      141
Woo, W. T., 164, 165, 171, 172, 173, 176,
      177, 178, 183
Workers. *See* Employment
Working age population, *141*
World Bank survey of Russian industrial
      firms, 82–83, 88, 94–96
Wu Bangguo, 170

Xu, C., 186, 191, 192, 194, 203, 205, 206,
      207

Youth unemployment, 145
Yugoslavia (former), banking, 99

Zhou, T.-H., 187, 188
Zhu, R., 154, 189
Zhuang, J., 191, 192, 205, 205, 206, 207
Zhu Rongji, 208
Zloty devalued, 35
Zukowski, R., 22, 23